D0042435

Evaluation
and
Social Work Practice

Evaluation
and
Social Work Practice

edited by

Ian Shaw and Joyce Lishman

SAGE Publications
London • Thousand Oaks • New Delhi

Chapter 1 © Joyce Lishman 1999
Chapter 2 © Ian Shaw 1999
Chapter 3 © William J. Reid and Pamela Zettergren 1999
Chapter 4 © Nick Gould 1999
Chapter 5 © Karen Dullea and Audrey Mullender 1999
Chapter 6 © Clare Evans and Mike Fisher 1999
Chapter 7 © Beth Humphries 1999
Chapter 8 © Ruth R. Martin 1999
Chapter 9 © Karen Tanner and Pat Le Riche 1999
Chapter 10 © Jan Fook, Robyn Munford and Jackie Sanders 1999
Chapter 11 © Roy Ruckdeschel 1999
Chapter 12 © Martin Bloom 1999
Chapter 13 © Maurice Vanstone 1999

First published 1999

All rights reserved. No part of this publication may be
reproduced, stored in a retrieval system, transmitted or
utilized in any form or by any means, electronic,
mechanical, photocopying, recording or otherwise, without
permission in writing from the Publishers.

SAGE Publications Ltd
6 Bonhill Street
London EC2A 4PU

SAGE Publications Inc.
2455 Teller Road
Thousand Oaks, California 91320

SAGE Publications India Pvt Ltd
32, M-Block Market
Greater Kailash – I
New Delhi 110 048

British Library Cataloguing in Publication data

A catalogue record for this book is available from the
British Library

ISBN 0 7619 5792 8
ISBN 0 7619 5793 6 (pbk)

Library of Congress catalog card number available

Typeset by Photoprint, Torquay
Printed in Great Britain by Redwood Books, Trowbridge, Wiltshire

CONTENTS

NOTES ON CONTRIBUTORS

Martin Bloom obtained a PhD in social psychology from the University of Michigan, USA, in 1963 after receiving a diploma in social study from the University of Edinburgh, UK (1958). He has been teaching in schools of social work for most of his career. Among his publications are *Primary Prevention Practices* (1996); *Successful Ageing* (1997, with Klein); and *Evaluating Practice: Guidelines for the Accountable Professional* (3rd edn, forthcoming). His current preoccupations include primary prevention, single-system evaluation, and his grandchildren – not necessarily in the order presented.

Karen Dullea is a doctoral student in the Department of Social Policy and Social Work at the University of Warwick, UK. Karen has worked in the past in international development and in Canadian Aboriginal communities. Both contexts have caused her to question power-over approaches to social development that serve to oppress those already silenced by injustice and exploitation. She therefore firmly believes in learning from the struggle and strength of others, and in supporting them to locate and respond to their own steps in their own direction towards self-determination and self-reliance.

Clare Evans is a disabled person with training and experience in social work and education. She has worked in community development with a range of voluntary organizations. She founded and directed Wiltshire and Swindon Users' Network – an example of good practice in user participation – and is currently Director of the Leonard Cheshire Disabled People's Forum, a British national user empowerment project. She is involved in managing the national user-controlled 'Shaping Our Lives' research project on user-defined outcomes in social care, and is an honorary fellow of the National Institute of Social Work in London. She is author of several publications on user involvement.

Mike Fisher is Director of Research at the National Institute for Social Work (London), and a former social worker and social work lecturer. He

currently directs two Department of Health funded research programmes on community care and on the social care workforce.

Jan Fook is Professor of Social Work at Deakin University, Australia. Her
main interests include the application of critical theories to social work
practice, the use of critical reflection in social work education, and the
development of professional expertise. Her publications include *Radical
Casework* (1993) and *The Reflective Researcher* (1996). She is currently
working on a number of books relating to critical social work practice.

Nick Gould is Director of Studies for Social Research and Senior
Lecturer in Social Work at the University of Bath, UK. He has been a
social work practitioner in local authority and forensic settings, and
maintains an involvement in mental health practice. He received a PhD
from the University of Bath and has current research interests in professional learning, information management and qualitative methodologies. Recent co-edited publications include *Reflective Learning for Social
Work* (1996) and *Effective Policy, Planning and Implementation: Information
Management for Social Services* (1997).

Beth Humphries has been in social work and social work education for
more than 20 years. She was a social worker in Northern Ireland,
Scotland and England. She carried out her doctoral research at Edinburgh University, and has taught social work in Newcastle upon Tyne,
Liverpool, and currently at Manchester Metropolitan University, UK. She
is a principal lecturer in the Department of Applied Community Studies,
with responsibility for research degrees co-ordination. Beth is co-editor
(with Carole Truman) of *Rethinking Social Research* (1994), and (with
Carole Truman and Donna Mertens) of *Research in an Unequal World*
(1999).

Pat Le Riche is a Lecturer in Social Work at Goldsmiths College,
University of London, UK. She has a PhD from the University of Bristol
and has worked in a range of social work agencies. Her teaching
experience includes working in a number of different roles within the
Open University and lecturing at the University of Kent at Canterbury.
Her work on developing practice models of observation undertaken with
Karen Tanner has resulted in several articles and a jointly edited book,
Observation and its Application to Social Work: Rather like Breathing (1998).

Joyce Lishman is Professor and Head of the School of Applied Social
Studies at the Robert Gordon University, Aberdeen, UK. Her practice
experience is with children and adolescents and their families and as a
Malcolm Sargent social worker with children with cancer and leukaemia
and their families. Her research has primarily been on client perceptions
of social work and the analysis of social workers' interviewing behaviour

and effectiveness. She was editor of the *Research Highlights in Social Work* series, including number 8, *Evaluation* (1984), and is currently general editor of the series.

Ruth R. Martin, MSW, PhD, is Professor and Associate Dean, University of Connecticut, School of Social Work, West Hartford, USA. Her practice experience includes work in family agencies, psychiatric and correction institutions and public schools. She teaches qualitative oral history research methods and their relationship to social work practice. The author of *Oral History in Social Work: Research, Assessment and Intervention* (1995), she is currently editing an oral history of the University of Connecticut School of Social Work (1998), and is writing a memoir. She has written several chapters, articles and monographs and made numerous presentations on the topic of oral history, its process, method and practice.

Audrey Mullender is Professor in Social Work at the University of Warwick, UK. She has produced over 70 publications in the social work field, including seven books, and is currently editor of the *British Journal of Social Work*. She is joint author of a research textbook (*Applied Research for Better Practice*, 1992, with Angela Everitt, Pauline Hardiker and Jane Littlewood), which highlights the value base of research and the scope for involving research 'subjects' in research design, conduct and dissemination. She has special interests in empowerment practice (explored in her joint book with David Ward, *Self-Directed Groupwork: Users Take Action for Empowerment*, 1991) and in gender issues (for example *Rethinking Domestic Violence*, 1996).

Associate Professor **Robyn Munford** is Head of the School of Policy Studies and Social Work at Massey University, Palmerston North, New Zealand. Robyn is currently involved in a research project (funded by a government social science foundation) which focuses on family well-being. She has recently completed (with Jackie Sanders) research on an agency providing family support services. This research examined the achievement of positive change and intervention strategies utilized by family support workers. Robyn teaches at the undergraduate and postgraduate level in a range of fields including: community development, feminism and social work, theory and practice in social work, research methods, disability studies and group work.

William J. Reid, DSW, is Distinguished Professor at the School of Social Welfare, University at Albany, State University of New York, USA, where he teaches research methods and clinical practice and chairs the PhD programme. He is the author or editor of 17 books on clinical practice and research. His most recent book (with Anne E. Fortune) is *Research in Social Work* (3rd edn, 1998).

Roy Ruckdeschel is a Professor of Social Work in the School of Social Service at St Louis University, USA. His academic training has been in both sociology and social work. Roy Ruckdeschel was an early advocate of the use of qualitative research methods in social work and has published a number of articles on this subject. His current research focus is on the application of qualitative methods to the evaluation of social work practice. He is also exploring ways in which computer technology can be used to facilitate qualitative research.

Jackie Sanders is the Research Director for the Barnardo's Child and Family Research Centre, New Zealand. Jackie has extensive management experience in the voluntary welfare sector, and in the provision of supportive and early childhood services to families in New Zealand. She is currently involved in several research projects which have children and families as their focus. The projects include research into the factors which were associated with positive change by families participating in a family support agency, and research into the factors associated with family well-being. The latter includes a specific focus upon the meanings and experiences of children in relation to family well-being. These research programmes have been funded by a government social science foundation.

Ian Shaw is a member of the Cardiff School of Social Sciences, Cardiff University, UK, where he teaches social work practice, evaluation, qualitative research methodology, and information technology. His research is in the fields of qualitative evaluation, homelessness, and children's involvement in prostitution. He is engaged in the development of computer assisted learning for social work. His recent books include *Evaluating in Practice* (1996) and *Social Care and Housing* (1998, with Susan Lambert and David Clapham). He has completed a methodology text on *Qualitative Evaluation* (1999)

Karen Tanner is a Lecturer in Social Work at Goldsmiths College, University of London, UK. She has practice experience in child protection and has worked with children suffering from life-threatening illnesses. She has a particular interest in child observation and is both a teacher and researcher in this area. Her work on developing practice models of observation undertaken with Pat Le Riche has resulted in several articles and a jointly edited book, *Observation and its Application to Social Work: Rather like Breathing* (1998)

Maurice Vanstone is a Lecturer in the School of Social Sciences and International Development at Swansea University, UK. He has also been a practitioner and manager in the probation service. He has researched and published widely on criminal justice issues, and in particular on cognitive behavioural work with offenders, probation day centres, voluntary prison aftercare, and sex offenders. He is joint author, with Professors Peter Raynor and David Smith, of *Effective Probation Practice* (1994); editor, with Mark Drakeford, of *Beyond Offending Behaviour* (1996); and co-author, with Matthew Colton, of *Betrayal of Trust* (1996). He is currently researching the history of probation practice methods.

Pamela Zettergren, MSW, is a doctoral student at the School of Social Welfare, the University at Albany, the State University of New York, USA. Her Bachelor's degree is in psychology; she graduated *summa cum laude* with departmental honours. Her experience of research includes work at the Social Phobia Clinic and on the Task Planner Project, both at the University at Albany. Her practice experience includes work with victims of domestic violence and with individuals diagnosed as mentally ill and chemically dependent.

1

INTRODUCTION

Joyce Lishman

Evaluation must be an integral dimension of social work and social care practice. While historically, evaluating practice has been problematic in social work, and the gap between direct practice and service provision, and research and evaluation continues to exist, we believe there are strong, if not imperative reasons why we should engage in the evaluation of both our practice and our service delivery. 'Evaluation examines our effectiveness and can help us to improve it, can increase our accountability to users and clients, develops our knowledge and identifies gaps in knowledge, and helps us develop new models of practice and service delivery' (Lishman, 1998: 101). Shaw (1996: 184) argues further that

> Evaluating in practice is not limited to determining whether social work is effective, but must be a means of empowerment and social change. . . . Evaluating in practice challenges social work to new understandings and new methodology. It recognizes throughout the significance of social workers' present evaluating as-it-is practices. More importantly, it holds the promise of keeping social work honest.

The contributors to this volume argue that it is both necessary and possible to maintain a commitment both to good practice and to rigour and conceptualization and indeed, that each enhances the other. While programme service evaluation and evaluation *about* social work are necessary for service development, they have often suppressed awareness of the necessity of evaluation as a part of practice, in a self-critical reflexive appraisal of process and outcome. We do not question that evaluation is essential as part of accountability to users and clients, and is required by the current culture and context of managerial and efficiency savings (Banks, 1995; Sheppard, 1995; Vanstone, 1995). However, the contributors address a rather different argument. They advocate and elaborate the importance of developing evaluation as an integral part of a professional commitment to social work. Our collective aspiration is to provide benchmark essays on evaluating as a dimension of direct practice both for and with service users. We invite our readers, whether students, academics, practitioners, project or service managers, researchers or senior managers to examine and develop that commitment.

What do we mean by evaluation? To evaluate is defined in the *Oxford English Dictionary* (*OED*) as:

> To work out the value of;
> to find a numerical expression for.

In a sense these apparently simple definitions encapsulate a debate within social work about how we address the fundamental issues of whether our activity is effective, for whom, and in what ways. There has often been a polarized division between quantitative and qualitative evaluation methodology, associated with a recurring tension between evaluation viewed as measurement ('to find a numerical expression for') and evaluation as judgement of moral or political merit ('to work out the value of'). We believe such polarizations are unhelpful if we are to develop appropriate evaluation and methodology in social work and social care.

When examining what we mean by evaluation we need to distinguish between evaluation and research. The *OED* defines research as:

> An investigation directed to the discovery of some fact by careful study of a subject;
> a course of critical or scientific enquiry.

Again these apparently simple definitions are problematic in relation to research in social work. While the concept of fact as a universal, objective truth has been challenged in the natural sciences (Popper, 1969), it is yet more problematic in the social sciences and social work, where individuals' perceptions, judgements, interpretations and meanings are valid and critical arenas of research.

The second part of the *OED* definition compresses debates found in both social work *research* and *evaluation*. A division between qualitative and pluralistic 'critical' inquiry (often the province of practitioners) and quantitative experimental research 'scientific' inquiry (carried out by academic researchers) is not helpful.

Research relevant to social work asks relatively broad questions about, for example, the origins and generation of social problems, the relationship of social class to life chances in health, employment and education, and the impact of structural characteristics (poverty, gender, ethnicity, disability and age) on access to and quality of service provision. Such research findings demonstrate the effect of structural characteristics on individual problems presenting to social work in child care, mental health, work with older people, and criminal justice. A weakness of such research for an individual practitioner is that the findings are probabilistic and do not demonstrate a necessary relationship, at an individual level, between structural characteristics and life chances and outcomes.

Research has frequently addressed the question of how social work provision may lead to more effective outcomes. In British child care, for example, the 'Looking After Children: Good Parenting, Good Outcomes' project (Scottish Office, 1997; Ward, 1995) uses child care research to inform assessment and good practice with children in care. In criminal justice McGuire (1995) demonstrated what kinds of work were most likely to be effective in reducing the risk of reoffending (Smith, 1998). However, as with survey-based research, research on effectiveness leads to conclusions which are about probabilities and this is problematic for the individual practitioner faced with decisions about risk prediction in relation to an individual user or client.

Research of this kind appears to be interlinked with, if not indistinguishable from evaluation. How may we separate them? In this volume Evans and Fisher draw a useful working distinction between research and evaluation. 'We see evaluation as in greater use amongst professional staff seeking to monitor the effectiveness of specific services in meeting their prescribed goals.' In contrast they take the term 'research' to mean the capacity of user inquiry to engage in conceptual exploration and theory development.

More generally the research/evaluation boundaries in this volume appear blurred. Reid and Zettergren locate empirical practice in the context of 'research methods' and a scientific mindset, but argue that research methods are part of case monitoring and evaluation, and of programme evaluation. In Chapter 2, Shaw, in addressing the distinction between research and evaluation, argues that the boundaries are indistinct and the ranges of methods overlap. He concludes: 'There are some methodological activities that are likely to be used mainly in research, some mainly in evaluation, and others in evaluating-in-practice. But some methods are used by practitioners in all three contexts.'

We disagree with those commentators who separate evaluation and research on methodological, discipline or professional grounds. Wherein, then, lies the distinctiveness of evaluation? In this volume the contributors focus on evaluation, which encompasses the examination (albeit tentative) of how effective social work or care intervention is for users – both clients and carers. Such examination/evaluation needs to take account of the contextual boundaries: legal, political, social and economic. Evaluation has to be set within a context of recognition of the roles and responsibilities of, and the resources available to, social workers and those engaged in the provision of social care.

However, evaluation is not simply about effectiveness of outcomes, with all the confounding variables and caveats identified. It must also encompass a developing understanding of how social workers themselves evaluate their practice (Shaw, 1996). Furthermore, evaluation cannot be confined within a model of resource accountability. It must address practice and process evaluation including needs assessment, reflection on and evaluation of process, empirically led theorizing about practice, and evaluation which leads to critiques of the political context in which practice and programmes develop and are provided. All of these are dealt with in this book.

We have argued that evaluation is an integral part of professional responsibility, accountability and development. In addition social work is increasingly subject to external review, inspection and audit.

> New managerialism in health and welfare has been accompanied, even strengthened by an array of what might be seen as research and development activities: monitoring, evaluation, inspection, performance review, output and outcome measurements and evidence based practice. (Everitt, 1998: 106)

Such developments tend to be externally imposed and based more on the requirements of managerial control and less on the professional responsibility to evaluate practice and policy and thereby increase their effectiveness.

We acknowledge the requirements of external audit and accountability, while maintaining a critical stance in relation to the effectiveness of audit and quality assurance (Adams, 1998). More importantly in social work and social care we need to own evaluation as part of direct practice and service provision, and to examine from within the effectiveness of what we do. We need to review and question both the value base and the methods of assessment and intervention in social work and social care, evaluate the effectiveness of our outcomes, and draw on wider evidence from evaluation and research about effective practice and service provision. As part of evaluation in practice we need to refer to and integrate techniques of reflective practice (Eraut, 1994; Schon, 1983, 1987).

To the editors and contributors to this volume the need for such evaluation seems self-evident. But evaluation in social work has enjoyed limited success, and despite established serious literature, the increase in evaluation journals and specialist postgraduate degrees in evaluation methodology, theorizing of evaluation in and for direct practice is weak. Why should this be so? It is possible to identify five reasons.

First, there has been a long-standing professional concern regarding the gap between research and social work. Proposed solutions such as curriculum changes or training in practitioner research skills affect only a minority of those involved in social work and social care. One reason for the gap between research and practice in social work and the health professions is the disparity of criteria of success between researcher and practitioner. The concerns raised by Davies a quarter of a century ago continue to have relevance in social work and health. He noted the emerging danger that caseworkers have to judge their practice by criteria selected by researchers and by cost conscious administrators and politicians (Davies, 1974). Practitioners may rightly be suspicious of research and evaluation if it is hijacked by political ideology and managerial control.

Secondly, evaluation in social work has sometimes been unhelpfully associated with sectional interests in terms of practice methods. For example, the benefits or otherwise of single-system designs are still the subject of lively debate, yet once evaluation becomes identified in the minds of practitioners with a particular practice stance it is unlikely to be accepted as part of the core of practice principles and methods.

Thirdly, evaluation interests have sometimes been pursued by different constituencies that appear ignorant of one another's existence. For example, while there would appear to be considerable potential for common ground between feminist evaluation and participatory forms of evaluation, feminist and participatory researchers rarely consult each other's work.

A fourth and rather different problem arises from responses to efforts to develop a theorized position regarding evaluation as part of direct, local practice. One major programme of work in this area has been carried out over three decades by Robert Stake (e.g. Stake 1991, 1994, 1995, 1997; Stake and Trumbull, 1982). His work on responsive evaluation, case study methodology, evaluation as service rather than critical analysis, his commitment to improving local practice, his work on stakeholder involvement, and his understanding of how case studies work in a complex world is highly relevant to social work evaluation. 'His arguments for case study methodology are complex, sophisticated and subtle – far more so than he is generally given credit for' (Shadish et al., 1990: 272). Yet most social workers seem unaware of the work of Stake, and of other evaluation theorists whose work is drawn on by Shaw in Chapter 2 of this volume.

Finally, evaluation of direct practice has suffered because it has not been seen as a professional competence in social work education. Even when a 'strong' position has been taken, it tends to become either a container for hermeneutic debates on just what is required to 'apply' the regulation (as in the case of the Council for Social Work Evaluation requirements), or it asks for what cannot be delivered, because it has no 'teeth'. Such requirements then rapidly become toned down to a more safe position, as in the case of the British rules and requirements for social work training (CCETSW, 1989, 1995).

There is an almost complete absence of theorizing by social workers on direct practice evaluation, as a result of these factors. This contrasts unhappily with the relatively rich base in social work of theorizing on policy and practice issues.

Almost all of the more general evaluation theorists have developed their work from an education background, and, as some of their number rightly complain, the constituent traditions within evaluation remain mutually insulated, and evaluators from within education tend to ignore work done in other disciplines (Cronbach et al., 1980). One consequence of this is that social work commentators are largely ignorant of the work done by several of the major evaluation theorists. Within the UK the work on the teacher as researcher identified mainly with the Centre for Applied Research in Education (CARE) at the University of East Anglia has a wide range of parallels in social work. Yet despite an extensive case-based literature this work is almost entirely unknown or ignored by social work practitioners and evaluators.

Historically, the extensive, if now rather neglected, evaluation of psychotherapy and social work in the period from 1945 to the mid-1960s led to few firm models for evaluation practice. Indeed early American evaluation studies reviewed by Fischer (1973), Mullen and Dumpson (1972) and Wood (1978) generally showed social work to have little positive effect for clients. What emerged from these early studies was that both practice theory and evaluation talked globally: the early studies asked 'Is Social Work [undefined] effective?' and the answer was no. Later evaluation studies asked the more specific question 'What kind of work, activity, or behaviour is effective for what client in what circumstances?'

After the early 1970s, while there continued to be problems in choosing appropriate methods of evaluation for social work, practice and methodology developed in parallel. A review of 18 controlled experimental studies of direct social work intervention pointed to the success of focused, time-limited methods with contract-based programmes and the use and adaptation of behavioural techniques (Reid and Hanrahan, 1981).

More recently, the empirical practice movement (which developed from the earlier identification of the relative success of time-limited, contract-based programmes) has provided an impressive body of work on its intellectual precedents, epistemological grounding and methodological repertoire (Bloom, Chapter 12 in this volume; Bloom et al., 1995; Reid, 1994 and Reed and Zettergren, Chapter 3 in this volume). In contrast Gould and Ruckdeschel identify in their chapters in this volume the increasing legitimization of qualitative methods in both social sciences and social work, and the theoretical underpinning of qualitative methodology. Humphries (Humphries and Truman, 1994; Humphries et al., 1998; and Chapter 7 in this volume) has developed the practice implications of a feminist evaluation research perspective. Mullender and Dullea (Chapter 5 in this volume) draw corresponding implications for evaluation from the broader literature on empowerment evaluation, and Fisher and Evans (Chapter 6) identify the practice implications of user-controlled research.

The field is developing but patchy – a position not dissimilar to that of nursing and the professions allied to medicine where a gap between research and practice also remains. Reasons for the lack of theorizing

about evaluation in social work may also apply to professional colleagues in health, although a further contributory factor may be the
influence of the medical profession (Rafferty and Traynor, 1997) which
sets the research priorities and the research paradigm of randomized
control trials, and remains less concerned to evaluate the broader experience of being a patient. It is interesting that in pharmacy research
contributing to evidence-based practice seems increasingly to include
patients' perceptions and views of their treatment (Cromarty, personal
communication, 1998).

We argue the necessity of evaluation in social work for service
effectiveness, responsiveness to users, and professional accountability.
We have suggested that theoretical approaches to evaluation are developing in social work in the countries represented by contributors to this
volume. Subsequent chapters address ways in which evaluation ought to
be an integral dimension of social work and social care practice. We
address a broad range of methodologies, including reviews of best
practice in Britain, North America and Australia, and engage in a critical
review of qualitative and quantitative approaches to evaluating.

Despite the weaknesses identified in the use and theorizing of evaluation in relation to social work and social care there has been a ground-
swell of interest in and development of the theoretical base of evaluation
in social work which this volume seeks to encapsulate. Many texts on
qualitative evaluation have been published, while the case for empirical
and quantitative methodology has been further developed.

Increasingly evaluation has been approached from a pluralistic perspective, using the concept of 'triangulation' (Denzin, 1989a, 1989b) and
seeking to utilize quantitative and qualitative approaches as appropriate.
Sherman and Reid (1994: 3) summarize the reasons for the growing use
of qualitative methodologies to complement and develop quantitative
evaluation.

> There was the recognition that the controlled and reductive procedures of
> quantitative research tended to selectively ignore much of the context of any
> study and thereby miss significant factors in the situation that more holistic
> qualitative observation and description might identify. There was also a
> recognition that the study and analysis of what goes on in the actual process of
> practice had been shortchanged in favour of measurable outcomes. Further, a
> need existed for more knowledge about the interactive and subjective experi-
> ence of the client in the clinical change process.

We have noted the ways in which external evaluations of social work
may be ideologically and politically driven. We recognize and indeed
applaud the overdue application to evaluation of concerns about
empowerment and participatory practice (see Dullea and Mullender,
Humphries, and Evans and Fisher in this volume). However, we are
concerned that there remain important weaknesses in the literature

which make it unlikely to have a far-reaching impact on the quality of practice.

There is a tendency for what have been called 'paradigm wars' to cloud a close assessment of the strengths and weaknesses of empirical and qualitative evaluation. Linked to a rigid defence of the paradigm stance and an equally unbending attack on alternative perspectives, this prevents a healthy and realistic assessment of the strengths and weaknesses of each methodology.

While there have been important developments within the empirical practice movement, these may have been at the expense of practice evaluation from the perspective of qualitative social science, with the costs identified by Sherman and Reid (1994).

Evaluation continues to be presented in the majority of the literature as something which is *applied to* practice rather than as a *direct dimension* of practice, and therefore there remains a gap, earlier identified, between practice and evaluation or research.

Finally, the language of discourse on evaluation has tended to distance it from the reality of everyday practice.

In this volume we attempt to address these concerns by presenting a healthy and realistic assessment of the strengths and weaknesses of both qualitative methodology and of the empirical practice movement, by examining evaluation as an integral dimension of practice, and by ensuring that the language of the debate is consistent with that of everyday practice. Each contributor was given the following guidelines:

- Contributors were asked to focus on evaluation as a *dimension of practice* rather than research/evaluation about practice.
- The book is about evaluation of the management and delivery of *social care* as well as direct practice in social work.
- While policy and programme evaluation are explicitly considered in some chapters, the central concern throughout should be *the implications of evaluation for practice delivery to service users* as well as professional accountability for effectiveness.
- Contributors were asked to set their conclusions in the context of the growth of the *performance culture, management culture* and *consumer accountability.*
- We asked contributors to develop a *cultural perspective* which was not blinkered by solely North American or British writing and experience.

Within these contextual constraints each contributor was asked to include a critical and reflexive assessment of the methodological position with which they are associated. We asked contributors to provide not a polemical assertion of the value of their position, but a critical account which acknowledges the challenge and contribution of competing methodologies. We are not sympathetic to evaluation debates conducted at the level of paradigm differences. But we are equally anxious to counter a premature, common denominator synthesis. We do not believe that social work will be advanced by mundane puzzle solving, but by the active, reflexive interplay of tenaciously held views. We did not wish to 'dumb down' any position represented. We also asked contributors to take not just an immediate perspective but to consider the overall gains and deficits of their approach in the medium term.

The volume begins by examining the broad theoretical, methodological and ethical frameworks of evaluation in social work and social care. In Chapter 2 Shaw introduces and critically evaluates the conceptual and theoretical base for the range of models of evaluation presented in this volume. In particular he draws on the literature from American evaluation theorists and from the field of education evaluation.

Reid and Zettergren then demonstrate the contribution of the empirical practice movement to social work's historical goal of creating a scientifically based profession but equally acknowledge its limitations. Perhaps its major value has been to strengthen the emphasis in social work education, training and practice on the use of evidence from research-based and validated intervention in practice. Such an emphasis is consistent with the current approach in the professions allied to medicine and in pharmacy, at least in Great Britain. Limitations of this approach are discussed, including the lack of attention to the richness of evidence derived from observation of the process. Further criticisms identified in this chapter relate to the limitations of evidence of effectiveness of empirical practice, its presumed theoretical neutrality, and its concept of accountability.

Gould examines critically the development of qualitative and reflective approaches to evaluation in Chapter 4. We have already acknowledged some of the gaps within empirical/quantitative-based methodologies, and the potential contribution of qualitative approaches to a more pluralistic evaluation of social work and social care. Gould addresses the gap between research and practice by demonstrating the synergy between social work practice as a 'form of qualitative enquiry, knowledge building and evaluation' and qualitative evaluation methodology. He argues that a qualitative methodology is essentially pluralistic and reflexive, that it makes a key contribution to empirical knowledge, but that its persuasiveness in contributing to policy making and choices needs to be enhanced.

In Chapter 5 Dullea and Mullender examine a different but potentially complementary strand in evaluation: the concept of participatory, bottom-up evaluation. Participatory evaluation sees individuals as the experts in their own lives and in the evaluation of the services they receive. This contrasts with the reflective practice perspective that the practitioner is the expert in the evaluation of practice, and with the empirical movement which has tended to emphasize researcher expertise through the measurement of behavioural and cognitive outcomes. The literature on participatory research argues that every marginalized group is now asking questions about policy, service delivery and practice which practitioners need to address in evaluating and informing their practice.

The field of disability politics research and service provision is an exemplar of an empowering and participatory coalition of researchers, activists and other users. Shakespeare (1996), Oliver (1990) and Morris (1991) show the way in which disability is construed as a personal problem, disabled people are pathologized, and services provided within this framework. As a result of critiques of research such as those by Oliver and Morris we have begun to see the development of social theories of disability and social policy.

From Chapter 6 onwards we provide examples of ways of evaluating practice of the kind we have advocated here. Evans and Fisher, in Chapter 6, consider the use and potential of user-controlled research. While based in the field of disability it addresses issues of power and control that have relevance to other aspects of community care, and indeed to work with criminal justice and child care. Humphries, in examining the role of feminist evaluation (Chapter 7), notes the danger that it will become one method of evaluation rather than underpinning and contributing to a range of evaluation methods. The same caveat applies to user-controlled research.

Both chapters emphasize the crucial importance of qualitative data, for example survey data about disability and employment and about women's subordination in economic activity (including part-time work and sex segregation). Both also stress the need to evaluate the experience and knowledge of users and clients and are critical of the scientific and technocratic rationality which excludes subjective experience and is easily hijacked by ideological and political rhetoric.

Chapters 8–10 consider rather more specific developments in research methods in social work evaluation. Martin explores the role of shared reflection on people's histories, reminiscence and recollection (an important component of social work) in evaluative practice. Tanner and Le Riche explore the use of observation in social work and social care. They stress the potentially oppressive nature of evaluation, as do Dullea and Mullender, Evans and Fisher, and Humphries. In particular they argue that differences in race, gender, class, sexuality and physical ability affect the power debates and discussion in evaluating practice.

Fook, Munford and Sanders examine interviewing, a core social work activity. They question the current obsession with measuring outcomes by quantitative methods and analyse the weaknesses of the contract culture with which this has become associated. They argue for the richness of qualitative methodologies and their value in measuring social services' responsibility rather than accountability.

Chapters 11–13 address the issues of evaluating outcomes of social work by discrete methods. Ruckdeschel, in common with Martin, Tanner and Le Riche, and Fook and colleagues, emphasizes the value of qualitative evaluation and the importance of understanding the richness of the data in interviews and in the voices heard and not heard in research and practice. He argues that the narrative mode is different from but as significant as the scientific or paradigmatic mode.

Bloom reviews the use of single-system designs and their relevance to individual practice, family work and service delivery. He addresses ethical concerns about client empowerment and demonstrates that in single-system design clients are involved in each step of the evaluation. Vanstone considers evaluations of the use of behavioural and cognitive interventions, specifically in relation to criminal justice and the development of evidence-based practice. He develops the argument that evaluation is in itself a critical and inseparable part of being an effective practitioner. He stresses the positive effects of cognitive behavioural work and the *What Works* evaluation literature (McGuire, 1995), but argues that this approach has minimized the impact in criminal justice of structural problems of poverty and unemployment on offending. Social work effectiveness has to be evaluated, as we have argued, within the constraints of structural components of individual problems.

The chapters in this volume represent diverse constituencies within the evaluation process and a wide range of methodologies and theoretical underpinnings. The stakeholders are users, practitioners, managers, policy makers, researchers and government. Top down research broadly reflects agendas of government and policy makers. Researchers and managers occupy a middle ground, responding to dictates from above but also asking questions about effectiveness from the outside. Practitioners, dealing with the mess of everyday life and the critical reports from official inspection processes and the press, may feel that evaluation and research is totally divorced from their daily experience of trying to provide services to clients, users and the courts, with inadequate staffing and resources. Users may see evaluation as dictated by political ideology or professional defensiveness.

In this volume we try to address honestly the different evaluation agendas, at least those of researchers, managers, practitioners and users. Some contributors argue for an integration of methodologies, the pluralistic use of methods, and an appropriate balance of quantitative and qualitative methodologies. Others are persuaded that the interests of social work, and more especially of those who are on the receiving end of social work services, are better served by some evaluation perspectives than by others. But all share a commitment to self-critical listening, reflexivity, mutual trust, and an acknowledgement that the problems associated with their position counterbalance the promises. We invite the judgement of readers, social workers, managers, policy makers and academics as to whether we have fairly reviewed the theoretical issues and practice implications relating to social work evaluation. We hope that readers will be encouraged and enabled to adapt and apply the methodologies analysed here to their own practice and service delivery, or to promote the overall stance developed in this book in teaching at all levels. Most importantly we hope that this text will provide some underpinning for evaluative, research-minded and evidence-based social work beyond the millennium.

References

Adams, R. (1998) *Quality Social Work*. London: Macmillan.
Banks, S. (1995) *Ethics and Values in Social Work*. London: Macmillan.
Bloom, M., Fischer, J. and Orme, J. (1995) *Evaluating Practice: Guidelines for the Accountable Professional*. Boston: Allyn & Bacon.
CCETSW (1989) *DipSW Rules and Requirements for the Diploma in Social Work*. London: Central Council for Education and Training in Social Work.
CCETSW (1995) *Assuring Quality in the Diploma in Social Work 1: Rules and Requirements for the DipSW*. London: Central Council for Education and Training in Social Work.
Cronbach, L., Ambron, S., Dornbusch, S., Hess, R., Hornik, R., Phillips, D., Walker, D. and Weiner, S. (1980) *Towards Reform of Program Evaluation*. San Francisco: Jossey-Bass.
Davies, M. (1974) 'The current status of social work research', *British Journal of Social Work*, 4 (3): 281–303.
Denzin, N.K. (1989a) *Interpretative Interactionism*. Newbury Park, CA: Sage.
Denzin, N.K. (1989b) *The Research Act*, 3rd edn. Englewood Cliffs, NJ: Prentice-Hall.
Eraut, M. (1994) *Developing Professional Knowledge and Competence*. London: Falmer Press.
Everitt, A. (1998) 'Research and development in social work', in R. Adams, L. Dominelli and M. Payne (eds), *Social Work: Themes, Issues and Critical Debates*. London: Macmillan.
Fischer, J. (1973) 'Is casework effective? A review', *Social Work*, 18 (1): 5–20.
Humphries, B. and Truman, C. (1994) *Re-thinking Social Research*. Aldershot: Avebury.
Humphries, B., Truman, C. and Mertens, D. (1998) *Research in an Unequal World*. Aldershot: Avebury.
Lishman, J. (1998) 'Personal and Professional Development', in R. Adams, L. Dominelli and M. Payne (eds), *Social Work: Themes, Issues and Critical Debates*. London: Macmillan.
McGuire, J. (ed.) (1995) *What Works: Reducing Offending: Guidelines from Research and Practice*. Chichester: Wiley.
Morris, J. (1991) *Pride against Prejudice: Transforming Attitudes to Disability*. London: Women's Press.
Mullen, E.J. and Dumpson, J.R. (eds) (1972) *Evaluation of Social Intervention*. San Francisco: Jossey-Bass.
Oliver, M. (1990) *The Politics of Disablement: A Sociological Approach*. London: Macmillan.

Popper, K. (1969) *Conjectures and Refutations: The Growth of Scientific Knowledge*. London: Routledge & Kegan Paul.

Rafferty, A.M. and Traynor, M. (1997) 'Quantity and quality', in *Research Policy for Nursing Research*, 2 (1): 16–17.

Reid, W. (1994) 'The empirical practice movement', *Social Service Review*, 68 (2): 165–184.

Reid, W.J. and Hanrahan P. (1981) 'The effectiveness of social work: recent evidence', in E.M. Goldberg and N. Connelly (eds), *Evaluative Research in Social Care*. London: Policy Studies Institute/Heinemann.

Schon, D.A. (1983) *The Reflective Practitioner*. New York: Basic Books.

Schon, D.A. (1987) *Educating the Reflective Practitioner*. San Francisco: Jossey-Bass.

Scottish Office Home Department (1997) *Looking after Children: Good Parenting, Good Outcomes*. Edinburgh: Scottish Office.

Shadish, W., Cook, T. and Leviton, L. (1990) *Foundations of Program Evaluation: Theories of Practice*. Newbury Park, CA: Sage.

Shakespeare, T. (1996) 'Rules of engagement: doing disability research', *Disability and Society*, 11 (1): 115–119.

Shaw, I. (1996) *Evaluating in Practice*. Aldershot: Ashgate.

Sheppard, M. (1995) *Care Management and the New Social Work: A Critical Analysis*. London, Whiting and Birch.

Sherman, E. and Reid, W. (eds) (1994) *Qualitative Research in Social Work*. New York: Columbia University Press.

Smith, D. (1998) 'Social work with offenders', in R. Adams, L. Dominelli and M. Payne (eds), *Social Work: Themes, Issues and Critical Debates*. London: Macmillan.

Stake, R. (1991) 'Retrospective on "The Countenance of Educational Evaluation"', in M. McLaughlin and D. Phillips (eds), *Evaluation and Education at Quarter Century*. Chicago: Chicago University Press.

Stake, R. (1994) 'Case study', in N. Denzin and Y. Lincoln (eds), *Handbook of Qualitative Research*. Thousand Oaks, CA: Sage.

Stake, R. (1995) *The Art of Case Study Research*. Thousand Oaks, CA: Sage.

Stake, R. (1997) 'Advocacy: a necessary evil?' in E. Chelimsky and W. Shadish (eds), *Evaluation for the 21st Century*. Thousand Oaks, CA: Sage.

Stake, R. and Trumbull, D. (1982) 'Naturalistic generalizations', *Review Journal of Philosophy and Social Science*, 7 (1): 1–12.

Vanstone, M. (1995) 'Managerialism and the ethics of management', in R. Hugman and D. Smith (eds), *Ethical Issues in Social Work*. London: Routledge.

Ward, H. (1995) *Looking after Children: Research into Practice*. London: HMSO.

Wood, K.M. (1978) 'Casework effectiveness: a new look at the research evidence', *Social Work*, 23 (November): 437–459.

2

EVIDENCE FOR PRACTICE

Ian Shaw

Social workers act or decline to act, feel confident or uncertain that they have a sound basis for their actions and decisions, draw prescriptions or confess agnosticism, and all in the light (or gloom!) of the best evidence they can reasonably assemble. Large parts of that evidence are in the form of descriptions and inferences regarding service users, and about previous interventions by colleagues, present and past, other welfare agencies, schools, law enforcement agencies, families and carers, and so on. But what is the status of such evidence? Can social workers safely act on the assumption that it provides a good enough approximation to reality, which will transfer to similar new situations? Or should they remain deeply sceptical of all similar information on the grounds that it is the contingent, relative product of a unique local context, and may also represent the interests and constructions of the powerful?

There is a welcome vigour in current advocacy of the need to make evidence 'work' for social work practice. The very phrase, 'evidence-based practice' captures a confident belligerence, a tone of 'prove-it-or-else'. The language of goals, objectives, outcomes and effectiveness challenges reliance on sentimentality, opinion-based practice, intuition or lay knowledge. The phrase, along with its companion question, 'What works?', has gradually crept into official formulations of social work and social care.[1] Although medicine is sometimes seen as the model that aspirants should emulate, teaching, nursing, policing, prisons, pharmacy and probation work all have their performance measured against evidence-based criteria.

There are both broad-stream and more narrow-stream versions of evidence-based practice. The broad-stream version is mainly practice driven. It includes an emphasis on accountability, close working relationships between researchers and practitioners, a general obligation to ground practice judgements in evidence, and an explicit drawing on research findings to support assessment and planning in, for example, reports to courts or care management plans. It also includes a pro-gramme to ease access to data, and to promote the dissemination of research findings in understandable form, an orientation to outcome issues in practice, and a twin stress on feasible and incremental practice development. These commitments represent a majority position within social work education in America, Australia and Britain, and provide a basis for more general versions of empirical practice in the USA, and for organizational initiatives such as 'Research in Practice' in Britain.

The more focused, narrow-stream version of evidence-based practice is largely academically driven, and is associated with the scientific practi-tioner, empirical practice movement in the USA, and with some behaviourist evaluation. This more restricted use of the term 'evidence-based practice' includes the features of the broader stream, but in addition typically entails advocacy of particular methods of practice intervention (often cognitive or behaviourally based) and on occasion some negativity towards qualitative evaluation methodology. The lit-erature is extensive, and is associated with the names of Scott Briar and Ed Thomas, through to the work of Martin Bloom, Fischer, Hudson and Tripodi, and more recently with Blythe and Thyer. Reid has been both a commentator on and contributor to aspects of the empirical practice movement. Robert Ross in Canada and McGuire, Sheldon and MacDonald in Britain have enriched this tradition. Reid and Zettergren, Bloom, and Vanstone review different aspects of these developments in this volume. Several of the discussions in this volume are relevant to developments in practitioner research, where there has been parallel but distinct work in Britain, America, Australia and Canada.

A different but equally enthusiastic commitment to rigour and evi-dence in social work is represented by the case for reflective practice. Donald Schon is perhaps the most well known name in this field, since his belated discovery by social work academics early in the 1990s (Schon, 1983, 1992, 1995). In addition, Elliot Eisner's work has been especially influential in education (Eisner, 1988, 1991a, 1991b), but has yet to be transferred to social work, and Heron's work has had influence in the counselling field (for example, Heron, 1996). In Britain, Reason has argued for and written extensively on participatory inquiry and 'new paradigm research' (Reason, 1988, 1994; Reason and Rowan, 1981), and has had some influence on critical theory through his earlier writing (Lather, 1991). Reason's work has also influenced a broader range of occupations including the professions associated with medicine. The implications of these writings for social work practice and research have been reviewed (Fook, 1996; Gould and Taylor, 1996; Mullen and Hess, 1995). England's earlier and original work – yet to be developed – illustrated the considerable potential of such approaches (England, 1986). Gould, Fook et al. and Ruckdeschel explore relective practice in this volume.

The progress and problems associated with evidence-based practice and reflective inquiry and practice have been reviewed from various positions, but their very difference from one another helpfully problematizes the notion of evidence in two ways. First, evidence-based practice and reflective inquiry both help promote the important assumption that some central issues of evidence are not special to social work but are shared by superficially very different professions. Evidence-based practice promotes this assumption by insistently asking the same core questions of all and sundry, and reflective inquiry promotes the assumption through a more inductive, bottom-up approach to understanding practice, shorn in part of prior assumptions that we already know what a given profession is really about. Social work needs to take this awareness much further. Secondly, reflective inquiry and evidence-based practice both force attention towards direct practice rather than broader programme evaluation strategies and agendas, which have dominated the theorizing of evaluation.

To evidence-based practice and reflective inquiry we need to add a third broad stance in relation to evaluation, represented by what is variously described as critical, empowerment or emancipatory evaluation. Social workers committed to empowerment models of evaluation are concerned less with the nature of the real world, and how we may know it, and more with their ideological stance. Such ideologically oriented evaluation includes neo-Marxist, most feminist, some participatory inquiry, and evaluation associated with the ideas of Paolo Freire. The chapters in this book by Reid and Zettergren, Gould, and Dullea and Mullender respond to each of these three broad stances in relation to evaluation.

The following chapters are planned as a multi-pronged response to the challenges facing evaluation which were outlined in the Introduction. We believe that debate and practice should be taken forward, but not by a lowest common denominator evaluation strategy, nor by the building of ever higher walls around our favoured battle lines. Rather, we need to proceed by a real if circumspect dialogue. This chapter briefly explores the background issues that shape debate and practice. They are posed, perhaps too simply, as a series of alternatives. Should evaluation be based on a particular worldview of evaluation practice, or on pragmatic, even opportunistic, initiatives? Where should we stand on the vexed issue of whether we can discover an objective, real picture of the world? Should evaluation be planned according to the demands of scientific rigour or practice relevance? How do we know if we are doing practice right? Are the results of evaluation research used through direct application to problems or through a more general process of enlightenment? How should our answers to these questions shape the methodology we use? In conclusion, we will risk guessing at the promising directions and likely dead ends for evaluation in practice near the turn of the century.

It is likely that practitioner readers of this chapter will have been educated, unwittingly for the most part, in an instrumental, scientific viewpoint. In addition, day to day practice is likely to be taken up with safe and quick administrative processes. Landing feet first in the language of paradigms, postpositivism, constructivism, and so on, could be read as academic escapism of the first water. I hope not. My personal agenda is to develop evaluation that is for and with service users, and that is both rigorous and practical (Shaw, 1996, 1997). In saying it must be practical, I echo the words of Schwab. 'I do *not* mean . . . the easily achieved, familiar goals which can be reached by familiar means', but refer to 'a complex discipline . . . concerned with choice and action' (Schwab, 1969: 1, 2).

The focus of this chapter is more broadly based than the following contributions, and is intended as an agenda of issues raised by evaluation of practice. I draw on two fields of literature in addition to direct writing on social work. These are the work of the major, mainly American, evaluation theorists, and the writing of those who have worked in the field of education evaluation. Social work has on the whole neglected both these sources of ideas and experience, and it is hoped that this chapter will begin to make up for this neglect. However, as a preamble to this discussion, a brief aside is needed on the relationship between research, evaluation, and everyday social work knowledge.

Evaluation, research and social work

Contributors to this book have written to a fairly focused brief, but they were given no definition of how evaluation should be understood in relation to either research or social work practice. Take the question of whether evaluation and research are the same or different activities. Strong views are expressed on either side of the question, and how evaluation is defined will telegraph the protagonists' answer in advance. The question can helpfully be clarified by asking it in different ways.[2]

1 *Can* research and evaluation be different?
2 *Should* evaluation and research be different?
3 *Is* evaluation different from research?

The first question is theoretical, the second one is normative, and the third is empirical.

Evaluation and research can often be distinguished only by general tendency and not by watertight categories. For example, *some* evaluation will involve theorizing and knowledge development (Greene, 1993), while probably *all* research will involve theorizing. Some evaluation will be focused on outcome measures, but we should not define evaluation in terms that necessitate an outcome orientation. Much evaluation will be focused on a programme or project, but to define evaluation in such a way as to preclude the evaluative dimension of professional practice illustrates one of the central problems addressed by this book. Furthermore, evaluation has fuzzy boundaries with policy research, and there will be substantially overlapping borders between evaluation and everyday discourse in social work. Evaluative *research*, evaluative *inquiry*, and evaluative *thinking* are different but not altogether dissimilar.

We live with ambiguity. Establishing hard and fast definitional boundaries has little to commend it. When it comes to methodologies, research and evaluation include a range of methods which overlap both with each other and with evaluative thinking in everyday practice. There are some methodological activities that are likely to be used mainly in research, some mainly in evaluation, and others in evaluating-in-practice. But some methods are used by practitioners in all three contexts.

Paradigms and pragmatism

'Paradigm' is a thorny word. Indeed, it has become a 'bucket word' (Popper) to hold undue diversity. If we take it in a general sense of 'a basic set of beliefs that guides action' (Guba, 1990: 17) we are only a little further forward. Even a mildly tendentious philosopher would have a field day with each of the five key words in this definition! Fortunately the particular question at issue is slightly more straightforward. If we take for a moment the distinction between quantitative and qualitative approaches to practice evaluation, is it the case that to be consistent, evaluators and practitioners must choose one or the other (Filstead, 1979)? Is there an inherent inconsistency in subscribing to the worldview of one approach but employing the methods of the other?

Hammersley distinguishes the elements of each pole as shown in Table 2.1 (Hammersley, 1992: Ch. 10).

Table 2.1   *Quantitative and qualitative paradigms*

	Quantitative	Qualitative
Data is	quantitative	qualitative
Fieldwork in	artificial settings	natural settings
Empirical focus is on	behaviour	meaning
Natural science model is	accepted	rejected
Analysis proceeds by	deduction	induction
Theorizing seeks	laws	patterns
Philosophy of	realism	idealism

Guba argues that all paradigms respond to three basic questions (Guba, 1990: 18):

- What is the nature of reality?
- What is the nature of the relationship between the knower (inquirer) and the known (or knowable)?
- How should the inquirer go about finding out knowledge?

We can discern four paradigm positions: positivism, postpositivism, critical evaluation, and constructivist evaluation. They correspond to the major developments in the philosophy of science. Each of these is present in social work evaluation and practice. For the *positivist*, 'the business of science is to discover the true nature of "reality" and how it "truly" works'. Positivism also has an objectivist epistemology, and the idea of an Archimedean point. Archimedes is said to have remarked that given a long enough lever and a place whereon he could stand, he could move the earth. 'Objectivity is the Archimedean point . . . that permits the inquirer to wrest nature's secrets without altering them in any way' (Guba, 1990: 19).

Despite claims to the contrary (for example by Everitt, 1996; Everitt et al., 1992), positivism has been in decline for at least 50 years. Social work attacks on fellow practitioners or academics as 'positivists' are generally ill-informed and damaging (Shaw, 1999). Indeed, it is difficult to find social work writers who believe there are absolute justifications of scientific assertions (although see Thyer, 1989, 1993). Phillips provides a lucid explanation of the reasons for the demise of positivism (Phillips, 1990). Although there are no *absolute* justifications, this does not mean there are *no* justifications. Yet while we may be warranted in holding particular views, we cannot assert that something is true, that our warrant is unchallengeable, or that it will for ever be warranted. This position is generally labelled *'postpositivist'*.[3]

The continuity between positivism and postpositivism should not be overemphasized. Phillips rightly insists, 'In no sense is [this] new philosophy of science . . . closely akin to positivism' (Phillips, 1990: 39). Postpositivist positions and those influenced by them (for example Reid and Zettergren in this volume), actively engage in partial trade-offs, of rigour to gain relevance, precision to gain richness, theoretical elegance to gain local applicability, and measures of outcomes to promote inquiry into process, meaning and local context.

Critical evaluation is a catch-all term to include neo-Marxist evaluation (Lather, 1991), some feminist positions (Dullea and Mullender, this volume; Humphries, this volume; Swigonski, 1993; Whitmore, 1990, 1994), the work of Paolo Freire, and some forms of participatory inquiry (Martin, 1994, 1996; Reason and Rowan, 1981). All approaches share an emphasis on the pervasiveness of values in practice. Critical evaluation takes a realist position, with the aim to eliminate false consciousness and energize and facilitate transformation. This is clearly expressed, for example, in feminist standpoint positions (Hartsock, 1983). Although there are instances of emancipatory *research*, full-blown critical evaluation positions are not common in social work evaluation (cf. Carr and Kemmis, 1986, for an influential example in the field of education).

The fourth paradigm, *constructivism*, is perhaps best known to social workers through Guba and Lincoln's book on *Fourth Generation Evaluation* (1989), but is also associated with the names of Smith and Schwandt. Schwandt seeks to recast evaluation in terms of practical acts of interpretation, often described for this reason as an interpretive or hermeneutic approach. He criticizes postpositivism on grounds of its alleged modernism.

> [We] resist three modernist tendencies: (1) . . . to conceive of knowledge only as the acquisition of power to control self, society and nature; (2) . . . to assume that method holds the key to knowledge; (3) . . . to define the individual knower as in complete control of self, nature and social arrangements. (Schwandt, 1997: 78)

The interpretive approach he advocates involves the positions

> (1) that the social world . . . can only be studied from a position of involvement 'within' it, instead of as an 'outsider'; (2) that knowledge of that world is practical-moral knowledge and does not depend upon justification or proof for its practical efficacy; (3) that we are not in an 'ownership' relation to such knowledge but we embody it as part of who and what we are. (1997: 75)

Constructivist evaluation involves emphases on the theory-ladenness of facts, the value-ladenness of facts, and the interactive nature of inquiry whereby the knower and the known are 'fused into a coherent whole' (Guba, 1990: 26). While a challenging variety of constructivist positions exists within social work and the disciplines on which it draws, the above quotations from Schwandt helpfully catch the recurrent motifs of paradigm-based constructivism. The position is gaining increasing voice in the evaluation journals, although these sources may perhaps be less influential with social workers in Britain than in the USA. The confessedly relativist position of writers such as Guba, Lincoln (1990), Smith (1993) and Schwandt poses special difficulties for social work practitioners and evaluators, deriving from the pressure on constructivist evaluators to seek guidelines and support for their work which will give it credibility and trustworthiness.

> Evaluators sense particular pressure to invoke such procedures because the contexts of program evaluation continue to demand assurances of methodological quality and data integrity in evaluative work. This work can make no contributions to social policy and program decision making unless it is perceived as credible and trustworthy. (Greene, 1994: 537)

To return to our initial questions, is it the case that to be consistent, evaluators and practitioners must choose one paradigm? Is there an inherent inconsistency in subscribing to the worldview of one approach but employing the methods of the other? Lincoln answers eloquently in the affirmative.

> The adoption of a paradigm literally permeates every act even tangentially associated with inquiry, such that any consideration even remotely attached to inquiry processes demands rethinking to bring decisions into line with the worldview embodied in the paradigm itself. (Lincoln, 1990: 81)

However, loud answers in the negative can be heard from different quarters. The mainstream stance of evaluation theorists is a mixture of postpositivist and pragmatic positions (Cook, 1985; Patton, 1990; Reichardt and Cook, 1979; Scriven, 1997; Shadish, 1995). Ethnographers have often taken a similar line. Hammersley, for instance, argues that for each of the seven elements of the divide between qualitative and quantitative methods (see Table 2.1), characteristics of each paradigm element can always be identified in examples of research conducted under the alternative paradigm.

Various kinds of *pragmatism* have been put forward by social work evaluators and practitioners as an alternative to paradigm thinking. The evaluation theorist whose work is perhaps most well known within social work puts the case for a 'paradigm of choices':

> A paradigm of choices rejects methodological orthodoxy in favour of *methodological appropriateness* as the primary criterion for judging methodological quality. (Patton, 1990: 38–39)

Pragmatism is attractive for a variety of reasons, and makes for some unexpected bedfellows. We can distinguish between *methodological pragmatism* and *philosophical pragmatism*. Methodological pragmatism rests on an impatience with philosophy and an emphasis on real world evaluation and practice, and it is claimed that methods (of evaluation or social work) can be separated from the epistemology out of which they have emerged. The emphasis is thus on practical utility and the credibility of the methods used.

In Britain a pragmatic evaluation stance has been carefully established through the work of Cheetham, Fuller and colleagues at the Centre for Social Work Research at Stirling University (Cheetham, 1998; Fuller and Petch, 1995). The guidelines and regulations for social work education in perhaps all the English-speaking countries take a broadly pragmatic stance, despite lobbying from specific evaluation constituencies. Evaluation with a strong action dimension also tends to take a pragmatic position on methodology. This is partly because ends are often regarded as more important than methodological means, and is partly due to the impatience with philosophizing that I mentioned a moment ago. For those who hold this position, 'the specific methodology employed is less important than the overall approach to action and research' (Kelly, 1985: 144).

Methodological pragmatism typically leads to a rejection of both epistemological and methodological 'purism', a contentment with a 'good enough' methodology, and a pluralist approach to specific methods. Thus, in complaining about the 'philosophically besotted', Scriven says

> it is better to build on what might conceivably be sand . . . than not to build at all. . . . It is a waste of time to try to solve the problems of epistemology without getting on with the job. (Scriven, 1997: 478, 479)

Reid argues similarly if more temperately for social work:

> Irreconcilable conflicts may indeed exist in the discourse of philosophers, but their perspectives are not essential to the task of resolving differences and building consensus in the practical worlds of social work. (Reid, 1994: 478)

Reid wants to 'redefine the nature of the mainstream so that qualitative methodology is part of it, not apart from it. . . . Neither method is inherently superior to the other, but rather each provides the researcher with different tools of inquiry' (1994: 477).

There are overlapping concerns between methodological pragmatism and *philosophical pragmatism*. However, there are important differences. Social work has too often been guilty of naïve pragmatism of the variety that says, 'if it works, it's true'. Philosophical pragmatism draws especially on the work of American philosophers, and has been invigorated by recent work by Richard Rorty, whose arguments are beginning to exercise a growing influence on social work thinking and practice (Rorty, 1979, 1991).

> When confronted with a knowledge claim the pragmatist is less concerned with whether it is right and asks instead, 'What would it be like to believe that?' 'What would happen if I did?' 'What would I be committing myself to?' . . . This shifts the focus of inquiry from verification and the appeal to method, to practice and an appeal to deliberation and conversation. (Schwandt, 1993: 18)

Reid applies some of these ideas in a provisional way to social work. He believes such a stance 'will take us further than grand epistemologies that trade in abstract assertions about Truth, Reality and so on', and locates himself 'within the tradition of American pragmatism, especially as it has been set forth in the writings of Pierce, James, Dewey and Rorty' (Reid, 1994: 472). He and Zettergren (this volume) develop the interesting idea of empirical practice as a *perspective* which allows an interchange with humanist and advocacy approaches.

Pragmatic arguments have also been used within some work on feminist postmodernism – one of the unexpected bedfellows referred to earlier. For example, given the radical's fear that pragmatism tends to political complacency (its 'orientation to decision making and hence to management', Greene, 1994, 532–533), it is interesting to observe Rorty's argument for a radical pragmatism (Rorty, 1991; cf. McLennan, 1995).

The application of more careful ideas of pragmatism to social work evaluation and practice is still in its infancy. But it has the potential to critically integrate aspects of postpositivist, constructivist and empowerment approaches to evaluation. My own position is a combination of a strong version of the *fallible* realism of postpositivism, the *constructed* character of reality, and the central role of political and personal *interests*. On paradigms, my premise is that 'the relationship between paradigms and methods is an empirical question' (Pitman and Maxwell, 1992: 732). Yet I think that Hammersley overstates the weakness of the relationship between epistemology, values and methods. People's actions, in evaluation as much as in any other activity, *are* shaped by values and worldviews, and paradigm positions do *not* inevitably tend to the intolerance suspected by Atkinson and colleagues (Atkinson et al., 1988). As early an advocate of paradigms as Filstead conceded that 'the middle ground of blending the assets of both approaches throughout an evaluation is optimal', and as enthusiastic a proponent as Guba allows there is now a 'more ecumenical stance' in the shared acknowledgement that both verification and discovery methods can go on in all paradigms (Filstead, 1979: 43; Guba, 1990: 23). Writing from a postpositivist position, Reichardt and Cook are probably safe to stop at the point that 'paradigms are not the sole determinant of choice of methods', and to conclude there is a 'real but imperfect linkage between paradigm and method' (Reichardt and Cook, 1979: 16).

The previous paragraphs have relevance to the evaluation of direct practice – to choices of methods of intervention, the criteria we draw on in judging whether we have done well in day to day practice, the choice of method for evaluation, even at the small scale level of personal practice, and for developing a rationale for feminist evaluation. In discussing paradigmatic approaches we have touched on issues of realism and relativism, trade-offs between relevance and rigour, and the uses of evaluation. This fairly extended discussion of paradigms has signalled the kinds of solution I am likely to suggest for each of these issues.

Realism and relativism

We opened the chapter with the dilemma of realism and relativism as it faces social workers in their daily practice. The problem runs through all social work and social care, and is not a special evaluation problem. Are practitioners working with fairly direct evidence of reality, relativist constructs, or the standpoints of the powerful? We will consider the first two alternatives – realism versus relativism – in this section of the chapter, and the third possibility when discussing validity and values. 'Realism', like 'paradigm', is a word that has attracted varied and differentiated meanings. Speaking of one variety of realism, Leplin wryly remarks that, 'Like the Equal Rights Movement, scientific realism is a majority position whose advocates are so divided as to appear a minority' (Leplin, 1984: 1).

Realism as applied to evaluation is usually assumed to demand an absolutist view of the role of evaluative inquiry, referred to as foundationalism. This involves a correspondence view of truth, that evaluation can represent realities independent of the inquiry process. In its strong, 'naïve' form, realism retains the positivist adherence to the role of observation as discloser of the true nature of reality, and a confidence in the objectivity of the evaluator. Strong versions of realism are present in some varieties of qualitative evaluation, as well as in positivist standpoints. Blumer and Harré are perhaps the best-known examples. For instance, Blumer argues that a constructivist view

> does not shift 'reality' . . . from the empirical world to the realm of imagery and conception. . . . [The] empirical world can 'talk back' to our picture of it or assertions about it – talk back in the sense of challenging and resisting, or not bending to, our images or conceptions of it. This resistance gives the empirical world an obdurate character that is the mark of reality. (Blumer, 1969: 22)

The counterpoint to a continuing commitment to a realist basis of evaluation is a radically relativist epistemology of evaluation, fashioned around assumptions that truth is a matter of consensus, facts do not have meaning except within some value framework, and causes and effects exist only in that they are imputed. Relativists believe that problems, findings and solutions from one context cannot be generalized to another. Evaluators are subjective partners with stakeholders in the literal creation of data, and act as orchestrators of a negotiation process. Hence, evaluation data have no special status, but represent simply another construction to be taken into account in the move to consensus. There are consequently multiple shapers of accountability, no one of which can be singled out for accountability (Guba and Lincoln, 1989; Rodwell and Woody, 1994).

The main criticisms of relativist evaluation are similar to those against social science relativism in general. It suffers from the well-known problem of being self-refuting, in that if it is true then it applies to itself. Truth is that which is believed to be true within some culture or community. It may therefore be regarded as true relative to that culture or framework of thinking, while it may properly be regarded as false from the perspective of a different culture. This can lead to stalemate, sometimes encountered in social work evaluation, where each side is able to claim that its views are 'true'. A particular problem connected with relativist evaluation is that constructions become divorced from any anchor point to structures and interests. They appear little more than personal, mental constructs, as when Guba concludes that 'realities exist in the form of multiple mental constructions. . . . It is the mind that is to be transformed, not the real world' (1990: 27). But reality is not simply and solely a mental product. It comprises social, collective acts, and these are material transactions with the world.

Relativism has also been troubled by practitioner struggles. Writing of qualitative evaluation Greene remarks that

> Many qualitative practitioners struggle with the dissonance invoked by the assumed mind-dependence of all social knowledge claims in the face of the contextual (as well as personal, ego-related) demands to 'get it right', to 'find out what's really going on in this setting'. (Greene, 1996: 280)

A critical or fallible realism is the stance of most contributors to this volume. In addition to those identified with the postpositivist position, and influential qualitative social scientists such as Blumer and Harré, it is also the position of the majority of evaluation theorists such as Scriven, Campbell, House, Cook, Shadish, and, with some ambiguity, Stake.

> The essence of this position is that, although a real world, driven by real natural causes, exists, it is impossible for humans truly to perceive it with their imperfect sensory and intellective mechanisms. (Cook and Campbell, 1979: 29)

A range of views co-exists within fallible realist evaluation. For example, some would be not very far from a strict positivist position in regard to their apparent belief that evaluation can provide an account closely approximating to reality. Others, such as the present writer, take the position that, while objectivity remains as a 'regulatory ideal' (Phillips, 1990: 43), evaluative processes and results are always significantly jeopardized by interests, the social location of the evaluator and powerful stakeholders, and the obdurate character of the world.

Such epistemological modesty does not necessarily lead to modest aspirations for social change. For example, Campbell's strong fallibilism is harnessed to a bold vision of an experimenting society, and from within social work Reid has asked, 'Is it better to make limited but well documented progress or to work toward more important goals with less certainty of what we have attained?' (Reid, 1988: 45). Yet fallible realist evaluators are less likely to pronounce confidently that they have got it right. They are likely to concur with Phillips when he admits that 'the objectivity of an inquiry does not guarantee its truth . . . *nothing* can guarantee that we have reached the truth' (Phillips, 1990: 43).[4]

Rigour or relevance?

Reid's choice between limited and well-documented goals, or working towards more important goals with less certainty, illustrates one of the central 'trade-offs' that appear to face practitioners and evaluators. Some have argued for objectivity and validity as the highest imperatives of the evaluator. For the outside evaluator, 'both distancing and objectivity remain correct and frequently achievable ideals' (Scriven, 1997: 483). Scriven's arguments for remaining distant, undertaking goal-free evaluation, the priority of summative evaluation over formative evaluation, and for dismissing 'so-called participatory design' as 'about as sloppy as one can get, short of participatory authoring of the final report' (1997: 486), are unlikely to find favour with most practitioners. I consider them either wrong-headed or other-worldly. But they remain important strands in the argument for evaluative rigour.

However, the wind has been blowing strongly in the direction of addressing issues of relevance as well as, and in some cases instead of, traditional ideas of rigour. Ironically it was the honest doubting of writers such as Campbell that opened the way for such changes. For example, writing in 1974 when 'many of our ablest and most dedicated graduate students are increasingly opting for the qualitative, humanistic mode', he expounded his insistence that qualitative, commonsense knowing is the building block and test of quantitative knowing:

> This is not to say that such common-sense naturalistic observation is objective, dependable or unbiased, But it is all that we have. It is the only route to knowledge – noisy, fallible and biased though it be. (Campbell, 1979: 54)

The mainstream among social work evaluators has for some time abandoned the claim that experimental and quasi-experimental designs, and single-system designs, can yield confident information about cause and effect. It is widely conceded that we are involved in 'social inquiry for and by earthlings' (Cronbach, 1986).

The possibility of rigorous evaluation has also been conditioned by loss of faith in the rationality of organizational decision making, and by the extensive work done first in the mid-1970s on the nature of policy making, and the ways in which information is used in such processes. This fed through to changed views about how evaluation is and can be used to change programmes, projects and practices. House has provided one of the most complete arguments for viewing evaluation as a form of persuasion (House, 1980). Where do we stand then on issues of relevance? The question involves several different aspects, and the contributors to this book address each of them from different standpoints.

First, relevance involves issues of how evaluation problems emerge and are agreed. Arguments for practitioner evaluation and action research are often based on claims of increased relevance, and that 'any losses in research rigour are more than compensated for by gains in the acceptability of the research' (Kelly, 1985: 148). The development of 'responsive evaluation' by Stake and others has also widened the involvement of stakeholders in practical agendas of problem setting.

Secondly, developments in how we think regarding the logic of evaluation have also helped to draw in practical criteria of relevance. There has been a welcome influence of ideas regarding practical reasoning, informal and working logic, and the stimulating impact of neo-Aristotelian ideas of practical reasoning. These developments all help promote a distinction between mainstream research rigour and more practical, everyday reasoning and logic, which also include ethical reasoning. Recent reflection on the place of practice wisdom in social work owes an indirect debt to these ideas.

Thirdly, the rigour and relevance question has been pulled in different directions by the unresolved question of whether evaluators should be concerned to develop theory, similarly to researchers. My own answer is, 'in some cases'. I do not accept the position of several theorists and writers on evaluation that theory development is the task of research, not of evaluation. But theory development raises special problems for evaluation. The question has been too little addressed by those working on the development of direct practice evaluation. Valuable work has been done in the field of education, for example, by Jennifer Greene (e.g. Greene, 1993). While she is mainly concerned with qualitative programme evaluation, the demand she makes that theory-related issues should be incorporated into evaluation poses big questions for practitioners and evaluators. She invites us to explicate our own theoretical predispositions, describe local programme theories ('locally meaningful theoretical perspectives on data interpretation': 1993: 38), attend to emergent theoretical issues, and integrate theory into evaluation conclusions and recommendations. The remaining problem acknowledged by Greene is how such theorizing should reflect contested evaluative purposes.

The fourth issue, that of changed ideas regarding the validity of evaluations, and the fifth – changed ideas of how evaluation is used – will now be considered.

Validity and values

In negotiating the trade-offs of rigour and relevance Cronbach employs a broadcasting metaphor of bandwidth versus fidelity, and always prefers bandwidth, i.e. less dependable answers about a broader range of questions. 'Scientific quality is not the principal standard; an evaluation should aim to be comprehensible, correct and complete, and credible to partisans on all sides' (Cronbach et al., 1980: 11). Our choices regarding rigour and relevance thus raise questions of the validity of evaluative work. Campbell's work on internal and external validity, and perhaps even more so his elucidation of the threats to validity, are the sounding board for all evaluative work, even where the original distinctions are at least modified, or even rejected.

The importance of validity issues is reflected in the place they are given by several contributors to this book. Evaluation writers take one of various orientations:

1 reliance on internal rigour and validity, including claims as to whether evaluation is dependable, confirmable and can be generalized;
2 reliance on broader criteria of plausibility, credibility, external validity and relevance;
3 interpretive criteria, which commence from the position that evaluation inquiry is not a technical task but a moral and practical activity;
4 validity judged according to fulfilment of a model of evaluation as service or reform;
5 openly ideological evaluation where the evaluation is judged according to its catalytic impact on the lives of the powerless, and by the fulfilment of an advocacy role by the evaluator.

Individual practitioners and evaluators may hold elements of more than one position. However, general distinctions can be made. Advocates of empirical or scientific practice, or the narrower version of evidence-based practice, have been associated with the first position. Mainstream ethnographic evaluators, postpositivist evaluators, and those committed to more pragmatic philosophical positions on evaluation are often characterized by the second position. However, this position is sometimes associated with rather different evaluative positions such as those of Guba, Lather and Reason. Helpful expositions have been given by Hammersley (1992: Ch. 4) and the Loflands (Lofland and Lofland, 1995: 168–177).

Others reject the relevance of the idea of validity. Smith (1993) is associated with this third position, which rests on a rejection of realism. In Smith's view no meaning has epistemic privilege and the 'validity' of evaluation is not concerned with understanding more accurately but with understanding more deeply and truly. Tests of good evaluation when applied to social work practice are in terms of fairness, an increased awareness of complexity in the practice environment, and an increased understanding of and respect for the values of others.

Evaluation as service is perhaps the most obvious way of distinguishing evaluation from research, in terms of its *purpose* rather than its *methodology*. This fourth general approach to evaluation and its corresponding stance on validity is summarized by Simon as 'a practical, particularistic, political, persuasive service' (Simon, 1987: 8). In Britain the work of Finch (1986) reflects this rejection of the view that the evaluator is a technician, and in the USA Greene has insisted that, 'No longer can we shroud our citizen-selves behind our scientific subjectivities. We must become scientific citizens' (Greene, 1996: 287).

Holders of this position often reason that evaluation should be educative and democratizing. Varying emphases on the role of advocacy can be found within this approach, from the pluralism of Cronbach and Stake to the reformist positions of House, Simon and Finch. An interesting example of this position within social work evaluation has been described by Bogdan and Taylor (1994). House has long been the advocate of a social justice criterion for evaluation, based on a concept of justice as fairness and impartiality. More recent work has aimed to develop ideas of justice as a criterion for judging evaluation (e.g. Altheide and Johnson, 1997; Kirkhart, 1995). While there are thorny questions to resolve regarding different philosophies of social justice, it is an area that will reward attention from social work evaluators.

Commitments to justice are also part of the fifth stance on evaluation and validity – that associated with openly ideological evaluation. A different response to the realist arguments discussed earlier is to shift the grounds of the debate away from the nature of the world, and how we may know it, to questions of values and morals, where debates about realism or relativism are replaced by the moral standpoints of the evaluator and practitioner. Evaluation practices which place moral considerations at the centre are discussed by Dullea and Mullender, and Humphries in this volume. Oliver's work in the field of disability research (Oliver, 1992) has also contributed to this debate in Britain. What place is there for advocacy through evaluation? Are Hammersley and Gomm right when they uncompromisingly claim that advocacy undermines public confidence in the impartiality of social evaluation and research? Furthermore:

> to the extent that such developments amount to redefining the goal of inquiry as the promotion of some practical or political cause, we see them as motivated bias, and believe they must be resisted by researchers. (Hammersley and Gomm, 1997: paragraph 5.4)

Lather has suggested an especially creative exploration of issues of validity in openly ideological evaluation and research. She confesses that, 'What I have found over and over again in the methodological literature of openly value-based research is a fuzziness on the need for data credibility checks' (Lather, 1986: 77). She concludes that the minimum standards that evaluation needs to build into its designs to address validity are:

- triangulation of *methods, data sources,* and *theories;*
- reflexive subjectivity (some documentation of how the researcher's assumptions have been affected by the logic of the data);

- face validity (established by recycling categories, emerging analysis, and conclusions back through at least a subsample of respondents);
- catalytic validity (some documentation that the research process has led to insight and, ideally, activism on the part of the respondents).

She warns that 'if we fail to develop these procedures, we will fail to protect our work from our own passions, and our theory building will suffer' (1986: 77).

A clutch of difficult issues remains on the table for social workers who wish to engage in valid evaluation. First, the crucial question of whether social work practitioners as evaluators should be partisan is not going to disappear. I have implied that there are four broad answers to this question (see Table 2.2).

Table 2.2 *Should social work evaluation be partisan?*

Solution	Associated with
Non-partisanship	Scriven, Hammersley
Multipartisan	Cronbach, Stake
Reformist	House, Finch
Radical partisan	Lather, Oliver

Secondly, social work has given too little attention to the question of whether the products of direct practice evaluation *generalize* to other settings. Problems of generalization from direct practice evaluating are discussed in this volume by, for example, Ruckdeschel. Cronbach's criticism of Campbell's arguments for internal validity has been widely accepted, although it is still far too little known and reflected on in social work evaluation in the countries represented by contributors to this volume (Cronbach, 1982; Cronbach et al., 1980; Shadish et al., 1990). Cronbach argues that ' "External validity" – validity of inferences that go beyond the data – is the crux of social action, not "internal validity" ' (Cronbach et al., 1980: 231). The consequences of his position are methodologically radical. He is convinced that Campbell's formulation of external validity is ultimately trivial, and that the issue for generalization is how we may generalize to people, interventions and settings *that were not sampled and are different*. Cronbach's work has valuable implications for practitioner forms of evaluation. Work by Eisner, and by Stake and Trumbull, is also apposite (Eisner, 1991a, Ch. 9; Stake and Trumbull, 1982). Relativist epistemologists have often rejected ideas regarding generalization, and believe that the local relevance of evaluation is all we have.

Thirdly, should social work evaluators and practitioners regularly recycle evaluation back to those who gave information? This is usually referred to as member validation. There are three basic possibilities, although they are not entirely mutually exclusive. First, we can opt for a realist understanding of member validation (and probably triangulation) as a method of validating data. Researcher and respondent views enable us to locate and position what is really happening. Secondly, it has been argued that this corroborative view of member validation is unduly naïve, and that member responses should be 'viewed instead as further important data, an occasion for extending and elaborating the researcher's analysis' (Bloor, 1997: 48). Thirdly, we may choose to retain a process of member feedback and response not on epistemological grounds but because of ethical and moral commitments to participatory, democratizing evaluation.

Fourthly, what value positions should be adopted by evaluators regarding the conclusions of their inquiry? The general divide on this issue is between those who take a descriptive position and those who adopt a prescriptive stance. In other words, these are the value positions and the possible consequences that appear to follow (descriptive), or, these are the conclusions regarding future action that we recommend (prescriptive). Reformist and radical evaluators are more likely to adopt a prescriptive position.

Fifthly, what ethical issues are posed by the process and validation of practice evaluation? Sensitive accounts have been given by Finch from her research on playgroups (Finch, 1985) and by Eisner (1991a, Ch. 10). Scriven helpfully underlines the distinction between the ethical issues raised by the practice or project being evaluated, and ethical issues raised by the evaluation as such – 'the problem of unethical practices in a programme with highly ethical objectives' (Scriven, 1996: 399).

Engineering or enlightenment?

Some vision of purpose is, at root, what guides evaluation practice. Close to the centre of that vision is a view of evaluation as having a usefulness for policies, services and practice. Until the 1970s that use was assumed to be relatively straightforward, and consisted of applying the results of evaluation in a direct instrumental or social engineering mode to the problem addressed by the evaluation. In the USA this was supported by the early work of Campbell and Scriven, and in Britain it was represented in the Fabian model of the researcher/policy maker relationship.

The shift in assumptions regarding the balance of rigour and relevance outlined earlier contributed to a new focus on the uses of evaluation. The key figure in these changes was Carol Weiss. In a ground-breaking paper first published in 1973 on 'Where politics and evaluation meet' (Weiss, 1987) she argued that political considerations intrude on evaluation in three ways. First, the programme and policies being evaluated are themselves the creatures of political decisions. They 'are not neutral, antiseptic, laboratory-type entities. They emerged from the rough and tumble of political support, opposition and bargaining' (1987: 49). Secondly, evaluation includes political considerations because its reports enter the political arena. This was an area to which she was to give detailed empirical attention later in the 1970s. Thirdly, politics is implicit in evaluation research. While the results of evaluation may question programme goals, 'when a social scientist agrees to evaluate a programme he or she gives an aura of legitimacy to the enterprise' (1987: 57). In general, most of the political implications of evaluation research 'have "establishment" orientations. They accept the world as it is; as it is defined in agency structure, in official diagnoses of social problems' (1987: 59–60).

Her empirical work led to more realistic theories of evaluation use. She introduced the ideas of 'decision accretion' and 'knowledge creep' to describe the way in which policy decisions are not made at a single point in time, but by the build-up of small choices, the closing of small options, and the gradual narrowing of available alternatives (Weiss, 1980). Rather than being made in the light of specific information, Weiss argued that policy makers' decisions reflect an enlightenment model of use, whereby there is a diffuse and indirect infiltration of research ideas into their understanding of the world. Ideas of use as enlightenment have become the established orthodoxy.

The view that social workers take on the use of evaluation will also affect how the task of dissemination of information takes place. There has been emphasis recently on the need to disseminate research findings. The work of Weiss and others suggests that we should not regard this as a matter of technical communication, but that it will raise issues of how we view social change. Social work, in Britain at least, has tended to treat dissemination and research utilization skills in an unproblematic fashion (Fisher, 1997).

We should not overdo the stress on enlightenment, and neither should we assume that ideas on use developed in the fields of programme evaluation and policy research will transfer easily to evaluation of social work projects and direct practice. *Enlightenment* models are best linked to longer-term change through evaluation research, to evaluation that aims to change the way people conceptualize their experience, to theorizing about the targets of evaluation, and to evaluation based within higher education. *Instrumental* views of evaluation are more likely to be associated with shorter-term, immediate applications, with little social science theorizing, and to evaluation that is agency based and may be carried out by 'insiders'. Evaluation of direct practice is unlikely to fall exclusively in one mode or the other, and enlightenment models of use will not provide sufficient frameworks for such evaluating in practice. The issue of use as a whole can be given too much emphasis. Chelimsky rightly points out that 'use is a good thing . . . but too much zeal about it will make us bland and innocuous when we really should be questioning prevailing policies, and challenging the status quo' (Chelimsky, 1997: 105, 108).

Methodology and methods

While this book is not offered as a text on the methodology and methods of evaluation, methodology and methods are among its central themes. The authors of Chapters 6 to 13 address ways in which specific evaluation approaches raise lessons and questions for social work practice, or how certain methods (interviews, observation and life histories) give a particular purchase on practice evaluation. The main reason for this approach is to move social work beyond the abstractness regarding methodology that characterizes much work on programme evaluation, and to explore ways in which methodologies for direct practice evaluation may be quite different from those for programme and policy evaluation.

The ambiguity surrounding methodology within evaluation theory is a mix of bane and blessing. We have seen that much of the work since the 1970s has served to underscore the idea that evaluation is not and should not be solely methodology driven. It has become orthodoxy – although not one shared universally in social work – that 'armed only with methodology, the evaluator is ill-prepared' (Shadish et al., 1990: 183). Yet this emphasis has its downside, as is apparent in Eisner's disparaging remark that 'in qualitative matters cookbooks ensure nothing' (Eisner, 1991a: 169). Part of this disdain for 'cookbooks' stems from the emphasis, especially within qualitative and constructivist evaluation, on the use of the self as instrument, and in the mistrust of methods as a modernist search for the key to knowledge. It also seems to follow from the shift to an enlightenment view of evaluation, where instrumental procedures take second place to wider political issues and trade-offs in evaluation. For these reasons the methodological leads that come from existing work are more general. For example, Scriven has laid great emphasis on the importance of a general *logic of evaluation*. This is helpful in that it ties the definition of evaluation to issues of purpose. The logic of evaluation is one area where social work can reflect on, adapt and colonize the debate, which has been reinvigorated by Scriven's advocacy of informal logic (Fournier, 1995; Scriven, 1995). Social workers are less likely, however, to follow Scriven in some of the key proposals he makes, for example on goal-free evaluation (see Scriven, 1997).

A different methodological lead follows from the *postpositivist shift* in mainstream evaluation. This has led to an emphasis on multiple methods ('critical multiplism', to use Cook's ugly phrase: Cook, 1985). There is a danger here in the current emphasis on a 'horses for courses' approach to evaluation design decisions. It is suggested, to caricature slightly, that quasi-experiments will still be right when measurement of effects and impacts is needed, whereas discovery methods and case studies will be fine when evaluators want 'bandwidth' rather than 'fidelity'. This is too comfortable and results in premature closure on debate about methods and methodology, influenced no doubt by the weariness with what in America have been called the 'paradigm wars'. Indeed, the central claim of this position is far from straightforward. For example, Campbell's own work on case studies 'constructs one of the strongest cases to date that qualitative methods can yield valid causal knowledge' (Shadish et al., 1990: 135).

Cronbach's work on *external validity* also has methodological consequences. It pushes him towards evaluation *within* programmes rather than evaluation *between* programmes. He is dragged by his conception of social program realities toward methodologically looser conceptions of evaluation designs, and 'does not want a particular conception of scientific method to trivialize the process of asking important questions' (Cronbach et al., 1980: 349). He views evaluation design as a series of 'artful trade-offs' (1980: 225), which are not solely technical but part of political accommodation. '*Leverage* is the bottom line. Leverage refers to the probability that the information – *if* believed – will change the course of events' (1980: 265; italics in original). For him this is not a move back to an instrumental view of how evaluation will be used, because 'the questions with the greatest leverage are the ones that contribute to insight' (1980: 266).

We have observed the ways that views about the uses of evaluation, its general logic, paradigm positions, and views about validity and generalization will give a special purchase on methodology. We also saw earlier in the chapter the way that Greene's wish to give *theory* a central place in evaluation steers us away from the view of evaluators as technical experts. Social work evaluators and practitioners need to be more self-conscious of where they stand on such issues. Only then are they likely to reach resolutions to the twin methodological questions for evaluation: what methods are most likely to meet the purposes of a given evaluation? and what special purchase and 'take' will evaluative purpose give to those methods?

Underlying this second question is a wider problem of how social workers view the relationship between evaluation/research practice and social work practice. It has frequently been argued, and by several contributors to this book, that the two kinds of practice are closely akin to one another (this has usually been in the form, 'social work is like evaluation/research' rather than the converse). This view has a long pedigree, as Reid and Zettergren point out in this volume, going back at least to Charles Loch, and his nineteenth-century vision of social work as scientific practice. The problem with such assertions is that they have been used to support a cluster of apparently incompatible claims – for management by effectiveness approaches, scientific practice, qualitative inquiry, and so on. Warnings against a naïve assumption of common purpose or method were given over 20 years ago by Thomas (1978), and are echoed by Ruckdeschel in this volume. Yet the idea is interesting, and social workers should continue to explore the correspondences and disjunctures of research and practice.

Conclusion

We have reviewed reasons why, notwithstanding the present vigour of debate on evidence and practice, social work remains chronically weak in its understanding of evaluation in and for direct social work practice. I have suggested that the groundwork for strengthening theorizing and practice should be done through

- empirical work on how social workers and members of cognate professions (and apparently very different professions: Schon, 1983), make evaluative sense of practice (Shaw and Shaw, 1997a, 1997b);
- fresh examination of the risks and benefits attached to paradigmatic commitments and to different forms of pragmatism;
- caution regarding both relativist and strongly realist assumptions about evaluation knowledge;
- disaggregation of global judgements about whether evaluation should emphasize rigour or relevance;
- new examination of the contribution of some evaluation theorists to arguments for the validity of evaluation;
- developing models of how evaluation may be used, tailored to the specific demands of evaluating and direct practice; and
- an understanding of how developments of this kind will promote strategic decisions regarding evaluation designs.

There are promising ways forward. Selective ploughing of some of the major evaluation theorists will repay effort. For myself, I find Cronbach, Weiss, House, Greene, and aspects of Stake's work to be especially fertile ground. I have not brought the work of evaluation theorists, education evaluators and social work evaluators into direct adjacency in this chapter, but dialogue, ideally face to face, will especially foster good evaluation within professional groups. This will require collaboration between practitioners and academics across national boundaries. The remark of Oscar Wilde, familiar to British ears, that 'the Americans and the British are two people separated by a common language', offers insight regarding the similarity and yet differences in the way practitioner evaluation of this kind has developed in each country.

The vigour of the debate on evidence-based practice ought to preserve us from monopolistic hegemonies regarding what counts as good practice. For example, there are emergent arguments in Britain by one of the contributors to this volume for what may be called 'knowledge-based practice' (Fisher, 1997), which may enable a wider incorporation of the different approaches to practice evaluation reviewed in this chapter.

Direct practice evaluation lives in interesting days.

Notes

I am grateful to Jenny Harrison and Colin Young – both of whom are reflective, enabling, evaluating practitioners – for comments on an earlier version of this chapter.

1 In Britain see for example Audit Commission (1996), and Wales Office of Research and Development for Health and Social Care (1998). The term was being used in the academic literature on evaluation research from at least 1980 (Weiss, 1980: 387). It was common currency in official reports in the USA by the mid-1980s (e.g. US Department of Education, 1986).

2 I am indebted here to Martyn Hammersley's discussion of the logically similar question of whether social research is political (Hammersley, 1995).

3 The prefix 'post' is used in different and potentially confusing ways. For example, in the term *postpositivism*, 'post' is used to convey that this is a position that keeps some of the key ontological/epistemological premises of positivism, with some more or less radical changes to doctrines of realism, subjectivity, etc. 'Post' serves to signal a greater or lesser element of *continuity* with the position it conditions. However, in the term *postmodernism*, 'post' is used to convey that the key motives and motifs of the modernist enterprise are challenged. What unites adherents to this position is what is challenged. 'Post' therefore serves to signal the element of *discontinuity* with the position it conditions.

4 The discussion here has been around critical, fallible realism. There are other strands of realist influence on evaluation, which I have not discussed. In particular, there is a gradual application to evaluation of ideas about scientific realism. House in America (e.g. House, 1991) and Pawson in Britain (Pawson and Tilley, 1997) are especially associated with these developments. Scientific realist evaluation places stress on the context of evaluation, and understanding causal mechanisms, and is a theory-driven model of evaluation.

References

Altheide, D. and Johnson, J. (1997) 'Ethnography and justice', in G. Miller and R. Dingwall (eds), *Context and Method in Qualitative Research*. London: Sage.

Atkinson, P., Delamont, S. and Hammersley, M. (1988) 'Qualitative research traditions: a British response to Jacob', *Review of Educational Research*, 58 (2): 231–250.

Audit Commission (1996) *Misspent Youth*. London: Audit Commission.

Bloor, M. (1997) 'Techniques of validation in qualitative research', in G. Miller and R. Dingwall (eds), *Context and Method in Qualitative Research*. London: Sage.

Blumer, H. (1969) *Symbolic Interactionism: Perspective and Method*. Englewood Cliffs, NJ: Prentice-Hall.

Bogdan, R. and Taylor, S. (1994) 'A positive approach to qualitative evaluation and policy research in social work', in E. Sherman and W. Reid (eds), *Qualitative Research in Social Work*. New York: Columbia University Press.

Campbell, D. (1979) 'Degrees of freedom and the case study', in T. Cook and C. Reichardt (eds), *Qualitative and Quantitative Methods in Evaluation Research*. Beverly Hills, CA: Sage.

Carr, W. and Kemmis, S. (1986) *Becoming Critical: Education, Knowledge and Action Research*. London: Falmer Press.

Cheetham, J. (1998) 'The evaluation of social work: priorities, problems and possibilities', in J. Cheetham and M. Kazi (eds), *The Working of Social Work*. London: Jessica Kingsley.

Chelimsky, E. (1997) 'Thoughts for a new evaluation society', *Evaluation*, 3 (1): 97–118.

Cook, T. (1985) 'Postpositivist critical multiplism', in R. Shotland and M. Mark (eds), *Social Science and Social Policy*. Beverly Hills, CA: Sage.

Cook, T. and Campbell, D. (1979) *Quasi-Experimentation*. Chicago: Rand McNally.

Cronbach, L. (1982) *Designing Evaluations of Educational and Social Programs*. San Francisco: Jossey-Bass.

Cronbach, L. (1986) 'Social inquiry by and for earthlings', in D. Fiske and R. Shweder (eds), *Metatheory in Social Science: Pluralisms and Subjectivities*. Chicago: University of Chicago Press.

Cronbach, L., Ambron, S., Dornbusch, S., Hess, R., Hornik, R., Phillips, D., Walker, D. and Weiner, S. (1980) *Toward Reform of Program Evaluation*. San Francisco: Jossey-Bass.

Eisner, E. (1988) 'Educational connoisseurship and criticism: their form and functions in educational evaluation', in D.M. Fetterman (ed.), *Qualitative Approaches to Evaluation in Education*. New York: Praeger.

Eisner, E. (1991a) *The Enlightened Eye: Qualitative Inquiry and the Enhancement of Educational Practice*. New York: Macmillan.

Eisner, E. (1991b) 'Taking a second look: educational connoisseurship revisited', in M.W. McLaughlin and D. Phillips (eds), *Evaluation and Education at Quarter Century*. Chicago: University of Chicago Press.

England, H. (1986) *Social Work as Art*. London: Allen & Unwin.

Everitt, A. (1996) 'Developing critical evaluation', *Evaluation*, 2 (2): 173–188.

Everitt, A., Hardiker, P., Littlewood, J. and Mullender, A. (1992) *Applied Research for Better Practice*. London: Macmillan.

Filstead, W. (1979) 'Qualitative methods – a needed perspective in evaluation research', in T. Cook and C. Reichardt (eds), *Qualitative and Quantitative Methods in Evaluation Research*. Beverly Hills, CA: Sage.

Finch, J. (1985) 'Social policy and education: problems and possibilities of using qualitative research', in R. Burgess (ed.), *Issues in Educational Research: Qualitative Methods*. London: Falmer Press.

Finch, J. (1986) *Research and Policy: The Uses of Qualitative Methods in Social and Educational Research*. London: Falmer Press.

Fisher, M. (1997) 'Research, knowledge and practice in community care', *Issues in Social Work Education*, 17 (2): 17–30.

Fook, J. (ed.) (1996) *The Reflective Researcher: Social Workers' Theories of Practice Research*. St Leonards, NSW: Allen & Unwin.

Fournier, D. (ed.) (1995) *Reasoning in Evaluation: Inferential Links and Leaps*. San Francisco: American Evaluation Association/Jossey-Bass.

Fuller, M. and Petch, A. (1995) *Practitioner Research: The Reflexive Social Worker*. Buckingham: Open University Press.

Gould, N. and Taylor, I. (eds) (1996) *Reflective Learning for Social Work*. Aldershot: Ashgate.

Greene, J. (1993) 'The role of theory in qualitative program evaluation', in J. Flinders and G. Mills (eds), *Theory and Concepts in Qualitative Research*. New York: Teachers College Press.

Greene, J. (1994) 'Qualitative program evaluation: practice and promise', in N. Denzin and Y. Lincoln (eds), *Handbook of Qualitative Research*. Thousand Oaks, CA: Sage.

Greene, J. (1996) 'Qualitative evaluation and scientific citizenship', *Evaluation*, 2 (3): 277–289.

Guba, E. (1990) 'The alternative paradigm dialog', in E. Guba (ed.), *The Paradigm Dialog*. Newbury Park, CA: Sage.

Guba, E. and Lincoln, Y. (1989) *Fourth Generation Evaluation*. Newbury Park, CA: Sage.

Hammersley, M. (1992) *What's Wrong with Ethnography?* London: Routledge.

Hammersley, M. (1995) *The Politics of Social Research*. London: Sage.

Hammersley, M. and Gomm, R. (1997) 'Bias in social research', *Sociological Research Online*, 2, 1. <http://www.socresonline.org.uk/socresonline/2/1/2.html>

Hartsock, N. (1983) 'The feminist standpoint: developing the ground for a specifically feminist historical materialism', in S. Harding and M. Hintikka (eds), *Discovering Reality*. Dordrecht: Reidl.

Heron, J. (1996) *Co-operative Inquiry: Research into the Human Condition*. London: Sage.

House, E. (1980) *Evaluating with Validity*. Beverly Hills, CA: Sage.

House, E. (1991) 'Realism in research', *Educational Researcher*, 20 (6) 2–9.

Kelly, A. (1985) 'Action research: what it is and what can it do?', in R. Burgess (ed.), *Issues in Educational Research*. London: Falmer Press.

Kirkhart, K. (1995) 'Seeking multicultural validity: a postcard from the road', *Evaluation Practice*, 16 (1): 1–12.

Lather, P. (1986) 'Issues of validity in openly ideological research', *Interchange*, 17 (4): 63–84.

Lather, P. (1991) *Getting Smart: Feminist Research and Pedagogy with/in the Postmodern*. New York: Routledge.

Leplin, J. (ed.) (1984) *Scientific Realism*. Berkeley, CA: University of California Press.

Lincoln, Y. (1990) 'The making of a constructivist: a remembrance of transformations past', in E. Guba (ed.), *The Paradigm Dialog*. Newbury Park, CA: Sage.

Lofland, J. and Lofland, L. (1995) *Analysing Social Settings*. Belmont, CA: Wadsworth.

Martin, M. (1994) 'Developing a feminist participative research framework', in B. Humphries and C. Truman (eds), *Rethinking Social Research: Anti-Discriminatory Approaches in Research Methodology*. Aldershot: Avebury.

Martin, M. (1996) 'Issues of power in the participatory research process', in K. de Koning and M. Martin (eds), *Participatory Research in Health*. London: Zed Books.

McLennan, G. (1995) 'Feminism, epistemology and postmodernism: reflections on current ambivalence', *Sociology*, 29 (2): 391–409.

Mullen, E. and Hess, P. (1995) *Practitioner–Researcher Partnerships*. Washington, DC: NASW Press.

Oliver, M. (1992) 'Changing the social relations of research production?', *Disability, Handicap and Society*, 7 (2): 101–114.

Patton, M. (1990) *Qualitative Evaluation*. Newbury Park, CA: Sage.

Pawson, R. and Tilley, N. (1997) *Realistic Evaluation*. London: Sage.

Phillips, D. (1990) 'Postpositivistic science: myths and realities', in E. Guba (ed.), *The Paradigm Dialog*. Newbury Park, CA: Sage.

Pitman, M. and Maxwell, J. (1992) 'Qualitative approaches to evaluation: models and methods', in M. LeCompte and J. Preissle (eds), *The Handbook of Qualitative Research in Education*. San Diego, CA: Academic Press.

Reason, P. (ed.) (1988) *Human Inquiry in Action*. London: Sage.

Reason, P. (ed.) (1994) *Participation in Human Inquiry*. London: Sage.

Reason, P. and Rowan, J. (eds) (1981) *Human Inquiry: A Sourcebook of New Paradigm Research*. Chichester: John Wiley.

Reichardt, C. and Cook, T. (1979) 'Beyond qualitative versus quantitative methods', in T. Cook and C. Reichardt (eds), *Qualitative and Quantitative Methods in Evaluation Research*. Beverly Hills, CA: Sage.

Reid, W. (1988) 'Service effectiveness and the social agency', in R. Patti, J. Poertner and C. Rapp (eds), *Managing for Effectiveness in Social Welfare Organisations*. New York: Haworth.

Reid, W. (1994) 'Reframing the epistemological debate', in E. Sherman and W. Reid (eds), *Qualitative Research in Social Work*. New York: Columbia University Press.

Rodwell, M. and Woody, D. (1994) 'Constructivist evaluation: the policy/practice context', in E. Sherman and W. Reid (eds), *Qualitative Research in Social Work*. New York: Columbia University Press.

Rorty, R. (1979) *Philosophy and the Mirror of Nature*. Princeton, NJ: Princeton University Press.

Rorty, R. (1991) 'Feminism and pragmatism', *Radical Philosophy*, 59: 3–14.

Schon, D. (1983) *The Reflective Practitioner: How Professionals Think in Action*. New York: Basic Books.

Schon, D. (1992) 'The crisis of professional knowledge and the pursuit of an epistemology of practice', *Journal of Interprofessional Care*, 6 (1): 49–63.

Schon, D. (1995) 'Reflective inquiry in social work practice', in P. Hess and E. Mullen (eds), *Practitioner–Researcher Partnerships*. Washington, DC: NASW Press.

Schwab, J. (1969) 'The practical: a language for curriculum', *School Review*, November: 1–23.

Schwandt, T. (1993) 'Theory for the social sciences: crisis of identity and purpose', in D. Flinders and G. Mills (eds), *Theory and Concepts in Qualitative Research: Perspectives from the Field*. New York: Teachers College Press.

Schwandt, T. (1997) 'Evaluation as practical hermeneutics', *Evaluation*, 3 (1): 69–83.

Scriven, M. (1995) 'The logic of evaluation and evaluation practice', in D. Fournier (ed.), *Reasoning in Evaluation: Inferential Links and Leaps*. San Francisco: American Evaluation Association/Jossey-Bass.

Scriven, M. (1996) 'The theory behind practical evaluation', *Evaluation*, 2 (4): 393–404.

Scriven, M. (1997) 'Truth and objectivity in evaluation', in E. Chelimsky and W. Shadish (eds), *Evaluation for the 21st Century*. Thousand Oaks, CA: Sage.

Shadish, W. (1995) 'Philosophy of science and quantitative–qualitative debates: thirteen common errors', *Evaluation and Program Planning*, 18 (1): 63–75.

Shadish, W., Cook, T. and Leviton, L. (1990) *Foundations of Program Evaluation: Theories of Practice*. Newbury Park, CA: Sage.

Shaw, I. (1996) *Evaluating in Practice*. Aldershot: Ashgate.

Shaw, I. (1997) *Be Your Own Evaluator: A Guide to Reflective and Enabling Evaluating*. Wrexham: Prospects.

Shaw, I. (1999) 'Seeing the trees for the wood: the politics of evaluating in practice', in B. Broad (ed.), *The Politics of Research and Evaluation*. Birmingham: Venture Press.

Shaw, I. and Shaw, A. (1997a) 'Keeping social work honest: evaluating as profession and practice', *British Journal of Social Work*, 27 (6): 847–869.

Shaw, I. and Shaw, A. (1997b) 'Game plans, buzzes and sheer luck: doing well in social work', *Social Work Research*, 21 (2): 69–79.

Simon, H. (1987) *Getting to Know Schools in a Democracy*. London: Falmer Press.

Smith, J. (1993) 'Hermeneutics and qualitative inquiry', in D. Flinders and G. Mills (eds), *Theory and Concepts in Qualitative Research: Perspectives from the Field*. New York: Teachers College Press.

Stake, R. and Trumbull, D. (1982) 'Naturalistic generalizations', *Review Journal of Philosophy and Social Science*, 7 (1): 1–12.

Swigonski, M. (1993) 'Feminist standpoint theory and questions of social work research', *Affilia*, 8 (2): 171–183.

Thomas, E. (1978) 'Research and service in single-case experimentation: conflicts and choices', *Social Work Research and Abstracts*, 14 (4): 309–325.

Thyer, B. (1989) 'First principles of practice research', *British Journal of Social Work*, 19 (4): 309–323.

Thyer, B. (1993) 'Social work theory and practice research: the approach of logical positivism', *Social Work and Social Sciences Review*, 4 (1): 5–26.

US Department of Education (1986) *What Works: Research about Teaching and Learning*. Washington, DC: US Department of Education.

Wales Office of Research and Development for Health and Social Care (1998) *A Research and Development Strategy for Social Care in Wales*. Cardiff: WORD.

Weiss, C. (1980) 'Knowledge creep and decision accretion', *Knowledge, Creation, Diffusion, Utilisation*, 1 (3): 381–404.

Weiss, C. (1987) 'Where politics and evaluation meet', in D. Palumbo (ed.), *The Politics of Program Revaluation*. Newbury Park, CA: Sage.

Whitmore, E. (1990) 'Empowerment in program evaluation: a case example', *Canadian Social Work Review*, 7 (2): 215–229.

Whitmore, E. (1994) 'To tell the truth: working with oppressed groups in participatory approaches to inquiry', in P. Reason (ed.), *Participation in Human Inquiry*. London: Sage.

3

A PERSPECTIVE ON EMPIRICAL PRACTICE

William J. Reid and Pamela Zettergren

Empirical practice, sometimes referred to as 'research-based' or 'scientific' practice, is an approach to social work with individuals, families and groups. This chapter builds on and updates an earlier review of the history and status of the empirical practice movement (Reid, 1994). Historically, the chief distinguishing characteristics of empirical practice have been (1) stress on case monitoring and evaluation through single-system designs (SSDs) and more broadly the application of scientific perspectives and methods in practice; (2) application, to the extent possible, of interventions whose efficacy has been demonstrated through research, and (3) the development of new knowledge by practitioner-researchers using SSDs.

In empirical practice the service provider functions as a practitioner-researcher who makes use of research methods and a scientific mindset to assess and specify the client's problem, record change in its course during intervention, and evaluate the success of intervention in resolving it. In this process case data are used as a basis for decision making and as a means of determining the practitioner's accountability to the client, the agency and funding sources.

Practice itself is shaped by the use of these methods as well as by the infusion of empirically tested intervention techniques. In addition at least some practitioner-researchers contribute to knowledge through disseminated studies involving their own cases.

There is little doubt that the empirical practice movement has been a major development in social work (Fischer, 1993; Reid, 1994; Witkin, 1991). Empirical practice is widely taught in schools of social work and has become the subject of a large literature of textbooks and journal articles. It has influenced social work practice, although the extent of this influence has been difficult to determine.

Early origins

In a sense, the origins of empirical practice can be traced to the scientific charity movement that preceded professional social work. The central tenet of that movement was that alms-giving could be placed on the same scientific footing as medicine or engineering. As C.S. Loch, Director of the London Charity Organization Society, succinctly put it, charity work is 'not antagonistic to science: it *is* science' (Loch, 1899: 11).

The belief in science as a basis for helping held fast as alms-giving transmuted into professional social work. The application of the scientific method to the study and treatment of individual cases was pioneered by Mary Richmond (1917). In her formulation, a social diagnosis was the product of a scientific process. Facts were gathered to serve as the basis for hypotheses, which were then to be tested by obtaining relevant evidence. As Thyer (1997) has noted, Richmond's use of scientific procedures closely anticipated specific features of single-system methodology. For example, she advised social workers of the time 'to ascertain whether abnormal manifestations are increasing or decreasing in intensity' (Richmond, 1917: 435). Although the psychoanalytic movement that began in the next decade introduced radically new theories and interventions for work with clients, it also adhered to the paradigm of study, diagnosis, and treatment following presumed scientific principles. As Hollis (1963: 13), a leading advocate of psychoanalytically oriented casework commented, 'Casework is a scientific art. Certainly since the days of Mary Richmond we have been committed to objective examination of the facts of each case. We draw inferences from those facts, we diagnose, we view the individual against a frame of reference which is itself the product of informal research. We constantly alert ourselves to sources of error.'

The formulations of Richmond and Hollis called for practice to be scientific in the sense of science as a rational, systematic, problem-solving activity. Their paradigms lacked the specific directives and procedures found in contemporary empirical practice, such as the collection of baseline data, the use of research instruments in initial assessment and to measure case progress and outcome, and the employment of research-based interventions. Nevertheless their paradigms were based on the notion that scientific methods were applicable to social work practice and set the stage for further developments in their application. Moreover they established a benchmark that can help determine whether or not a given sample of contemporary practice presumed to be 'empirical' does indeed differ from practice that is scientific in the sense of being simply a rational, systematic, problem-solving activity.

The beginnings of modern empirical practice

The evolution of these earlier paradigms into contemporary empirical practice began in the early 1960s. From its inception, the empirical practice movement has been led by social work practitioner-researchers and researchers based in academic settings. In this respect the evolution of empirical practice has differed markedly from that of other major practice movements in social work. To be sure, other movements, such as psychodynamic, family and crisis therapies, were well represented by social work academics, but these movements were also firmly embedded in the practice community, which provided much, and in some instances most, of the intellectual leadership. In the USA, empirical practice was largely the creation of research-oriented academics who had entered doctoral programmes in schools of social work in the 1950s and early 1960s. (For a more detailed account, see Reid, 1994.) This was a period of rapid development of such programmes and the beginning of a major shift in academic leadership from master's to doctoral-trained faculty, especially in the direct practice area.

Many of these new empirically minded faculty had been trained in psychodynamic approaches, which, at the time, held a virtual monopoly of direct social work practice. While they may have questioned the weak scientific bases of these approaches, they had little choice but to accept them. Their doctoral training did not provide alternatives but did stimulate scepticism about such approaches. Moreover their training reinforced their research-mindedness, exposed them to developments in the social sciences, and equipped them with tools to study practice. In short, their training had prepared them to search for new practice alternatives.

One soon appeared on the horizon. In the mid-1960s, faculty and doctoral students at the University of Michigan School of Social Work, under the leadership of Edwin Thomas, began to experiment with the new behavioural methods that had begun to emerge a decade earlier in clinical psychology and psychiatry. In a series of dramatic and controversial presentations at the 1967 Annual Program Meeting of the Council of Social Work Education, this group unveiled their 'socio-behavioural' approach to social work (Thomas, 1967).

The socio-behavioural and other behavioural models presented attractive, if not compelling, alternatives to those with a research orientation to social work intervention. The models were the product of experimental research, drew upon the well-tested tenets of learning theory, made use of measurable treatment and outcome variables, and, perhaps of greatest significance, contained a rigorous research methodology for guiding and evaluating intervention in the single case. They were clearly models with which researchers could feel at home.

As they continued to spread, behavioural approaches became the leading form of empirical practice. But at the same time a more general conception of empirical practice began to emerge. This conception was built around the methods of assessment, case monitoring and outcome evaluation that were used in single-system designs (SSDs) in behavioural approaches. It was assumed that SSDs could be applied to any form of direct social work practice. They could not only guide practice in individual cases but could be used in more rigorous forms by practitioner-researchers to test the effectiveness of practice models. Knowledge from such research as well as other kinds of research-based knowledge should then be used as a base for selecting methods of intervention. Finally the use of SSDs could help establish the effectiveness of social work practice as well as enabling practitioners to establish their accountability to funding sources and other constituencies. In this way the profession could respond to criticisms that its methods lacked effectiveness (Fischer, 1973, 1976; Mullen and Dumpson, 1972) and that its practitioners were not providing evidence that they were fulfilling their mandates (Briar, 1973).

The empirical practice movement emerged as a complex combination of a practice model and a research agenda. In important ways, it defined how practice should be done – for example by defining goals in measurable terms and by using research-based interventions. It also prescribed a method of doing practice research in which a central role would be played by social workers functioning as both researchers and practitioners. It became a distinct approach to practice, one that absorbed the measurement technology of behaviour modification without wedding itself to its technology for effecting change.

In the USA the principles and methods of empirical practice were developed in a number of books that appeared between the late 1960s and the early 1980s (for example Bloom and Fischer, 1982; Briar and Miller, 1971; Hudson, 1982; Jayaratne and Levy, 1979; Pinkston et al., 1982; Thomas, 1967; Tripodi and Epstein, 1980; Wodarski, 1981).

In the UK, the empirical practice movement had a different evolution and character. Although the behavioural approach was introduced into the UK through the work of Jehu (1967) at about the same time as it made its appearance in American social work, it had less immediate impact on practice. Moreover, there was no movement, as in the USA, to extract SSD methodology from behavioural models for use as a practice evaluation tool. However, as the evaluation of social work practice began to assume greater importance, empirically oriented models were incorporated into the British social services (Goldberg and Robinson, 1977; Sheldon, 1978, 1982, 1983). Thus in the UK aspects of empirical practice relating to the use of research-based or validated intervention assumed greater salience than aspects related to the use of SSD methods in case evaluations or to the practitioner-researcher as a generator of knowledge.

Subsequent developments in the empirical practice movement, primarily in the USA, will be examined in relation to each of its core components – application of research methods in practice, use of demon-strably effective interventions, and knowledge building by practitioner-researchers. Although to separate these interrelated facets may be somewhat artificial, there are advantages in so doing since each has evolved in a somewhat different manner and each presents its own distinctive set of issues.

Research methods in practice

The main idea driving the empirical practice movement was use of research methods to guide and evaluate service in individual cases. Although this approach was meant to be used by social work practi-tioners, wholesale adoption by this group did not seem to be in the offing. The most likely route to dissemination seemed to be through social work educational programmes.

An educational strategy

Beginning in the early 1970s, content on empirical practice, emphasizing SSDs, was introduced into research and practice courses, mostly the former, or into integrated practice/research courses. As part of their coursework, students were usually required to apply empirical practice methods to one of their own cases (Briar, 1979; Siegel, 1983) in their field placements or employing agencies.

As this educational movement gained momentum, its adherents con-vinced the Council of Social Work Education (in the USA) to require social work education programmes, both graduate and undergraduate, to prepare students to evaluate their own practice. The Council's action (in 1984) provided further stimulus to the movement. By the late 1980s, a comprehensive survey revealed that the research offerings of a third of the graduate schools of social work in the USA *emphasized* SSDs and own practice evaluation, with additional schools having substantial content of this kind in their curricula (Fraser et al., 1991). Integrated formats for teaching practice and research were reported by almost 40 per cent of the schools.

There was a comparable development in the UK. The ability to carry out an evaluation of an intervention was made a core competency in social work training in 1989. Although little was done to implement this requirement and it was subsequently weakened, aspects of empirical practice began to emerge in the curricula of qualifying and post-qualifying programmes.

Studies of practice

Has this educational strategy for dissemination of empirical practice met with any success? Since the early 1980s, a number of US studies have attempted to provide some answers to this question (Cheatham, 1987; Gingerich, 1984; Kirk and Penka, 1992; Millstein et al., 1990; Penka and Kirk, 1991; Richey et al., 1987). In these studies samples of graduates of particular programmes or of practitioners in general have been asked to respond to questionnaires covering the extent to which they have used specific components of empirical practice. By and large the studies have reported substantial use of such components as specifying target problems and goals, describing goals in measurable terms, and monitoring client change over time. Small, but not always inconsequential, minorities of subjects have reported use of more time-consuming or intrusive operations such as graphs to measure change, standardized instruments, or controlled (withdrawal or multiple baseline) SSDs.

Lack of time and agency support as well as interference with practice have been cited by practitioners as major reasons for not using research methods in their cases (Cheatham, 1987; Gingerich, 1984; Millstein et al., 1990; Penka and Kirk, 1991; Richey et al., 1987), while Tolson (1990) and Kagle (1982) have noted as obstacles the turbulence of many settings and the brief, crisis nature of much social work practice.

As has been suggested by Briar (1990) and others, the results can be interpreted as evidence that the educational programmes in empirical practice are having some impact. A number of empirical practice components are being widely used, and there are at least some practitioners who appear to be making significant use of more complex SSD methodology. Further, the amount of exposure to empirical practice content appears to be correlated with the extent to which these components are used (Cheatham, 1987; Kirk and Penka, 1992).

Although the studies suggest that a beginning has been made in the dissemination of empirical practice, their results must be interpreted with some reservations. As Richey, Blythe and Berlin (1987: 18) have pointed out, 'semantic differences in descriptions and definitions of component evaluation activities may result in the underreporting and overreporting of such activities'. For example, Penka and Kirk (1991) found in their study of NASW members, two-thirds of whom had little or no exposure to SSDs in their graduate education, that subjects reported using such components as 'operationalizing target problems' or 'monitoring client change' with over three-quarters of their clients on the average. Are many of the practitioners in these studies interpreting such components in ways that would be hard to reconcile with conceptions of empirical practice? For example, is it possible to interpret 'monitoring client change' as simply asking clients about their progress in the course of a clinical interview? Are some of the practitioners using the kind of scientific orientation advocated by Richmond and Hollis, one that is not unique to empirical practice? Are practitioners who report use of AB (baseline followed by intervention) designs using largely reconstructed baselines? To what extent are their responses influenced by a wish to appear 'scientific', especially on a questionnaire sent to them by researchers? In a sense the subjects may be hitting the semantic ball back to the empiricists' court, forcing them to come up with more discriminating measures of empirical practice components. At some point such measures need to be applied to actual samples of practice. Also there is need for more up-to-date research. To our knowledge no published studies of the type reviewed above have been *conducted* since the beginning of the 1990s.

Agency projects

Another strategy for the dissemination of empirical practice approaches has consisted of projects in which training in use of empirical practice as well as instruments and other materials are provided to practitioners in agencies, usually by academic researchers (see for example, Kazi and Wilson, 1996a ,1996b; Kazi et al., 1997; Mutschler, 1984; Mutschler and Jayaratne, 1993; Toseland and Reid, 1985). The most extensive projects have been carried out by Kazi and his colleagues in the UK and Finland (Kazi et al., 1997). These projects, as well as their predecessors, have been successful in getting practitioners to use elements of SSD methodology, such as putting targets of intervention into operational form, collecting baseline (often retrospective) data, and using data for decision-making and evaluation purposes. The more time-consuming and demanding the procedure, the less likely it is to be used, and little use of controlled designs is reported.

The extent to which SSDs were used post-project has varied from little or no use to a high level of continued implementation. A key variable appears to be agency support. For example, in one project (in Finland) practitioners, left to their own devices, stopped using the designs at six months follow-up (Kazi et al., 1997), but in another, at the Kirklees Council, single-case evaluation became a standard feature of agency practice (Kazi and Wilson, 1996a). Despite their limitations, it appears as if initiatives of this kind may provide a way of helping empirical practice become established in supportive agency settings.

Issues

The use and advocacy of empirical practice in student and professional work with clients has evoked a good deal of critical reaction. The critics appear to agree on one point: that students and practitioners could better spend their time doing things other than learning about and implementing empirical practice methods. Beyond that, the critics are likely to part company, since they represent rather diverse camps. On the one hand are those, such as Heineman (1981, 1994) and Witkin (1991, 1996) who have been critical of the epistemological foundations of mainstream research. For them empirical practice represents an unwarranted extension of a faulty science paradigm into the world of social work practice. On the other are those such as Bronson (1994), Wakefield and Kirk (1997), Rubin and Knox (1996) and Thomas (1978) who seem to have no problems with the epistemological foundations of mainstream research but who have objected to empirical practice on a variety of grounds having to do with the application of that mode of research. The issues raised by critics in both camps can be subsumed under two broad questions: (1) Does empirical practice adversely affect services to clients? (2) Does it add sufficiently to these services, or to their evaluation, to justify the effort put into it?

POTENTIAL ADVERSE EFFECTS An issue voiced over the years by a number of critics (Bronson, 1994; Heineman, 1981; Thomas, 1978; Wakefield and Kirk, 1996) has concerned ethical conflicts in practitioners' use of SSDs as a part of ordinary practice. The battle has been joined chiefly in relation to use of controlled designs. To use such intrusive designs in a practice context may improperly confound research and service objectives. The interests of the client may become subordinate to the requirements of the study.

However, this issue has been softened in recent years by the emerging recognition that controlled designs are not often used in ordinary practice. Moreover, most empirical practice advocates no longer see these designs as an integral part of practitioner use of SSD methods. As Blythe and Rodgers (1993) have put it, 'Over time, we came to realize that many designs, such as the withdrawal and multiple baseline designs were inappropriate for practice . . . and began to emphasize simpler designs.' Although even recent texts produced by empirical practice advocates provide a basis for the continuance of such criticisms – for example, controlled designs are described in detail and ways in which they can be used by practitioners are discussed (Bloom et al., 1995; Blythe et al., 1994), it is clear from the advocates' pronouncements that the use of such designs is a minor and probably expendable ingredient in their current view of empirical practice. Since the designs are not being used anyway by practitioners, the argument becomes academic, in a quite literal sense.

Perhaps the only remaining aspect of this issue – one that has not been dealt with much in the literature – concerns the type of baseline used in SSDs. Although advocates of empirical practice allow for reconstructed or retrospective baselines, prospective baselines, in which intervention is delayed until baseline data are collected, appear to be favoured. For clients actively seeking help, delaying intervention while baseline data are collected could activate the conflict between research and service interests. While the issue merits more analysis, it is likely to occur in only a small fraction of cases. Given their current tendencies toward retrenchment, most empirical practice advocates would probably concede the appropriateness of reconstructed baselines in such cases.

THEORETICAL NEUTRALITY   A second issue has to do with the 'theoretical neutrality' of SSDs. Advocates take the position that such designs
can be used with any kind of practice model. To support their argument
they can point to a variety of 'non-behavioural applications', including
communications approaches (Nelsen, 1978); psychodynamic practice
(Broxmeyer, 1978; Dean and Reinherz, 1986), and narrative therapy
(Besa, 1994). Critics counter that the assumptions, or metatheory, underlying empirical practice inevitably impart a certain direction to work
with clients regardless of the model ostensibly used (Kagle, 1982; Wakefield and Kirk, 1996; Witkin, 1996). For example, problems tend to be
seen in terms of specific behaviours of the client rather than as a result of
failure of the client's environment or social systems. The reliance on
practitioner-engineered measurement to guide treatment decisions may
lessen the client's sense of autonomy; it may empower the practitioner
rather than the client.

Advocates of empirical practice, and we include ourselves among
them, may be better off abandoning the notion of theoretical neutrality
and recognizing that they are operating within a metatheoretical framework, with its own set of assumptions about epistemology and practice .
By being explicit about this framework, we can better articulate its
rationale and broaden its scope.

It may make sense to construe empirical practice as a 'perspective' on
intervention, comparable to the generalist, feminist or ecosystems perspectives. Perspectives, like intervention models, take theoretical positions and contain practice guidelines. Specifically, in empirical practice,
primacy is given to research-based knowledge, and practitioners are
enjoined to collect data on change and to use them for decision making.
But in perspectives the theoretical positions and guidelines are general.
Unlike models, perspectives are not spelled out in detailed protocols.
They are designed, in fact, to be used in conjunction with more specific
intervention approaches, although they may make a difference to how
these approaches are used.

Defined as a perspective with a clear statement of its basic principles
and requirements, empirical practice might be used in combination with
approaches in which it is not normally employed. Some examples
may provide clarification. At first glance, an empirical perspective may
appear to be incompatible with certain humanistic therapies. Thus the
empirical perspective does direct practitioners to help clients define their
problems in specific, measurable terms, a directive that might run
counter to the manner in which such therapies are often conducted. But
there is no inherent reason why specificity, measurement and other
requirements of empirical practice cannot be met without violating the
fundamentals of humanistic practice. The application, cited previously,
of an empirical perspective to a test of narrative therapy (Besa, 1994) is a
good case in point. Or an empirical perspective could be used with
participatory research approaches in which practitioners and clients

could work together on a more egalitarian and collaborative basis than one customarily finds in empirical practice. This might involve some educating of clients in empirical methods as well as willingness to accredit client ideas about measurement, data collection and the like that might not fit conventional research notions. Nor is there any reason why an empirical practice perspective could not be used with advocacy research, even though the practitioner-researcher might need to forgo his or her 'neutrality'. Thus in work with a tenants' group systematic collection of baseline data about housing conditions could serve to demonstrate a need for change. Advocacy interventions designed to improve conditions could be implemented and their effects monitored. As these examples may illustrate, an empirical perspective could be combined with a range of approaches that may appear in some ways incompatible with it. The key to such combinations would be the development of adaptations on both sides. The empirical practice may depart from that used in conventional SSDs and the approach with which it is used may differ from routine applications of it. But the result may be a stronger and better evaluated intervention.

The much-needed development of qualitative methods for empirical practice (Reid and Davis, 1987) would facilitate its use with other approaches. This is especially true in applications to interventions with complex outcomes that may be difficult to quantify, such as those associated with humanistic practice. Care should be taken, however, to develop and use rigorous methods that can be distinguished from the more impressionistic 'qualitative' data collecting and evaluation that is part of routine clinical practice.

COST-BENEFIT CONSIDERATIONS Empirical practice involves an expenditure of time and effort on the part of both practitioner and client – in operationalizing targets, collecting baseline data and repeated measures of change, constructing and analysing graphs, and so on. Is it worth these outlays? Advocates argue that the benefits far outweigh the costs. The procedures used enable the practitioner to make data-informed decisions about case planning, to help clients understand change processes, and to serve purposes of accountability to agency and community. Not necessarily so, say the critics. They point to the lack of studies demonstrating the effectiveness of empirical practice procedures over traditional methods (Wakefield and Kirk, 1996). Moreover, the critics suggest that data collected may be open to question. Standardized instruments, often developed with samples from the white middle class, may give misleading results with poor and minority clients (Wakefield and Kirk, 1996). Graphs of the client's progress frequently yield ambiguous pictures of change (Rubin and Knox, 1996).

Lack of evidence that the use of SSDs does enhance outcome is admittedly a limitation of the empirical practice approach. The only experimental study to our knowledge addressed to this question

(Slonim-Nevo and Anson, 1998) did show some positive effects. Israeli delinquents who received treatment accompanied by SSD methods (for example, targeting of specific problems, collection of baseline data, tracking change through scales, self-monitoring, and graphing) were compared with a presumably similar group who were treated alike, but without the addition of the SSD methods. The SSD group showed statistically better outcomes on self-reports of arrests and school or work participation than the controls at a 9–12 months follow-up. However, no differences between the two groups were found on a variety of standard-ized scales, including measures of self-esteem, anger, and relationships with parents. Although the two groups were comparable on pre-test measures, allocations to the experimental or contrast groups were made by the probation officers who treated the youth, raising the possibility of selection as an explanation of the findings.

The study illustrates both the feasibility of an experimental test of SSD methods and the difficulties inherent in such a test. SSD methods must be used in conjunction with some intervention approach, which would be expected to produce most of the outcome effects. The added effects produced by the SSD methods might be difficult to detect. Moreover, the treatment models used in experimental and contrast groups would need to be similar. Models already incorporating features of SSD methods, such as those targeting specific problems, would create difficulties in such testing.

Pending the results of more rigorous experiments, the outcome-enhancing effects of SSDs remains an open question. Even if effects prove to be minor or non-detectable, SSDs can be justified on other grounds, such as their role in determining accountability and practitioner self-development (both discussed below).

ACCOUNTABILITY According to its critics, empirical practice even fails on its central claim that it provides a powerful method of establish-ing professional accountability. It fails to do so because the methods customarily used cannot isolate the practitioners' interventions as a cause of whatever changes have been measured. Moreover, account-ability is not just a question of determining the effectiveness of the methods that have been tested. It is also a question of ascertaining if a treatment is appropriate or if it is superior to alternatives (Wakefield and Kirk, 1996). If one chooses to step outside the empirical practice meta-theory, and there is no one happier to do so than Witkin, then account-ability is open to a limitless range of interpretations, including being accountable to oppressed clients by challenging existing forms of oppres-sion (Witkin, 1996).

The critics have added some new dimensions to the accountability question. As they suggest, professional accountability is more than demonstrating practice effectiveness (even when that is possible). It involves showing that the practitioner has used the best possible methods for the case at hand in the most suitable way – that he or she has engaged in 'appropriate practice' (Ivanoff et al., 1997). This larger (albeit fuzzier) concept of accountability should replace the one-track idea of accountability as measurement of change.

Nevertheless, the monitoring of client change and its evaluation on a case by case basis is certainly an important aspect of accountability, and it happens to be one that is within our grasp through SSDs, however imperfectly we may attain it. If such accountability data can be collected systematically, this should prove far superior to traditional agency practices of presenting 'success stories'. It may also satisfy demands of funding and managed care organizations using performance-based evaluation systems for accountability purposes. Evidence reviewed earlier has suggested that agency support is needed if SSD methodology is to be systematically implemented. Providing such support may be to the agency's advantage when competing for funds in a resource-stingy and evidence-demanding environment.

Benbenishty's (1996, 1997) proposal to recast accountability and empirical practice as an agency responsibility merits consideration in this context. Results from single-system evaluations could be fed into a service-oriented, computerized information system which could not only serve some of the agency's accountability needs but also provide useful feedback to managers and practitioners. Developments in computer-based instrument packages should facilitate this effort (Nurius and Hudson, 1993).

STUDENT AND PRACTITIONER SELF-DEVELOPMENT   One aspect of the use of SSDs has been glossed over in the debates about their efficacy, contribution to accountability and so on, and that is their role in student and practitioner self-development. Accurate feedback from one's own cases can be an important source of learning for both beginning and experienced social workers. It is reasonable to suppose that SSDs can facilitate this through the case data they provide, although evidence needs to be gathered on this point. Studies of how practitioners actually evaluate their own cases , such as Shaw and Shaw's (1997) qualitative investigation of the kinds of evidence social workers use to determine whether their work has 'gone well', are especially needed to optimize the fit between the outputs of SSDs and styles of practitioner self-evaluation.

Demonstrably effective interventions

During the past two decades a number of reviews and meta-analyses have identified a sizeable body of demonstrably effective practice methods used by social workers (de Schmidt and Gorey, 1997; Gorey, 1996; MacDonald et al., 1992; Reid and Hanrahan, 1982; Rubin, 1985;

Sheldon, 1986; Videka-Sherman, 1988). These methods are part of a much larger set of interventions of proven efficacy available to the helping professions. For example, the first author reviewed 42 meta-analyses (in 31 problem areas) that examined the results of several thousand experimental tests of interventions in the helping professions that are (or could be) used by social workers (Reid, 1997). The vast majority of studies in these meta-analyses reported positive effects. Although behavioural and cognitive-behavioural methods predominated in the reviews and meta-analyses referred to, positive effects were found for a wide variety of approaches. Moreover, some methods proved more effective than others for particular problems. Certainly an ample body of research-based methods exists as a base for a substantial amount of practice, especially for well defined problems, such as anxiety, depression and child behaviour difficulties. However, it is difficult to determine the extent to which such methods are being used in practice or to what extent their use preserves the substance of the methods actually tested. There is evidence that empirically based interventions are being taught in practice courses (LeCroy and Goodwin, 1988). Self-report surveys of social work practitioners have suggested that heavily tested methods, such as behavioural, cognitive and cognitive-behavioural are widely used (Jayaratne, 1982; Jensen et al., 1990; Strom, 1992), though not as much as those less research-based, such as psychodynamic, approaches.

In the UK there has been increased use of cognitive-behavioural, task-centred, and other empirically based methods in social work practice. A particular area of application of such methods has been in work with offenders (see McGuire, 1995 and Vanstone, Chapter 13 in this volume).

Issues

Not everyone agrees that research provides a better basis for selecting interventions than other sources of knowledge, such as practice wisdom. Witkin (1991) has argued that lack of objective criteria for determining empirical validation and limits on generalizing findings nullify the presumed superiority of research-based methods. Chandler (1994) has also questioned the utility of research-based interventions, given the typical lack of correspondence between their supporting studies and the clinical situations faced by practitioners.

These arguments take a rather purist position about the application of research-based methods. For example, there may be risks of error in applying methods to client populations that differ from those used in the studies that determined their effectiveness. There may be added risks because of flaws in the studies. But even so, the evidence supporting the research-based method may provide a more persuasive case for its use than whatever rationale might be supporting an alternative approach.

Research-based methods may then offer the practitioner the 'best available knowledge' (Reid, 1994) or 'best available information'(Klein and Bloom, 1995) as a basis for intervening.

This position certainly does not exclude the use of methods that lack empirical verification. As Berlin and Marsh have observed, 'Despite the importance of empirical knowledge, it is insufficient for guiding practice' (1993: 230). Practitioners must frequently, if not usually, use methods that lack an empirical base. It is always a matter of using research-based methods to the extent feasible as a way of enhancing practice effectiveness.

To the use of research-based methods in empirical practice, one should also add the use of research-based knowledge relating to assessment and human functioning and their connection to intervention (MacDonald, 1994). For example, research findings on factors contributing to resistance to delinquency in high-risk youth (Smith et al., 1995) can guide intervention at different levels. In this connection it is important to remember that empirical practice is always a matter of degree. Practice that may not be normally thought of as empirical, becomes such to a degree when research is used to inform theories that guide it. For instance, when a psychodynamic practitioner makes use of research on female development to correct traditional object relations theory and thus to inform treatment of a lesbian client (Goldstein, 1998), he or she has stuck a toe in the empirical practice waters.

If we assume that there is a sufficient quantity of research-based knowledge related to interventions and to human problems and behaviour to make a substantial difference in most social work practice, then the question of utilization arises. How can up-to-date knowledge be made available to practitioners in such a form that they will use it properly? Although social workers appear to be making use of research-based knowledge, there is no assurance that they are using more than a fraction of what is available, or that their usage is in accordance with the best or most recent of the research findings. This lack of utilization of research-based knowledge by social work practitioners has been well documented (Kirk, 1990). Better ways need to be found to put such knowledge into their hands.

In developing the necessary diffusion technology, it would pay us to take note of the 'evidence-based medicine' movement, which is gaining adherents in both the UK and the USA, (Sackett and Rosenberg, 1995; Whynes, 1996). Problems of non-utilization of research by practitioners plague medicine as well as social work, despite the former's vastly larger base of scientific knowledge. Evidence-based medicine is an effort to make available to physicians research that would inform their treatment. A key component is a large scale worldwide effort, the Cochrane Collaboration, which is creating computerized data bases of research evidence of what works and what doesn't in medical practice. The information is being made available in consumer-friendly form in journals, on CD ROMs, and on the Internet. A similar initiative might be thought of for social work; in fact, one such project, which provides evidence-based practice and policy information to 50 child welfare services, has been developed in the UK (Marsh, 1998).

Knowledge building

At the beginning of the empirical practice movement it was hoped that agency-based practitioner-researchers, using controlled SSDs, would be major producers of disseminated practice knowledge (Briar, 1979) – the third component in empirical practice developments. This hope has not been realized. Agency practitioners have published only a handful of such studies over the past two decades.

Although the idea of practitioner-researchers as contributors to social work knowledge has remained dormant in the social agency, it has come to life in academic settings. Practitioner-researchers in such settings are likely to be faculty members (or doctoral students) with practice experience and who teach or supervise practice. They may also be involved in some form of direct practice activity. Much of their research takes the form of developing and testing innovative service approaches, which may in itself involve direct contact with clients or the supervision of practitioners who provide services. Usually these approaches are tested in agency settings.

The published work of such practitioner-researchers began to appear in the 1970s. Some of it has taken the form of SSDs (see, for example, Besa, 1994; Jensen, 1994; Pinkston et al., 1982; Tolson, 1977). The rate of production of SSDs, however, has been modest – probably not more than about three studies a year. (In his comprehensive meta-analytic review of social work effectiveness studies, Gorey, 1996 found nine published SSDs during the 1990–94 period.) There has been little evidence of the use of replication series (Barlow et al., 1984) as a means of establishing generality of results.

A more influential form of research has consisted of group experimental tests of programmes academic practitioner-researchers themselves have designed and directed. This style of research represents a major departure from the types of experiment dominant in social work research prior to the 1970s. Such experiments were exemplified by *Girls at Vocational High* (Meyer et al., 1965) and *Helping the Aged* (Goldberg, 1970) in which researchers were cast primarily in the role of evaluators with little involvement in the design and operation of the service programmes. Indeed the majority of service experiments reported in the social work literature have followed the practitioner-researcher model (MacDonald et al., 1992; Reid and Hanrahan, 1982; Rubin, 1985). A particular strength of this model is that it enables researchers to design and shape their own interventions together with the means of testing them.

In contrast to earlier experiments, most of the single-system and group experiments conducted during the past two decades have had positive outcomes (Gorey, 1996; MacDonald et al., 1992; Reid and Hanrahan, 1982; Rubin, 1985; Videka-Sherman, 1988). Although the effects have often been limited – modest changes in circumscribed problems – and investigator allegiance (experimenter bias) is a concern in the practitioner-researcher model, the studies have begun to produce the kinds of demonstrably effective intervention that empirical practice so badly needs.

Admittedly the reliance on academics using largely group experiments rather than on agency practitioners using single-system experiments to build knowledge is quite a departure from earlier conceptions of the empirical practice movement. In fact it could be argued that such a departure should not properly be subsumed under the rubric of empirical practice. We would argue that it should be when the experiments, whether group or single system, are carried out by persons, whether school or agency based, who are actively involved in designing the interventions tested and who can thus be considered practitioner-researchers. This conception would also include exploratory experimental work in developmental research (Fortune and Reid, 1998; Rothman and Thomas, 1994).

In the UK, there have been even fewer instances than in the USA of practitioner-researchers using SSDs to generate knowledge, although there have been some recent UK projects by Kazi and associates, as noted earlier. The UK has not seen the emergence of a cadre of academic practitioner-researchers who develop and test their own intervention approaches. There has been, however, interest in fostering agency-based practitioner-researchers who conduct small scale programme evaluations (Cheetham et al., 1992; Cheetham and Kazi, 1998).

Conclusions

In the USA, the empirical practice movement has contributed to social work's historic pursuit of the goal of creating a scientifically based profession. Teaching students how to use research methods in case monitoring and evaluation has become well established in social work education, and there is evidence of applications of these methods in agency practice. There appears to be greater emphasis on research-based interventions and knowledge in teaching and practice. Practitioner-researchers have been active in designing and testing practice methods.

In empirical practice, as in most movements in American social work, accomplishments have fallen short of expectations and are sometimes difficult to discern or accredit. Its hallmark methodology – the single-system design – has not become well rooted in agency practice and there is little reason to assume that its occasional use has made much of a difference in agency efforts to evaluate practice or establish account-ability. However, its use may increase, or it may facilitate related applications, as agencies become more concerned about evaluation in a managed care and performance-based funding environment. Significant advances have been made in the incorporation of research-based inter-ventions into education and practice, but such interventions provide only a portion of the knowledge that is needed, and the extent of their use has not been adequately described.

Contrary to the vision of early advocates, there have appeared no significant numbers of agency-based practitioner-researchers who have contributed to intervention knowledge through SSDs. On the other hand, academic practitioner-researchers have made contributions using these designs. Further, the single-system methods, with their bonding of research and practice, may have stimulated the new look in group experimental designs, which began in the 1970s – designs in which academic practitioner-researchers develop and test intervention models.

The empirical practice movement has taken a different course in the UK. The use of empirically based methods and practitioner training and involvement in practice evaluation have been definite features. Practi-tioner own-case evaluations through SSDs have not been common, although recently some projects promoting such evaluations have been reported.

There is by no means consensus that the empirical practice movement, at least the US version, represents an advance. From its beginnings the movement has been criticized by those who reject the tenets of main-stream research on epistemological grounds. More recently, and perhaps more seriously, some mainstream researchers have called into question its central component – the use of single-system methodology in practice. They have faulted this as a dubious application of unproved benefits and possibly adverse effects. Although their criticisms appear somewhat overdrawn and perhaps directed at positions that advocates of empirical practice no longer hold, they have nevertheless raised some valid issues concerning evidence for the effectiveness of empirical practice, its pre-sumed theoretical neutrality, and its conception of accountability.

In light of these criticisms and with consideration to other needs of the empirical practice movement, we would recommend the following for both the USA and UK:

1   Empirical practice should be seen as a perspective, like the generalist or feminist perspective, that will make a difference to how inter-vention is carried out, rather than as a theoretically 'neutral' methodology.

2   In appraising the benefits of use of research methods in practice more stress should be placed on their potential value in student and practitioner self-development.
3   Conceptions of accountability should be broadened to reflect the idea of appropriate practice (Ivanoff et al., 1997) and not simply be demonstrations of client change or the effectiveness of whatever interventions happen to be used.
4   There should be greater emphasis on connecting single-system methodology to agency concerns with programme evaluation and accountability, with aggregation of results of case evaluations into computerized agency information systems (Benbenishty, 1996, 1997).
5   Efforts should be made to develop and apply rigorous qualitative methods within an empirical practice framework.
6   Research is needed to obtain a clearer and updated picture of the use of single-system methodology in practice and research-based interventions by practitioners, as well as to ascertain the effects of the use of empirical practice components.

References
Barlow, D.H., Hayes, S.C. and Nelson, R.O. (1984) *The Scientist Practitioner: Research and Accountability in Clinical and Educational Settings*. New York: Pergamon Press.
Benbenishty, R. (1996) 'Integrating research and practice: time for a new agenda', *Research on Social Work Practice*, 6 (1): 77–82.
Benbenishty, R. (1997) 'Outcomes in the context of empirical practice', in E.J. Mullen and J.L. Magnabosco (eds), *Outcomes Measurement in the Human Services*. Washington, DC: NASW Press. pp. 198–203.
Berlin, S.B. and Marsh, J. C. (1993) *Informing Practice Decisions*. New York: Macmillan.
Besa, D. (1994) 'Evaluating narrative family therapy using single-system research designs', *Research on Social Work Practice*, 4 (3): 309–325.
Bloom, M. and Fischer, J. (1982) *Evaluating Practice: Guidelines for the Accountable Professional*. Englewood Cliffs, NJ: Prentice-Hall.
Bloom, M., Fischer, J. and Orme, J.G. (1995) *Evaluating Practice: Guidelines for the Accountable Professional*, 2nd edn. Boston: Allyn & Bacon.
Blythe, B.J. and Rodgers A.Y. (1993) 'Evaluating our own practice: past, present, and future trends', *Journal of Social Service Research*, 18 (1/2): 101–119.
Blythe, B., Tripodi, T. and Briar, S. (1994) *Direct Practice Research in Human Service Agencies*. New York: Columbia University Press.
Briar, S. (1973) 'The age of accountability', *Social Work*, 18 (2): 3–4.
Briar, S. (1979) 'Incorporating research into education for clinical practice in social work: toward a clinical science in social work', in A. Rubin and A. Rosenblatt (eds), *Sourcebook on Research Utilization*. New York: Council on Social Work Education. pp. 132–140.
Briar, S. (1990) 'Empiricism in clinical practice: present and future', in L. Videka-Sherman and W.J. Reid (eds), *Advances in Clinical Social Work Research*. Washington, DC: NASW Press. pp. 1–10.

Briar, S. and Miller, H. (1971) *Problems and Issues in Social Casework*. New York: Columbia University Press

Bronson, D.E. (1994)'Is a scientist-practitioner model appropriate for direct social work practice? No', in W.W. Hudson and P.S. Nurius (eds), *Controversial Issues in Social Work Research*. Boston: Allyn & Bacon. pp. 79–86.

Broxmeyer, N. (1978) 'Practitioner-research in treating a borderline child', *Social Work Research and Abstracts*, 14: 5–10.

Chandler, S.M. (1994) 'Is there an ethical responsibility to use practice methods with the best empirical evidence of effectiveness? No', in W.W. Hudson and P.S. Nurius (eds), *Controversial Issues in Social Work Research*. Boston: Allyn & Bacon. pp. 105–111.

Cheatham, J. (1987) 'The empirical evaluation of clinical practice: a survey of four groups of practitioners', *Journal of Social Service Research*, 10: 163–177.

Cheetham, J. and Kazi, M. (1998) *The Working of Social Work*. London: Jessica Kingsley.

Cheetham, J., Fuller, R., McIvor, G. and Petch, A. (1992) *Evaluating Social Work Effectiveness*. Buckingham: Open University Press.

Dean, R. and Reinherz, H. (1986) 'Psychodynamic practice and single system design: the odd couple', *Journal of Social Work Education*, 22: 71–81.

De Schmidt, A. and Gorey, K.M. (1997) 'Unpublished social work research: systematic replication of a recent meta-analysis of published intervention effectiveness research', *Social Work Research*, 21 (1): 58–62.

Fortune, A.E. and Reid, W.J. (1998) *Research in Social Work*, 3rd edn. New York: Columbia University Press.

Fischer, J. (1973) 'Is casework effective?: a review', *Social Work*, 18: 5–20.

Fischer, J. (ed.) (1976) *The Effectiveness of Social Casework*. Springfield, IL: Charles Thomas Press.

Fischer, J. (1993) 'Empirically-based practice: the end of ideology?' *Journal of Social Service Research*, 18 (1/2): 19–64.

Fraser, W., Lewis, R.E. and Norman, J.L. (1991) 'Research education in M.S.W. programmes: an exploratory analysis', *Journal of Teaching in Social Work*, 4 (2): 83–103.

Gingerich, W.J. (1984) 'Generalizing single-case evaluation from classroom to practice', *Journal of Education for Social Work*, 20: 74–82.

Goldberg, E.M. (1970) *Helping the Aged*. London: Allen & Unwin.

Goldberg, E.M. and Robinson, J. (1977) 'An area office of an English social service department', in W.J. Reid and L. Epstein (eds), *Task-centered Practice*. New York: Columbia University Press. pp. 242–269.

Goldstein, E.G. (1998) 'Psychology and object relations theory', in R. Dorfman (ed.), *Paradigms of Clinical Social Work*, Vol. 2. New York: Brunner/Mazel. pp. 19–44.

Gorey, K.M. (1996) 'Effectiveness of social work intervention research: internal versus external evaluations', *Social Work Research*, 20 (2): 119–128.

Heineman, M.P. (1981) 'The obsolete imperative in social work research', *Social Service Review*, 55: 371–397.

Heineman, M.P. (1994) 'Science, not scientism: the robustness of naturalistic clinical research', in E. Sherman and W.J. Reid (eds), *Qualitative Research in Social Work*. New York: Columbia University Press. pp. 71–88.

Hollis, F. (1963) 'Contemporary issues for case-workers', in H.J. Parad and R.R. Miller (eds), *Ego-oriented Casework*. New York: Family Service Association of America. pp. 110–116.

Hudson, W.W. (1982) *The Clinical Measurement Package: A Field Manual*. Homewood, IL: Dorsey Press.

Ivanoff, A., Blythe, B.J. and Briar, S. (1997) 'What's the story, morning glory?' *Social Work Research*, 21 (3): 194–196.

Jayaratne, S. (1982) 'Characteristics and theoretical orientations of clinical social workers: a national survey', *Journal of Social Service Research*, 4: 17–29.

Jayaratne, S. and Levy, L. (1979) *Empirical Clinical Practice*. New York: Columbia University Press.

Jehu, D. (1967) *Learning Theory and Social Work*. London: Routledge & Kegan Paul.

Jensen, C. (1994) 'Psychosocial treatment of depression in women: nine single-subject evaluations', *Research on Social Work Practice*, 4 (3): 267–282.

Jensen, J.P., Bergin, A.E. and Greaves, D.W. (1990) 'The meaning of eclecticism: new survey and analysis of components', *Professional Psychology: Research and Practice*, 21 (2): 124–130.

Kagle, J. (1982) 'Using single-subject measures in practice decisions: systematic documentation or distortion?' *Arete*, 7 (2): 1–9.

Kazi, M.A.F. and Wilson, J. (1996a) 'Applying single-case evaluation methodology in a British social work agency', *Research on Social Work Practice*, 6 (1): 5–26.

Kazi, M.A.F. and Wilson, J. (1996b) 'Applying single-case evaluation in social work', *British Journal of Social Work*, 26: 699–717.

Kazi, M.A.F., Mantysaari, M. and Rostila, I. (1997) 'Promoting the use of single-case designs: social work experiences from England and Finland', *Research on Social Work Practice*, 7 (3): 311–328.

Kirk, S.A. (1990) 'Research utilization: the substructure of belief', in L. Videka-Sherman and W.J. Reid (eds), *Advances in Clinical Social Work Research*. Washington, DC: NASW Press. pp. 233–250.

Kirk, S.A. and Penka, C.E. (1992) 'Research utilization and MSW education: a decade of progress?' in A.J. Grasso and I. Epstein (eds), *Research Utilization in the Social Services*. New York: Haworth Press. pp. 407–419.

Klein, W.C. and Bloom, M. (1995) 'Practice wisdom', *Social Work*, 40 (2): 799–807.

LeCroy, C.W. and Goodwin, C.C. (1988) 'New directions in teaching social work methods: a content analysis of course outlines', *Journal of Social Work Education*, 24: 43–49.

Loch, C.S. (1899) 'Christian charity and political economy', *Charity Organization Review*, 6 (November): 10–20.

MacDonald, G. (1994) 'Developing empirically-based practice in probation', *British Journal of Social Work*, 24: 405–427.

MacDonald, G., Sheldon, B. and Gillespie, J. (1992) 'Contemporary studies of the effectiveness of social work', *British Journal of Social Work*, 22 (6), 625–643.

Marsh, P. (1998) *Report on Research in Practice Phase Two – for Association of Directors of Social Services*. Sheffield: University of Sheffield.

McGuire, J. (ed.) (1995) *What Works: Reducing Reoffending, Guidelines from Research and Practice*. Chichester: John Wiley.

Meyer, H., Borgatta, E. and Jones, W. (1965) *Girls at Vocational High*. New York: Russell Sage Foundation.

Millstein, K.H., Regan, J. and Reinherz, H. (1990) 'Can training in single subject design generalize to non-behavioral practice?' Paper presented at the Annual Program Meeting of the Council of Social Work Education, Reno, Nevada, 3–6 March.

Mullen, E.J. and Dumpson, J.R. and Associates (1972) *Evaluation of Social Intervention*. San Francisco: Jossey-Bass.

Mutschler, E. (1984) 'Evaluating practice: a study of research utilization by practitioners', *Social Work*, 29: 332–337.

Mutschler, E. and Jayaratne, S. (1993) 'Integration of information technology and single-system designs: issues and promises', in M. Bloom (ed.), *Single-system Designs in the Social Services: Issues and Options for the 1990s*. New York: Haworth Press. pp. 121–145.

Nelsen, J.C. (1978) 'Use of communication theory in single-subject research', *Social Work Research and Abstracts*, 14 (12): 12–19.

Nurius, P.S. and Hudson, W.W. (1993) *Human Services: Practice, Evaluation, and Computers*. Pacific Grove, CA: Brooks/Cole.

Penka, C.E. and Kirk, S.A. (1991) 'Practitioner involvement in clinical evaluation', *Social Work*, 36: 513–518.

Pinkston, J.L., Levitt, G.R., Green, N., Linsk, L. and Rzepnicki, T.L. (eds) (1982) *Effective Social Work Practice*. San Francisco: Jossey-Bass.

Reid, W.J. (1994) 'The empirical practice movement', *Social Service Review*, 68 (2): 165–184.

Reid, W.J. (1997) 'Research on task-centered practice', *Social Work Research*, 21(3): 132–137.

Reid, W.J. and Davis, I.P. (1987) 'Qualitative methods in single case research', in N. Gottlieb (ed.), *Proceedings of Conference on Practitioners as Evaluators of Direct Practice*. Seattle: School of Social Work, University of Washington. pp. 56–74.

Reid, W.J. and Hanrahan, P. (1982) 'Recent evaluations of social work: grounds for optimism', *Social Work*, 27: 328–340.

Richey, C.A., Blythe, B.J. and Berlin, S.B. (1987) 'Do social workers evaluate their practice?' *Social Work Research and Abstracts*, 23: 14–20.

Richmond, M. (1917) *Social Diagnosis*. New York: Russell Sage Foundation.

Rothman, J. and Thomas, E.J. (eds) (1994) *Intervention Research: Design and Development for Human Service*. Binghampton, NY: Prentice-Hall.

Rubin, A. (1985) 'Practice effectiveness: more grounds for optimism', *Social Work*, 30: 469–476.

Rubin, A. and Knox, K.S. (1996) 'Data analysis problems in single-case evaluation: issues for research on social work practice', *Research on Social Work Practice*, 6 (1): 40–65.

Sackett, D.L. and Rosenberg, W.M.C. (1995) 'On the need for evidence-based medicine', *Health Economist*, 4: 249–254.

Shaw, I. and Shaw, A. (1997) 'Game plans, buzzes, and sheer luck: doing well in social work', *Social Work Research*, 21 (2): 69–79.

Sheldon, B. (1978) 'Theory and practice in social work: a re-examination of a tenuous relationship', *British Journal of Social Work*, 8 (1): 1–22.

Sheldon, B. (1982) *Behaviour Modification: Theory, Practice and Philosophy*. London: Tavistock Publications.

Sheldon, B. (1983) 'The use of single-case experimental designs in the evaluation of social work', *British Journal of Social Work*, 13: 477–500.

Sheldon, B. (1986) 'Social work effectiveness experiments: review and implications', *British Journal of Social Work*, 16: 233–242.

Siegel, D.H. (1983) 'Can research and practice be integrated in social work education?' *Journal of Education for Social Work*, 19 (3): 12–19.

Slonim-Nevo, V. and Anson, Y. (1998) 'Evaluating practice: does it improve treatment outcome?' *Research in Social Work*, 22 (2): 60–74.

Smith, C., Lizotte, A.J., Thornberry, T.P. and Krohn, M.D. (1995) 'Resilient youth: identifying factors that prevent high-risk youth from engaging in delinquency and drug use', *Current Perspectives on Aging and the Life Cycle*, 4: 217–247.

Strom, K. (1992) 'The effect of third party reimbursement on services by social workers in private practice'. Doctoral dissertation, Cleveland, Ohio, Case Western Reserve University.

Thomas, E.J. (ed.) (1967) *The Socio-behavioral Approach and Applications to Social Work*. New York: Council on Social Work Education.

Thomas, E.J. (1978) 'Research and service in single-case experimentation: conflicts and choices', *Social Work Research and Abstracts*, 14: 20.

Thyer, B.A. (1997) 'Who stole social work?' *Social Work Research*, 21 (3): 198–201.

Tolson, E.R. (1977) 'Alleviating marital communication problems', in W.J. Reid and L. Epstein (eds), *Task-centered Practice*. New York: Columbia University Press. pp. 100–112.

Tolson, E.R. (1990) 'Synthesis: why don't practitioners use single-subject designs?' in L. Videka-Sherman and W.J. Reid (eds), *Advances in Clinical Social Work Research*. Silver Springs, MD: NASW Press. pp. 58–64.

Toseland, R.W. and Reid, W.J. (1985) 'Using rapid assessment instruments in a family service agency', *Social Casework*, 66: 547–555.

Tripodi, T. and Epstein, I. (1980) *Research Techniques for Clinical Social Workers*. New York: Columbia University Press.

Videka-Sherman, L. (1988) 'Meta-analysis of research on social work practice in mental health', *Social Work*, 33: 325–338.

Wakefield, J.C. and Kirk, S.A. (1996) 'Unscientific thinking about scientific practice: evaluating the scientist-practitioner model', *Social Work Research*, 20 (2): 83–95.

Wakefield, J.C. and Kirk, S.A. (1997) 'Science, dogma, and the scientist-practitioner model', *Social Work Research*, 21 (3): 201–205.

Whynes, D.K. (1996) 'Towards an evidence-based national health service?' *Economic Journal*, 105: 1702–1712.

Witkin, S. (1991) 'Empirical clinical practice: a critical analysis', *Social Work*, 36: 158–165.

Witkin, S. (1996) 'If empirical practice is the answer, then what is the question?' *Social Work Research*, 20 (2): 69–75.

Wodarski, J.S. (1981) *The Role of Research in Clinical Practice: A Practical Approach for the Human Services*. Baltimore, MD: University Park Press.

4

QUALITATIVE PRACTICE EVALUATION

Nick Gould

One definition of evaluation given by the *Oxford English Dictionary* is, 'to express in terms of the known', and so qualitative evaluation might be broadly understood as the expression of that which can be known through the analysis of spoken words, texts or observable behaviour. It seeks to interpret and find meaning within these phenomena as means towards the assessment of intervention. The focus of analysis will depend upon judgement, choice and interpretation as part of an inferential process by which categories, typologies and explanations are derived from phenomena which are usually studied in natural environments. Social work practice is itself strongly characterized by such forms of procedure. When a mental health social worker interviews a person to determine whether compulsory hospital admission is warranted they are making an assessment based on data constructed from observation and interpretation of behaviour and speech. The group worker constructs and tests hypotheses based on social interaction. As part of a review process a child care worker is likely to be synthesizing a range of documentary evidence based on reports and other texts. Qualitative inquiry is an inalienable element of practice.

In recent years some writers have pointed to a crisis of the professions, within which social work is implicated (Gould, 1996). Elements within this crisis are a withdrawal of public confidence in professional decision making, scepticism about value for money and claims of a lack of accountability; an effect of these is to promote defensive, procedurally driven practice. An alternative response in some areas has been to 'take a qualitative turn', seeking reconstructed forms of accountability and evaluation which go with the grain of practice, which recognize its qualitative character, being both reflexive and hermeneutic. Reid has argued that social work knowledge is 'a network of propositions with origins both in practice experience and research' (Reid, 1994: 475). This chapter will similarly argue that qualitative practice evaluation is emerging from the synthesis of the reconceptualization of practice as a reflective process of evaluation and learning, the reconstruction of the understanding of expert practice as an inductive process, and the contribution of qualitative research, from both within and without social work. Because this is still a perspective in formation the concepts of research and evaluation will be treated as having a permeable interface.

Although this process may have accelerated in recent years, qualitative inquiry stands on the shoulders of various intellectual projects within and around social work. At the risk of over-simplification it may be helpful to think of three illustrative lines of development in qualitative inquiry:

- Social scientists who have taken social work as a topic of inquiry. This literature reflects the evolution of theoretical and methodological concerns within their different disciplines, for instance Polsky's (1962) participant observation study of residential care for delinquent boys *Cottage Six*. In the United Kingdom Dingwall, Eekelaar and Murray's (1983) ethnographic study of risk management in the field of child protection was influential. More recent preoccupations with poststructuralism have led to a reinterpretation of the discourse of social work, such as Stenson's analysis of social work interviews (Stenson, 1993).
- Social work researchers who have drawn pragmatically on qualitative methods to illuminate issues which are of contemporary professional concern. An example would be the qualitative research concerned with the articulation of service user perspectives on the process of intervention and the consumption of services (e.g. Fisher, 1983; Howe, 1993; Mayer and Timms, 1970; Rees, 1978).
- Social work practitioner research (whether conducted by academics or practitioners) which is concerned with the development of qualitative forms of practice evaluation. Much of the early social work academic literature took the form of descriptive single case studies and indeed Sherman and Reid (1994) have suggested that the form of case study described by Mary Richmond in *Social Diagnosis* (1917) was a form of qualitative research. More recently academics and practitioners have adopted qualitative methods as tools for the direct evaluation of practice, such as Fook and colleagues' (1997) use of critical incident analysis, Hall's (1997) use of narrative and life story methods to give voice to children, and Shaw's (1996) overview of qualitative methods as evaluation strategies.

The emergence of qualitative inquiry reflects and is contemporaneous with a re-energizing of qualitative domains in various areas of the social sciences utilizing a range of methods including ethnography, grounded theory, discourse analysis, case studies and narrative inquiry. A brief overview can only indicate selectively some of these directions. Psychology has become highly preoccupied with discourse and textual analysis (Billig, 1991; Edwards and Potter, 1992; Soyland, 1994); in sociology and political science there are new approaches to case studies (Yin, 1994); in anthropology, ethnography maintains its central position but has incorporated poststructuralist interests in the construction of power (Miller, 1997); feminist studies reflect postmodernist approaches to the deconstruction of cultural forms (Walby, 1990). Social work sometimes has a laggardly relation with social science and social theory (Gould, 1990) but collections of writing have begun to emerge bringing together social work research which builds on these developments in the various qualitative domains (e.g. Riessman, 1994; Sherman and Reid, 1994). The boundary between research and evaluation is not always clear – and this chapter does not seek to hold to a rigid distinction – but the incorporation and legitimization of qualitative approaches in social work now seem to support a climate within which qualitative evaluation becomes part of the evaluative repertoire (Shaw, 1996).

It would be premature to argue that anything exists as tangible or capable of delineation as a qualitative practice movement. In contrast, the emergence and history of the empirical practice movement is something which can be described in terms of its institutional base, intellectual antecedents, key personnel, methodological contributions, relationship to practice and knowledge building (Reid, 1994). We cannot identify an equivalent pedigree for qualitative practice or evaluation though we can begin to map the territory in terms of epistemology, methods and knowledge building. Although, as will be discussed later, the term 'qualitative' subsumes a plurality of perspectives, philosophically it implies a rejection of unmodified positivism. This includes the assertion that the only valid forms of scientific inquiry follow the procedures of experimental and quasi-experimental design, from which objective observations of relations between phenomena lead to universalizable laws and the possibility of control and prediction. The debate around positivism has become particularly difficult in social work because of two linguistic elisions. One is the implication that only quantitative research is synonymous with scientific inquiry. The other is the incorporation by the empirical practice movement of the term 'empiricism' when what is often being promoted is positivism. This is presumably a response to the frequently pejorative connotations of positivism (Silverman, 1993), which is often replaced by a more neutral term such as 'empirical', but this obscures the fact that there are many forms of empirical knowledge, including that derived from qualitative inquiry.

Thus, the provenance of this chapter will be the interlocking perspectives that comprise the qualitative domain in social inquiry. Put together, none of this constitutes a unified movement or school. Rather like Denzin and Lincoln's general characterization of qualitative research, it is still 'primarily defined by an essential series of tensions, contradictions and hesitations' (Denzin and Lincoln, 1994: 15).

Reflection, expertise and qualitative practice

This emergent qualitative perspective in social work and other practitioner domains argues that practitioners are involved in the construction of forms of knowledge which have a distinct structure and epistemology (Fook, 1996; Gould and Harris, 1996). This critique addresses three domains – the forms of knowledge used in practice, the context of practice and the nature of problem-setting.

Forms of knowledge

It is widely recognized that even good practitioners are unable to give explicit accounts of their practice in terms of formal or propositional knowledge derived from positivist research. They may be able to demonstrate a form of intervention which has a positive outcome but not say why or how it works (Jarvis, 1983). There is no direct correlation between the acquisition of propositional knowledge and effectiveness in practice, despite the implicit presumptions of some champions of the latest positivist nostrum, evidence-based practice (see Neate, 1997). Indeed, it is clear from research evidence that what distinguishes expert from inexpert judgement is not the ability to make rule-based inferences from abstract problem representations. Though a universal characterization of expertise is elusive or unattainable because of the importance of context, expert performance often correlates with the practitioner's accumulation of experientially developed templates for pattern recognition (Boreham, 1988).

The context of practice

The traditional view of practice as applied formal knowledge fails to recognize the context of practice as a formative influence in knowledge-use and creation by practitioners. Professional knowledge is created and revealed through a range of sources but only has meaning – in common social work parlance 'becomes owned' – through use in specific situations. Despite the presumptions often made in social work education, knowledge-in-use is very context specific and learning is not generally directly transferable (Whittington, 1986). Usable knowledge is interpretive, requiring adaptation and explication in the context of practice.

Problem-setting

A third line of critique of conventional epistemologies of practice has been to challenge the mistaken belief that problems are pre-defined, or somehow pre-exist and await discovery. This fallacy reflects a pre-

Popperian belief that observation can take place independently of theoretical assumptions. Problems are constructed and labelled through selective perception from an open-ended field of data. Positivism suggests that practitioners have a repertoire of approaches which can be matched to a pre-given problem. This (to paraphrase Schon, 1983) is a view from the high ground which is at odds with the practitioner's experience of life in the swampy lowlands where situations are encountered which have unique (even if patterned) features that require analysis and review to determine what is the problem.

As indicated, much of this critique is brought forward in Donald Schon's elaboration of reflective practice (Schon, 1983). He locates his model of reflective practice in a critique of technical rationality, which he sees as underpinning a positivist hegemony in academic institutions. This legitimizes the authority of forms of knowledge and scientific practice supporting 'pure' academic research, and devalues applied and performance-based forms of knowledge creation and expertise. Social work academicians will readily identify with Schon's portrayal of marginalized disciplines where tenure of employment may be difficult to secure. In the UK social work is not recognized by government research councils as a discipline, and in Europe social work education largely lies outside the university sector (Lorenz, 1994). One response to promote the 'respectability' of social work is to emulate the scientific paradigm and this is still indicated by the emphasis in student research textbooks on quantitative methodologies. As random examples from mainstream social work literature, a 1991 North American textbook on research methods for social work contains one chapter on qualitative methods out of a total of 13 (Royse, 1991), and a more recent volume includes one chapter out of 17 (Mark, 1996).

The case for qualitative evaluation of practice is also supported by developments in understanding of the nature of expertise. There is a reasonable consensus that practitioner expertise does not reside in the ability to complete more efficiently the same cognitive problem-solving strategies as novices. Experts, particularly in complex fields such as professional practice, use different strategies and bring to bear different kinds of knowledge at higher levels of problem solving and task performance (Ericsson and Oliver, 1995). Dreyfus and Dreyfus (1986) showed that skilled performance lies in the domain of tacit knowledge. This has been elaborated in other professional areas, notably in Benner's qualitative study of nursing, which showed how the development of expertise mirrored the Dreyfuses description of the development of non-rule-governed-inference (Benner, 1984). Briefly, their thesis is that it is only novice practitioners who are guided by rules based on formal theoretical knowledge, with little ability to adapt practice to local contextual variations. As the practitioner becomes more expert, this mechanistic application of theory becomes more situated in the context of practice, more consciously selected, and increasingly based on recognition of prior problem-solving experience. In this way expertise becomes more implicit and seemingly 'intuitive' and unlike the technical rationality, which underpins the notion of expertise, assumed by empirical practice. More recently, Fook and colleagues have begun to apply similar analyses to social work and find similar validations of a conceptualization of expertise which resides in experientially based inductive processes rather than the deductive application of propositional knowledge (Fook et al., 1997).

Taken together, there is now a substantive body of empirical and theoretical work that characterizes practice as itself a form of qualitative inquiry, knowledge building and evaluation. Although Schon is a key figure in this debate, much of the intellectual underpinning derives from the American pragmatic tradition and subsequent research in the field of experiential learning (Gould, 1989). John Dewey is undoubtedly an important influence in the emergence of this perspective. For Dewey, experience is the organizing focus for learning, which in turn synthesizes observations and actions with conceptual ideas, so providing the basis for higher order purposeful action. However, postponement of immediate action is necessary until 'observation and judgment have intervened' (Dewey, 1938 quoted Gould, 1989: 11). This cyclical formulation is echoed in Kurt Lewin's work (Lewin, 1951) in which he argues that experience initiates a feedback loop to the individual in which experience is transformed through observation into abstract concepts and generalizations which are retested in new situations. Kolb drew together the work of Dewey and Lewin in formulating a learning cycle linking concrete experience, reflective observation, abstract conceptualization and active experimentation (Kolb, 1984).

There are direct parallels between these theories of experiential learning and Schon's model of reflective practice. Both see practice as a form of ongoing inquiry and evaluation that produces new knowledge. This perspective inverts the conventional understanding of the relationship between theory and practice by acknowledging that practitioners operate within an 'indeterminate zone of practice' where problems have to be constructed out of messy, fluctuating circumstances, often presenting themselves as unique cases falling outside the existing categories of theory and technique, and containing inherent conflict between value systems.

> These indeterminate zones of practice – uncertainty, uniqueness and value-conflict – escape the canons of technical rationality. . . . And in situations of value conflict there are no clear and self-consistent ends to guide the technical selection of means. (Schon, 1987: 6)

This reconstruction of the epistemological base of practice equates learning with the construction and development of self-evaluation and the

construction of usable theories of practice. This is not to dismiss positivist approaches or formal theory out of hand but to recategorize them
as additional resources for the critical review or reframing of practice.
Eraut draws the radical implication of this position that the practitioner
is validated as the expert in the evaluation of practice – the academic or
researcher no longer has primacy as a producer of knowledge. The
implication is that the 'outsider' such as the academic should perceive
her or himself as 'enhancing the knowledge creation capacities of individuals and professional communities' (Eraut, 1985: 117).

The paradigm debate

The qualitative approach is essentially pluralistic, as is congruent with an
epistemological position which is provisional, inductivist, relativist and
pragmatic. In a highly influential contribution to the qualitative evaluation debate Lincoln and Guba distinguish between positivism, postpositivism, critical theory and constructivism (Guba and Lincoln, 1989,
1994), all of which with the exception of positivism they regard as being
at a formative stage. Each can be identified on dimensions of ontology
(what is reality and what can be known about it?), epistemology (what is
the relationship between the knower and what can be known?) and
methodology (how can the inquirer go about finding out whatever can
be known?). Lincoln and Guba's argument is that the evaluator is forced
to choose a position, and the position taken on any one of these three
questions implies a stance on the other two. The adoption of a paradigm
has important consequences not only for the conduct of the inquiry but
also for the interpretation of findings and policy choices. Briefly stated,
they outline the paradigms as follows:

Positivism

The aim of inquiry is to explain phenomena, leading to their prediction
and control. An external reality is assumed to exist which can be
apprehended. The evaluator is separate from the object of inquiry and
findings can be taken to correspond directly to objectively observable
reality. Legitimate processes of inquiry will follow experimental design,
usually to produce quantified data.

Postpositivism

This modified view of positivism still views the nature of external reality
as unproblematic, but accepts that research will reveal partial and
incomplete apprehensions of that reality. Postpositivism accepts a
modified form of dualism: that the observer and observed are separate

but that objectivity is sought through peer review and commensurateness of findings with preceding bodies of knowledge. Knowledge building proceeds through quasi-experimental methods and 'triangulation' (study of the same phenomenon using different methods).

Critical theory

This paradigm takes structures and processes to be experienced as 'real' but views them as produced through historical, cultural, gender and ethnic experiences. The evaluator and evaluated are regarded as inextricably linked, so that findings are mediated by their social positions. The implied methods for inquiry are dialogue and critique: these are used to transcend false or illusory accounts of social life and to reveal underlying relations of domination, exploitation and power.

Constructivism

Realities are taken to be local, specific and experiential, dependent for their emergence and development on groups or individuals. These constructions are not more or less true in any final or universal sense. Findings of research are iteratively created through the interactions of researcher and researched. Constructions are elicited by interaction between the inquirer and co-inquirers or respondents which are deconstructed by hermeneutic exploration.

There is a long-standing debate within the social sciences as to whether they are 'pre-paradigmatic', as well as some debate in the social work literature on the validity of the concept of paradigm in relation to social work knowledge (see, for instance, Stenson and Gould, 1986; Shaw, Chapter 2 in this volume). For the purposes of this discussion it suffices to say that we can probably locate most social work research and evaluation within one of the last three categories even though authors may not explicitly assign their practice to a 'paradigm'.

For the practitioner seeking to develop a method for incorporating evaluation within practice this plethora of schisms and positions can become a predicament of almost medieval theological complexity. As Lincoln and Guba state, the metaphor of a 'paradigm war' is overstated but the problems of commensurability of paradigms are significant. This is not least at the level of epistemology where it is difficult to reconcile people who assert there is an external reality with those who believe that all social life is a construction. However, the purposes of a practice-based (albeit intellectually complex) endeavour such as social work may enable practitioners to find bases for consensus, whilst suspending claims for ultimate definitions of reality. The attempt here will be to suggest a provisional overview which synthesizes the main 'orthodoxies' within qualitative practice evaluation, but which hopefully does not do too great an injustice to more specific perspectives. I take the common themes to be threefold. First, the process of inquiry and evaluation is cyclical rather than linear. We have talked about the relationship between learning cycles and evaluation, rather than the linear process of positivism that moves from hypothesis to finding. Secondly, the researcher rejects a Cartesian distinction between observation and action and takes a reflexive position towards his or her own subjective responses. Thirdly, methodology does not depend upon standardized measurement but upon the improvisation and adaptation of tools which are contextually appropriate.

Following the action-learning cycles discussed above this may be characterized as a four-stage process. The cycle may be repeated as many times as is desirable or practicable until the iteration seems to be complete – no further useful understanding or change can be produced – or practical limitations of time or other resources are exhausted.

The first stage is concrete experience: the immersion of the worker in the situation as it presents itself, the lived reality of the service user. In conventional models of the social work process this is the engagement and assessment phase when a shared definition is sought with the service user of what constitutes the problem, how it has arisen, its context, contributory factors and their effects. This is likely to proceed through the processes of interview, dialogue and the collection of relevant information from other data sources. Out of this engagement and involvement, or reflection-in-action, emerges a provisional perspective on the situation, its boundaries and significance.

In the second stage reflective observation, or reflection-on-action becomes the dominant mode of inquiry. This may take various paths including dialogue with significant actors, supervision, internal mental reflection, or more formalized events such as family network conferences. Assimilation and synthesis of information characterize this stage.

Thirdly, a preliminary conceptualization of the problem emerges. This may take various forms and need not be a highly intellectualized, abstractly represented view of the issues. It may also be expressed in metaphor, imagery, or in terms of patterns or schemas which are based in previous experience. Whatever the form or medium, the conceptualization of the problem suggests forms of action which might be effective in producing change.

Finally, the insights gained through reflection-on-action and conceptualization are translated into new prescriptions for action and are tested out in practice. This is equivalent to Kolb's phase of active experimentation, which leads back into concrete experience and further review of whether the problem has improved or changed. At no stage does this preclude the use of methods from empirical clinical practice (such as those espoused by Walter Hudson), derived from behavioural or cognitive approaches. Indeed, there may be a good case for establishing baseline measures of a problem at the initial concrete experience stage. But the critical point of qualitative practice is that there is recognition that all this takes place within a hermeneutic circle unavoidably involving what Gadamer has called interpretive understanding. The meanings of things can 'only be grasped through the circle of understanding, a circle that presupposes the fore structures that enable us to understand' (Usher and Bryant, 1989: 34).

Towards transparency, consensus and validity

Since its emergence from anthropological and sociological forms of inquiry there has been a sense that the qualitative approach constitutes an 'outsider' perspective – the reactionary academic jibe that the qualitative is just about 'nuts, sluts and perverts'. This has reflected not only the empirical content of sociological inquiry, particularly within the sociology of deviance, but also the criticisms of reliability and validity which are faced by those who depend primarily on qualitative methods. Empirical practice promotes itself as validated by the rigour of experimental design based on scientific principles. There is now persuasive evidence within the sociology of scientific knowledge to show that the natural sciences themselves proceed in knowledge building through socially constructed and interpretive practices (e.g. Collins, 1985; Woolgar, 1985). Even the seemingly unassailable practice of mathematics can be argued to be a form of social practice which is constructive (Livingston, 1987).

As the common ground and convergence of positivist research and qualitative inquiry become understood so the case emerges for accepting that we might find some shared perspectives for making judgements about standards in quantitative and qualitative research and evaluation. Indeed, and as Reid has also argued, many of these criteria correspond surprisingly closely to the judgements social workers make as part of skilled practice: corroboration, bias, generalization, theory validity and task relevance (Reid, 1994: 471). In many ways validity is achieved in qualitative evaluation through transparency in setting out the process of inquiry (Altheide and Johnson, 1994).

Sometimes qualitative evaluators and researchers seem to be suggesting that the demands by positivists that they (the qualitative camp) show how they demonstrate validity are part of a reductionist, anti-humanist conspiracy. In fact empirical practitioners ask reasonable questions about the validation of knowledge which – particularly in social work – will have a significant impact on people's lives. As Miles and Huberman have argued:

> Our view is that qualitative studies take place in a real social world, and can have real consequences in people's lives; that there is a reasonable view of 'what happened' in any particular situation (including what was believed, interpreted, etc.), and that we who render accounts of it can do so well or

poorly, and should not consider our work unjudgable. In other words, shared understandings are worth striving for. (Miles and Huberman, 1994: 277)

Patton has suggested three areas into which can be subsumed questions about standards in evaluation (Patton, 1987, 1990). The first is whether data of high quality have been carefully collected and analysed in terms of reliability, validity and triangulation. The second are the qualifications and credibility of the evaluator herself, whether she is adequately trained, experienced and skilled in evaluation. Thirdly is the coherence of the theoretical and philosophical underpinning of the evaluation, whether there is congruence between the epistemological and onto-logical assumptions made by the evaluator, the forms of inquiry initiated by the evaluation and the claims made in the outputs.

In the first instance, although there are very many typologies of validity and reliability, some common definitions will be considered here. *Confirmability* is the issue of whether the evaluation is acceptably neutral and free from researcher bias. This will be judged by criteria such as whether the process has been recorded fully and can be followed clearly and unambiguously. Given that most qualitative evaluators will reject the possibility that evaluation can be value free, are the assump-tions, feelings and biases of the practitioner openly stated? *Reliability* refers to the stability of intervention over time, the quality control of intervention and care taken. Again, there are questions which can be asked by the practitioner about whether the objectives of the evaluation were clear and the intervention congruent with them. *Internal validity* has been described as the crunch question: the truth value. Were predictions of outcomes made, and were they confirmed? Are the findings judged to be true by participants, including service users? Was negative evidence actively sought and have alternative explanations of events been con-sidered and tested against the evidence? *External validity* considers the generalization of findings to other contexts. It is in the nature of much social work evaluation that the findings will be essentially local; the orthodox consideration of qualitative research of whether generalization can be made from sample to population will be too ambitious. However, analytic (theory-connected) and case-to-case generalizability will be of relevance. Does intervention from a certain theoretical perspective con-firm prior theoretical claims of the perspective? Is the description of a case sufficiently precise and full to allow transfer of the intervention to other cases which fall within similar categories? *Utilization*, or pragmatic validity, is of particular relevance to social work where there is a commitment to making a difference to the quality of service users' lives. This may involve follow-up to see whether gains made are sustained or, in the instance of evaluation relating to programmes, whether managers and policy makers have incorporated recommendations or new insights from the evaluation.

The second area by which qualitative evaluation is justified relates to the standing of the evaluator. In social work there has been a long struggle towards the recognition of evaluation as an important element of practice (Shaw, 1996). In the United Kingdom, qualification as a social work practitioner is not tied to any academic level and many practitioners will not have had the opportunity to receive an explicit research or evaluation training over and above the modest requirements of the Diploma in Social Work curriculum. However, there have been developments in social work education towards the establishment of forms of good practice which may not have the formal label of 'qualitative evaluation' but which could, if established, be part of a more qualitative evaluation practice. Requiring that students elicit user feedback on the intervention they have received is part of the reflective evaluative dialogue. This may be more or less formalized as a process ranging from a conversation to the completion of a written questionnaire. The use of supervision is also an established part of the culture of social work and can be an opportunity for evaluation, provided that there is a shared willingness to move beyond the narrower organizational agendas towards a more reflective analysis and dialogue about the efficacy of methods of intervention and their outcomes. Not least is the adoption within social work education of forms of pedagogy which are inherently inductive and qualitative such as problem-centred learning, inquiry and action learning, and self-directed learning and reflective learning (Burgess, 1992; Gould and Taylor, 1996; Yelloly and Henkel, 1995).

Thirdly, is there internal consistency between the theoretical and methodological aspects of an evaluation? The suggestion in this chapter is that practitioners can develop a generic and pragmatic approach to qualitative evaluation. However, it is a central tenet of an inductive approach to evaluation that this activity cannot be value free and inevitably reflects some assumptions about the nature of reality, causal relationships and judgements of relevance. In other domains, particularly education, there is extensive debate about the extent to which distinct paradigms of qualitative evaluation can be discerned, and social work might learn from this. Although social work may be, in the well-used term from the sociology of knowledge, pre-paradigmatic, we may well see a more explicit future debate about the theoretical positions around which social work practitioner-evaluators may organize their evaluative activity. Were the debate to follow the terms established in education by Lincoln and Guba then we would expect some distinctions to emerge. These could include postpositivists who accept a realist position about external reality and mirror the approach of positivists towards evaluation in practice. A critical theory position might emerge drawing on neo-Marxism, feminism, participatory inquiry and an approach essentially based on the emancipatory potential of critical dialogue. We might also see the establishment of a constructivist paradigm drawing on discourse theory, postmodernist deconstruction and other hermeneutic approaches to the analysis and reconstruction of practice. Each paradigm has its own internal logic. Part of the totality which comprises the credibility of qualitative evaluation is consistency of evaluation in ontology, epistemology and method.

Moving the debates forward

There is a tendency in Western cultures to polarize debate and reduce alternatives to bipolar constructs (Haste, 1993) and social work is no exception. This has been the thrust of debates around empirical practice in social work, and the debate may become even more polarized because of the more recent emergence of evidence-based practice. The latter is uncritically imported from medicine where the objective has been to encourage clinicians to use techniques for which there is research-based validation. Usually this means the availability of research evidence based on narrow criteria of experimental method, especially randomized controlled trials. In the UK the Department of Health has now made a major financial investment in the establishment of a university-based centre to promote an evidence-based approach in social work. Social work will soon have to consider whether it also wants to be driven by this positivist agenda, or whether we want to assert the importance to practice of evaluation-based knowledge which includes qualitative approaches that have a particular synergy with social work practice.

This is not to reject the importance of quantitative methods in evaluation. There are established procedures in qualitative research for analysing the frequency of events or entities to confirm or refute hypotheses. Similarly, quantitative and experimental methods are themselves forms of social practice which depend upon social processes to produce knowledge. As W. David Harrison has argued, exemplary social work practitioners use information and paradigms in an integrated and flexible way (Harrison, 1994: 411). Propositional knowledge, sometimes including quantitative data, constructs part of the frame of analysis in which practice may be qualitatively assessed. As an example from my own experience, an evaluation of team practice in family centres included a statistical mapping of family need as a guide to identifying aspects of the service which were to be evaluated both quantitatively and qualitatively. Quantitative measures and numerical data can inform the reflective cycles of qualitative practice evaluation. Rather than fall into the trap of constructing the dichotomy we have just been criticizing, part of the paradigmatic synthesis will be a multiple perspective which accepts that qualitative, reflective evaluation will when appropriate incorporate quantitative techniques.

This is particularly true of programme evaluation (Rutman and Mowbray, 1983). Whereas we have primarily been concerned with reflective evaluation of practice by single practitioners, a programme is a set of activities designed to achieve external objectives, for instance to meet a social need or solve a social problem. A programme is likely to involve the co-ordination of several players, perhaps a project team within an agency and sometimes a multi-agency approach. The complexity of a programme is likely to require for the purposes of evaluation a multi-method approach designed to capture the effects of the multiple elements within it. Likewise different stakeholders may have different views of what success could mean in terms of programme outcomes. The combination of quantitative measures of effectiveness with qualitative analysis arguably deepens and enriches the evaluation, and may also support a more pluralistic inquiry which addresses the concerns of a range of constituencies (Smith and Cantley, 1985).

There are political agendas behind some of the façades of seemingly technical debates about methodologies. Some sociologists, drawing on the insights of poststructuralism into the relationship between knowledge and power, have excavated the relationship between behavioural positivism and technologies of social control (Cohen, 1985). Nevertheless, it would be naïve to assume that by inference qualitative evaluation must always be on the side of the ideological angels. It is as well to remind ourselves of the powerful critique of social interactionism as a qualitative tradition in social science: that it was inherently conservative because of its focus on micro analysis and ignored the wider construction of relationships of power. Similarly there is a case to be heard that the reflective practice movement and other related approaches still suffer from a theoretical and methodological individualism and as a result make no serious contribution to the central contemporary concerns of social work to challenge oppressive social structures. The models of action-learning cycles which are generic to much of the qualitative practice evaluation literature are essentially psychological models which foreground the learning process of the individual and leave in the background the relationships of power and inequality which impact on the emancipatory potential of the individual. Some recent writers on reflective practice, particularly those writing from a feminist perspective such as Amy Rossiter (1996), reassert the relationship between the personal and the political. Others such as Charles Rapp have argued for the capacity of qualitative methods to give a voice to stakeholders who normally would not have a platform to articulate their concerns, such as users of mental health services (Rapp et al., 1994). Rapp's thesis is not qualitative versus quantitative methods, but to remind us that one fundamental question to ask is: what emancipatory values are advanced by the evaluation strategy? The connections with emancipatory values need to be sustained as part of qualitative evaluation if it is not to retreat into an inherently disempowering impasse of subjectivism and relativism.

In the coming years qualitative evaluation, to consolidate its position as a useful perspective, will have to confront various issues many of which relate to the tendency of closed communities, whether of academics or practitioners, to speak only to themselves and the initiated:

- At the epistemological level it is important to avoid the slippery slope on which anti-oppressive practice slides into a radical form of relativism within which all perspectives are equally valid. Any evaluation makes reference to some external criteria. Social work may be assisted by referring to recent attempts in social policy to delineate universal – qualitative and quantitative – definitions and measurements of need (particularly Doyal and Gough, 1991).
- At the methodological level it needs to be accepted that empirical practitioners ask important questions about the robustness and stability of findings from qualitative inquiry. Qualitative methodology has reached a stage of development where there are coherent principles for testing reliability and validity but these need to be more consciously integrated into evaluation practice.
- It will not be helpful for social work either to become stuck in a 'paradigm war' where the followers of a particular school are locked into a single perspective, or to fall back on an atheoretical pragmatism where anything goes.
- Policy makers remain more receptive to quantitative data as forms of persuasion in making policy choices (Majone, 1989; Rist, 1994; though see Ruckdeschel, Chapter 11 in this volume). Raising the plausibility of qualitative findings partly depends on the previous point about validity but there is also work to be done in demonstrating the relevance and plausibility of the analysis, not least by the continuing development of mixed method approaches.
- Evidence-based practice is a persuasive discourse that offers the practitioner the illusion of certainty, but practitioners need to remember that 'evidence' is a contested and complex concept, which can incorporate qualitative knowledge.
- Accountability to both funders and service users cannot now be taken off the agenda. Practitioners of qualitative inquiry will need to be responsive to their multiple constituencies by communicating their principles and methods in forms and language that are found to be relevant and intelligible. It also requires a continuing effort to establish processes for involving service users in the design, execution and dissemination of evaluation.

References

Altheide, D.L. and Johnson, J.M. (1994) 'Criteria for assessing interpretive validity in qualitative research', in N.K. Denzin and Y.S. Lincoln (eds), *Handbook of Qualitative Research*. Thousand Oaks, CA: Sage.

Benner, P. (1984) *From Novice to Expert: Excellence and Power in Clinical Nursing Practice*. Menlo Park, CA: Addison-Wesley.

Billig, M. (1991) *Ideology and Opinions: Studies in Rhetorical Psychology.* London: Sage.

Boreham, N.C. (1988) 'Models of diagnosis and their implications for adult professional education', *Studies in the Higher Education of Adults,* 20 (2): 95–108.

Burgess, H. (1992) *Problem-Led Learning for Social Work: The Inquiry and Action Approach.* London: Whiting and Birch.

Cohen, S. (1985) *Visions of Social Control.* Cambridge: Polity Press.

Collins, H.M. (1985) *Changing Order: Replication and Induction in Scientific Practice.* London: Sage.

Denzin, N. and Lincoln, Y.S. (eds) (1994) *Handbook of Qualitative Research.* Thousand Oaks, CA: Sage.

Dingwall, R., Eekelaar, J. and Murray, T. (1983) *The Protection of Children: State Intervention and Family Life.* Oxford: Basil Blackwell.

Doyal, L. and Gough, I. (1991) *A Theory of Human Need.* Basingstoke: Macmillan.

Dreyfus, H. and Dreyfus, S. (1986) *Mind Over Machine: The Power of Human Intuition and Expertise in the Era of the Computer.* Oxford: Basil Blackwell.

Edwards, D. and Potter, J. (1992) *Discursive Psychology.* London: Sage.

Eraut, M. (1985) 'Knowledge creation and knowledge use in professional contexts', *Studies in Higher Education,* 10 (1): 117–137.

Ericsson, K. and Oliver, W. (1995) 'Cognitive skills', in N. Mackintosh and A. Colman (eds), *Learning and Skills.* London: Longman.

Fisher, M. (ed.) (1983) *Speaking of Clients.* Sheffield: University of Sheffield Joint Unit for Social Services Research.

Fook, J. (ed.) (1996) *The Reflective Researcher: Social Workers' Theories of Practice Research.* St Leonard's, NSW: Allen & Unwin.

Fook, J., Ryan, M. and Hawkins, L. (1997) 'Towards a theory of social work expertise', *British Journal of Social Work,* 27 (3): 339–417.

Gould, N. (1989) 'Reflective learning for social work practice', *Social Work Education,* 8 (2): 9–20.

Gould, N. (1990) 'Political critique of Kantian ethics: a contribution to the debate between Webb and MacBeath, and Downie', *British Journal of Social Work,* 20 (6): 495–499.

Gould, N. (1996) 'Social work education and the "crisis of the professions" ' in N. Gould and I. Taylor (eds), *Reflective Learning for Social Work.* Aldershot: Arena.

Gould, N. and Harris, A. (1996) 'Student imagery of practice in social work and teacher education: a comparative research approach', *British Journal of Social Work,* 26 (2): 223–238.

Gould, N. and Taylor, I. (eds) (1996) *Reflective Learning for Social Work.* Aldershot: Arena.

Guba, E.G. and Lincoln, Y.S. (1989) *Fourth Generation Evaluation.* Newbury Park, CA: Sage.

Guba, E.G. and Lincoln, Y.S. (1994) 'Competing paradigms in qualitative research', in N.K. Denzin and Y.S. Lincoln (eds), *Handbook of Qualitative Research.* Thousand Oaks, CA: Sage.

Hall, C. (1997) *Social Work as Narrative: Storytelling and Persuasion in Professional Texts.* Aldershot: Avebury.

Harrison, W.D. (1994) 'The inevitability of integrated methods' in E. Sherman and W.J. Reid (eds), *Qualitative Research in Social Work*. New York: Columbia University Press.

Haste, H. (1993) *The Sexual Metaphor*. New York: Harvester Wheatsheaf.

Howe, D. (1993) *On Becoming a Client*. London: Sage.

Jarvis, P. (1983) *Professional Education*. London: Croom Helm.

Kolb, D.A. (1984) *Experiential Learning: Experience as the Source of Learning and Development*. Englewood Cliffs, NJ: Prentice-Hall.

Lewin, K. (1951) *Field Theory in the Social Sciences*. New York: Harper & Row.

Livingston, E. (1987) *Making Sense of Ethnomethodology*. London: Routledge & Kegan Paul.

Lorenz, W. (1994) *Social Work in a Changing Europe*. London: Routledge.

Majone, G. (1989) *Evidence, Argument and Persuasion in the Policy Process*. New Haven, CT: Yale University Press.

Mark, R. (1996) *Research Made Simple: A Handbook for Social Workers*. Thousand Oaks, CA: Sage.

Mayer, T.E. and Timms, N. (1970) *The Client Speaks: Working Class Impressions of Casework*. New York: Atherton Press.

Miles, M.B. and Huberman, A.M. (1994) *Qualitative Data Analysis*. Thousand Oaks, CA: Sage.

Miller, G. (1997) 'Building bridges: the possibility of analytic dialogue between ethnography, conversation analysis and Foucault', in D. Silverman (ed.), *Qualitative Research: Theory, Method and Practice*. London: Sage.

Neate, P. (1997) 'Face facts', *Community Care*, 1181 (17–23 July): 18–19.

Patton, M.Q. (1987) *How to Use Qualitative Methods in Evaluation*. Newbury Park, CA: Sage.

Patton, M.Q. (1990) *Qualitative Evaluation and Research Methods*. Newbury Park, CA: Sage.

Polsky, H.W. (1962) *Cottage Six: The Social System of Delinquent Boys in Residential Treatment*. New York: Wiley.

Rapp, C.A., Kisthardt, W., Gowdy, E. and Hanson, J. (1994) 'Amplifying the consumer voice: qualitative methods empowerment and mental health research', in E. Sherman and W.J. Reid (eds), *Qualitative Research in Social Work*. New York: Columbia University Press.

Rees, S. (1978) *Social Work Face to Face*. London: Edward Arnold.

Reid, W.J. (1994) 'The empirical practice movement', *Social Service Review*, 68 (2): 165–184.

Richmond, M. (ed.) (1917) *Social Diagnosis*. New York: Russell Sage Foundation.

Riessman, C.K. (ed.) (1994) *Qualitative Studies in Social Work Research*. Thousand Oaks, CA: Sage.

Rist, R. (1994) 'Influencing the policy process with qualitative research', in N.K. Denzin and Y.S. Lincoln (eds), *Handbook of Qualitative Research*. Thousand Oaks, CA: Sage.

Rossiter, A. (1996) 'Finding meaning for social work in transitional times: reflections on change', in N. Gould and I. Taylor (eds), *Reflective Learning for Social Work*. Aldershot: Arena.

Royse, D.D. (1991) *Research Methods in Social Work*. Chicago: Nelson-Hall.

Rutman, L. and Mowbray, G. (1983) *Understanding Programme Evaluation*. Beverly Hills, CA: Sage.

Schon, D. (1983) *The Reflective Practitioner*. London: Temple Smith.

Schon, D. (1987) *Educating the Reflective Practitioner.* San Francisco: Jossey-Bass.

Shaw, I. (1996) *Evaluating in Practice.* Aldershot: Arena.

Sherman, E. and Reid, W.J. (eds) (1994) *Qualitative Research in Social Work.* New York: Columbia University Press.

Silverman, D. (1993) *Interpreting Qualitative Data: Methods for Analysing Talk, Text and Interaction.* London: Sage.

Smith, G. and Cantley, C. (1985) 'Policy evaluation: the use of varied data in a study of a psychogeriatric service', in R. Walker (ed.), *Applied Qualitative Research.* Aldershot: Dartmouth.

Soyland, A.J. (1994) *Psychology as Metaphor.* London: Sage.

Stenson, K. (1993) 'Social work discourse and the social work interview', *Economy and Society,* 22 (1): 42–76.

Stenson, K. and Gould, N. (1986) 'A comment on "A Framework for Theory in Social Work" by Whittington and Holland', *Issues in Social Work Education,* 6 (2): 41–46.

Usher, R. and Bryant, I. (1989) *Adult Education as Theory, Practice and Research: The Captive Triangle.* London: Routledge.

Walby, S. (1990) *Theorizing Patriarchy.* Oxford: Basil Blackwell.

Whittington, C. (1986) 'Literature review: transfer of learning in social work education', *British Journal of Social Work,* 16 (5): 571–577.

Woolgar, S. (ed.) (1985) *Knowledge and Reflexivity: New Frontiers in the Sociology of Knowledge.* London: Sage.

Yelloly, M. and Henkel, M. (eds) (1995) *Learning and Teaching in Social Work: Towards Reflective Practice.* London: Jessica Kingsley.

Yin, R.K. (1994) *Case-Study Research: Design and Methods.* Thousand Oaks, CA: Sage.

5

EVALUATION AND EMPOWERMENT

Karen Dullea and Audrey Mullender

Service evaluation in social work settings is typically a managerially driven enterprise emphasizing techniques of measurement and monitoring, rather than an empowering value base. This is not inevitable. There are evaluatory traditions far more in tune with the philosophy of social work – even overlapping with some areas of practice intervention, notably group and community work – which draw those on the receiving end of services into full participation at every stage of the process, from deciding what should be evaluated to working out how this should be done, what the resulting information means, and what should happen as a result. They are democratizing in intent, and they stress the fact that something *should* happen – that some action or change should flow from research and evaluation into policy and practice.

The most obvious methodologies that lend themselves to such an approach are participatory research and feminist research (see Humphries, Chapter 7 in this volume for a fuller exposition of feminist research). Combining their strengths – and responding, also, to some more recent challenges – offers a transformative model of evaluation with a natural home in empowerment models of social work practice.

Participatory research: the generation of transformative knowledge

Rejecting 'top down' expertise

Participatory research is democratic inquiry into the social, political and economic pressures that sustain oppression. Systems of authority and influence have traditionally claimed to know best what people need and have been reflected in officially sanctioned processes of knowledge creation (research, policy formulation and so on). These teach people 'to believe that they cannot adequately understand their own lives' (Maguire,

1987: 36) so that outside experts must be brought in to provide the answers. A similar tendency engendered amongst service users by top down, non-consultative social work services has more recently been challenged by models of empowerment practice (Lee, 1994; Mullender and Ward, 1991) and, over a far longer timescale, by social and community action (Coyle, 1980). Participatory research, like empowerment practice, is a strongly value-based attempt to build on strengths and to work with people who are taking control of their lives by understanding and tackling oppression and injustice. It is unusual amongst research methods in that it contains these specific elements of previously disempowered people *taking control* and *taking action*.

Participatory research has developed in a context of recognizing unjust social structures (Anderson, 1996; Hick, 1997). There is a practice-based parallel in empowerment, in the recognition that the problems service users face 'can never be fully understood if they are seen solely as a result of personal inadequacies' (Mullender and Ward, 1991: 31) and in the need to base intervention on a wider questioning of the causes (for example Mullender and Ward, 1991: 18). The social structures in question not only control our lives in practical terms but also affect the way we perceive ourselves, through processes of internalized oppression (Freire, 1972: 23; Lee, 1990: 24).

Both social work intervention and its evaluation get caught within systems of top down authoritative knowledge. Whenever social work and health professionals paternalistically take care of people or judge the outcomes of the services they receive, believing they know what is best (Cornwall and Jewkes, 1995: 1674), they collude with keeping people in a position of supposed inferiority. Prescribing cures or services, expecting individuals to adjust to that which they cannot control (including socially constructed disability, and restrictive and demeaning images of ageing), and pathologizing natural responses to injustice and inequality (Anderson, 1996: 72), are all variants of this process. In the mixed economy of welfare, 'consumers' may be told they have choice, but the persistently service-led, professional definitions of individual need in a context of scarce resources are light years away from collective user control over the design and delivery of services.

Precisely similar traps exist in social science research and in the evaluations which draw upon its techniques. Traditionally the realm of the academic and now increasingly of the contract researcher, social science inquiry pursues answers to questions which are generated either in detached theorizing or in pursuit of the profit (or 'value for money') motive. Academics, paid researchers and evaluators typically descend on their research sites to gather data, then write reports the format of which is not relevant to the research 'subjects' – and which are not made available to them in any case. Some multiply deprived areas are repeatedly visited by research teams but derive no benefit. As a black woman who had experienced this phenomenon once remarked (personal communication), 'We spill our beans but nothing changes'.

The evaluation of public services, including the personal social services, thus draws on two top down traditions: the expertise models of social work practice and of social science research. Empowerment practice and participatory research stand in opposition to these trends. Though they may resonate oddly in the UK, in an era of managerialism and performance targets, their practice is playing a key role in various parts of the globe.

The participatory research tradition

Participatory research has been most fully developed in parts of the globe labelled the 'Third' or 'Developing World'. It is particularly rooted in Freirian analysis (Anyanwu, 1988: 12). Freire used literacy classes to help Brazilian peasants reach their own social understanding and find their own voice. His resultant concept of 'conscientization' (1972) links oppression in a dialectical relationship with education, personal and collective empowerment, and hence with community development (Hope and Timmel, 1984) and social action groupwork (Mullender and Ward, 1991). Participatory research follows the same threefold process of seeking to develop critical consciousness, improve participants' lives, and transform social structures and relationships (Maguire, 1987: 196). The involvement of local people in the evaluation of development programmes, in ways appropriate to their own lives, is a notable strand in this tradition (Feuerstein, 1986).

Participatory research attempts to bring knowledge and action within the reach of people who have hitherto been silenced. They may choose to join together on their own around an issue affecting their lives, or an outside researcher or professional may initiate contact to 'help formulate an identifiable problem to be tackled' (Park, 1993: 8). This must be someone who wants to work ' "with" rather than "for" oppressed people' (Maguire, 1987: 28) and to be an 'ally' of the people (Anderson, 1996: 78–79). The professional does not bring knowledge to bestow but engages in a partnership of investigation at the grass roots, offering facilitation of a jointly owned process (Cornwall and Jewkes, 1995; Ward and Mullender, 1991).

Working with, rather than for, people means sharing fears, aspirations, pain and struggle in a subject–subject relationship, not the familiar subject–object one where researchers study people (or evaluate the impact of services upon them) for their or their funders' own purposes. The researcher has to be willing to get emotionally involved, to be humbled, to self-question. He or she must also have an abiding faith in people's ability to take control of their lives and communities (Maguire, 1993) and to put the knowledge generated through participatory research to good use (Hall, 1993).

How it works

Participatory research (or participatory action research – the terms will be used interchangeably) – involves familiarization with the context and with prospective participants, identifying the key problem they want to tackle, deciding and pursuing *together* the most appropriate ways of finding out answers, learning together what those answers might mean, and acting together upon the conclusions (Maclure, 1990: 5–6). A briefer formulation sometimes offered is investigation, education and action (Hick, 1997). Neither the education nor the action element of this process is emphasized to the same extent in any other research method. Participants share their hopes, struggles, ideas, perceptions and experiences in a relationship of dialogue and mutual reflection, then undertake together a consciousness-raising journey into critical thinking and collective action (Vargas Vargas, 1991).

There is no 'right way' to do participatory research: 'There is a need for a variety of solutions, a multiplicity of tactics and strategies in different settings' (Anderson, 1996: 79, writing about the related concept of empowerment). The learning is in the doing (Maguire, 1987). Participatory research is dynamic and organic, responding to the range of communities and human need (Hick, 1997). It demands sensitivity and a self-conscious willingness on the part of the 'outsider' to respect the wisdom of 'ordinary people' (Rahman, 1991: 20).

Whatever shape the process takes, the action component is always seen as integral, and gives participatory research its closest affinity with social and community action – to the point where they may appear indistinguishable (see, for example, the account of working with a women's group in Maguire, 1993). What makes this 'research' is the emphasis on *collecting and analysing information* and on generating new knowledge; people recognize and name their own experiences, then augment what they come to understand by this means with factual evidence (which they accumulate themselves by learning relevant techniques). Typically, this grassroots knowledge is subsequently used to set up an oppositional voice to that of the politicians, policy makers or professionals.

Examples of generating information for empowerment

Participatory research is based on the belief that people can do research. They are capable of gathering data, analysing them, and using them to take action based on the research findings, even in a world where what constitutes knowledge is normally defined by the 'experts' (Gaventa, 1993). People in a community in Colombia (de Roux, 1991), for example, had been organizing around an unreliable electricity supply, using multimedia popular action including a 'march of lights'. When they noticed that increasingly erratic bills appeared to rise most steeply when the company was known to have large costs to meet, localized users' committees collected the monthly statements and recruited help to translate them into simple graphs which were then analysed in community assemblies. This community-generated knowledge gave people power through control of the information:

> The graphs made it obvious that the company's 'computer' was generating incoherent data. . . . In some communities . . . total electricity consumption has doubled – according to the computer – from one month to the next. (de Roux, 1991: 48)

Armed with this solid evidence, the people were able successfully to confront the company and its computer, which the company had said 'does not make mistakes' (1991: 42).

A similar, though unpublished example occurred on a British council estate where a community worker met with families, all on social work caseloads, who were at risk of having their power supply cut off as a result of non-payment of bills. In this case, the tenants were able to gather hard information to demonstrate that faulty housing design was causing some rooms to be exceptionally hard to heat and to put pressure on the local authority to institute improvements to the insulation and some back-dated remission of rent.

Through their own actions, these 'ordinary' people in Europe and Latin America realized they could reframe and investigate problems in order to find solutions. The development of a wider understanding of injustice and disempowerment made these the acts of people reclaiming their self-respect, dignity and control over aspects of their lives – a transformation through critical understanding.

> In other words, it was not only a matter of generating knowledge on the electricity problem . . . [the] methodology . . . must be capable of unleashing people's pent-up knowledge . . . thus stimulating their creativity and developing their analytical and critical capacities. (de Roux, 1991: 44)

Who participates in the action

It is important to note that action in itself need not necessarily be empowering since it may be practitioner rather than participant or service user oriented and led. Nevertheless, the tradition of action research in the public sector, including the health and social services (Hart and Bond, 1995), offers a useful literature and methodology and does include some examples of working collaboratively with service users. The approach has deeper roots in education (Carr and Kemmis, 1986) where democratic evaluation continues to be actively developed, for example through the work of CARE, the Centre for Action Research in Education, at the University of East Anglia.

Action research rests on a cyclical process of information–action–reflection which can become a working routine and which, interestingly, has also been presented as 'enquiry, intervention and *evaluation*' (Hart and Bond, 1995: 3; italics added). It certainly has a long history of being seen as an integral part of direct empowerment practice in social work and community development contexts (Hart and Bond, 1995; Hope and Timmel, 1984; Lees and Smith, 1975; Mullender and Ward, 1991). Currently in British social work, it is engendering a participatory stream in groupings such as the Participatory Inquiry and Action in Social Practice Network (http://www.anglia.ac.uk/sphs/piasp/), whose philosophy emphasizes not only collaboration with service users, but also the empowerment of participants and the nature of inquiry and action as integral to practice. Further afield, participatory action research has combined with a self-help tradition in the voluntary sector in Melbourne, Australia, to emphasize local groups' ability to undertake evaluations themselves, to their own, rather than funders' agendas of what is efficient, effective and appropriate (Wadsworth, 1984, 1991).

All these groupings can trace a line of descent from the development of action research in social psychology, and from the American Anti-Poverty Program of the 1960s (Lewin, 1948; see Hart and Bond, 1995, Ch. 2 for an account of this history). However, in social and community work settings it tends to be the *participatory* action research model which is stressed. This leaves well behind the model's partial origins in social engineering and functionalist organizational change and focuses, instead, on its potential for empowerment.

Potential obstacles

MOTIVATION AND TIMESCALE   Of course, the process of participatory research does not always go smoothly. It can take time even to motivate people into meeting together (Cornwall and Jewkes, 1995; cf. Maguire, 1987). The very idea of doing 'research' is alien to most people. Academics do research, but why should *they*? Conversely, people may join a project with initial enthusiasm and expect amazing results, only to be disillusioned when the going gets tough and there is little to show in return.

Motivation and timing are about being sensitive to the moment – when an issue of genuine concern may arise – and not being worried about numbers or capabilities. A group of no more than six Aboriginal women in Manitoba, Canada, recognized sexual violence as a community problem. When opened up to wider discussion, this led to the reinstitution of the traditional Circle of Healing, both to change the behaviour of the abuser and to support the victims and families involved, first on this one reserve and later across the South-East Tribal Council Region (Match International Centre, 1990). It is important to recognize how different this latter approach was from the mainstream one, where social workers, from agencies managed many hundreds of miles away, were too often responding by cutting across traditional practices and using child protection procedures to intervene in communities they did not understand (Dullea, 1992).

CONFLICTS OF INTEREST Professionals come with varied reasons to a participatory research project. Someone in a broadly social work role would have the clear advantage of a sustained presence in and knowledge of the area. They might well be able to use their networks to spark off a participatory process, or lend it their support, or take on board its results. At the same time, there would be other issues to resolve, such as how far the professional could be trusted and whether they would be serving two sets of interests. As Anderson (1996: 76) suggests: 'For professionals to effectively facilitate empowerment education it is necessary for them to subvert the bureaucratic structures of which they are a part.' Social workers, in particular, walk a fine line between wanting to 'empower' service users while being called upon to control their lives, their choices or their behaviour (Central Council for Education and Training in Social Work, 1995) – between being answerable to supervisors and agency mandates and wanting to be accountable to the people they serve.

HOW PARTICIPATORY? Participatory researchers should expect to be judged on how participatory they really are. Professionals and academics can, intentionally or unintentionally, assume control. Local people may follow the expectations of a lifetime and accede control to the outside 'expert' (Martin, 1994), or to certain authoritative voices and dominant discourses, even where the views express conflict with the evidence of their own eyes (Pottier, 1997). Evaluators with hidden agendas or who are seeking to produce quick and easy solutions to complex problems may collude with or exploit the tendency to defer to authority. Nor does it necessarily imply a denial of social agency on the part of service users to note such power dynamics in operation. Everitt and Hardiker (1996: 114) point out that various groups of service users learn to talk 'strategically' when asked to give their views on a service, so as not to risk its withdrawal. It may take time and care to hear their voices as distinct from the 'prevailing discourses' which maintain existing power relations.

Even where researchers have put time and respect into striving for equality – and appear on the surface to have achieved it – asking themselves hard questions can reveal that disagreements or resistances have been concealed, or that differences in educational and social backgrounds run so deep that people are on different wavelengths (Martin, 1994; Whitmore, 1994). It requires a considerable commitment to anti-oppressive values and to honest reflexivity in research, together with a certain postmodern and poststructural sophistication, to peel away and acknowledge the layers of diversity and difference so as to build trust and mutual understanding. These are manifested not just in finding a shared language, but also in learning what motivates or scares people, and what a particular project means to them in the context of their lived experience (Whitmore, 1994). In so far as this last sentence sounds closer to good social work than it does to traditional research, social workers may have a head start here, provided their belief in shared participation is genuine.

Certain people within the community may also control the process for others, so that some voices remain submerged. Participatory research has not, for example, traditionally listened to women or focused on their issues. Maguire speaks of the absence of women at the time when she came to the subject in the mid-1980s: 'In the most widely circulated participatory research literature of that time, the voices and observations of women participants were largely unheard' (1993: 162). This made her wonder: if participatory research was about empowering people, then *which* people? Women's subjugation within the home or 'double day' workload frequently makes their full participation impossible in practical terms unless special efforts are made, so participatory research in an undeveloped form is no more likely to involve women on an equal basis than is any other social context. If women or any other group are not included, their needs will not be considered important and will not be met. Hall highlights this contradiction of the undemocratic democracy, in concluding that 'Our early assumption that women were automatically included in terms such as "the people" or "community" or "the oppressed" has rendered them invisible in important ways' (Hall, 1993: xvi).

The contribution of feminist research

Feminist writings have offered increasingly sophisticated discussions about what it means to give women a voice. For example, Ribbens asks how feminist researchers can hear the more muted voices 'even amongst women' (1998: 24), while Standing (1998) reflects on the dilemmas of writing up the spoken word with accuracy yet respect. These are some of the key dilemmas of feminist research: how to 'listen' to what women are saying; how to 'hear' what women are saying; and then how to write what women are saying without losing the meaning and the distinctiveness of the voices, while at the same time not patronizing women by the way their words are recorded or excluding them by the way they are theorized (Standing, 1998).

It is now widely recognized that oppressed groups are unlikely to speak freely in mixed settings or fully to explore the central issues of their lives (Rahman, 1990). Patricia Maguire (1993) joined with a group of women, all of whom had left violent, abusive relationships, in order to undertake a piece of feminist participatory research. Not only was the women's opportunity to develop an understanding of abuse as an expression of male domination and control dependent on a women-only context, but so was their undertaking of their own solution building, for example in collecting and presenting information to try and influence policy and practice. At one point, they commented on an agency proposal to involve men as on-call volunteers for women reporting incidents of abuse and put forward the group's fully debated view that this would not be appropriate. The top down discourses both of clinical social work and of quantitative research were turned against them. The researcher who worked with the group was told by the agency manager that the women's thinking was 'paranoid and neurotic' (Maguire, 1993: 170) and that their views had not been 'scientifically collected'. One of the women from the group stood by their subjective expertise as a valid source of knowledge: 'It's because they don't know how it is. They've never been beaten up' (1993: 171).

Commonalities between participatory research and feminist research

Participatory research and feminist research share many ideals that can inform empowering evaluatory practice. Both consider that 'knowledge ... is power' (de Roux, 1991: 48; Maguire, 1993: 163) and that it should be demystified. Learning to question and to think critically, as occurs in the classic feminist technique of 'consciousness raising' and in participatory research's use of 'conscientization', is fundamental to a process of dialogue and reflection. Feminist research is never politically neutral and nor is participatory research, within which 'an analysis of oppressive social structures is in itself a political act' (Lee, 1990: 22).

Both forms of research are typically concerned with social change – not reform, but personal and social transformation (see, for example, de Roux, 1991 for participatory research, and Maguire, 1987, for feminism). Both research traditions seek to bridge the gap between the 'researcher' and the 'subjects of research' (Maclure, 1990: 3; Maynard, 1994: 15–16) so that the latter are truly heard, and both have acknowledged that power dynamics may creep back in. Both traditions attempt to be non-hierarchical and non-exploitative (Hick, 1997; Maynard, 1994). Although feminism is widely credited for its recognition that the researcher, as an 'outsider', inevitably brings his/her subjective self into the research, this is also an issue in the participative and wider ethnographic tradition (May, 1993). This 'reflexivity' acknowledges not only that any claims to complete objectivity in research (including evaluation) are unrealistic, but also that the reflections of, and responses to, the researcher within the research process generate valuable data in their own right. Both participatory and feminist research also stress the importance of the subjectivities and sociocultural contexts of the research participants (Maclure, 1990; Maynard, 1994), whose own perspectives and under-standings both constitute and frame the knowledge being sought.

Not surprisingly, given these shared emphases, important work has been done to bring the two traditions together into a model of feminist participatory research (Maguire, 1987, 1993; Martin, 1994; Wolf, 1996). There remains a need for far more work in this area, however.

Participatory feminist research

Taking the best from both traditions means that, at the same time as women gain a voice in their own issues, a stake in their own questions and an agency in their own solutions, there are further gains from the participatory research traditions of overcoming *distance* in research through shared ownership and flexible methods, and of a commitment to *action*. Evaluation certainly has much to gain from these combined strengths.

Overcoming distance

Feminist participatory research, or participatory research from a feminist perspective, challenges traditional approaches which still retain the 'researcher'/'researched' divide. It has, for example, been noted that much of feminist research still takes place within an individual, face-to-face interview format (Kelly et al., 1994), even though this has evolved to include two-way dialogue, information exchange and relationship formation (Maguire, 1987).

Feminist researchers engaging in participatory research work at decreasing not just their distance but their control over the agenda, process and results of research (McCarl-Nielson, 1990; Wolf, 1996). The possibility then arises of a mutually liberating and educative research partnership which strives to be open, honest and inclusive: 'If participants "own" every dimension of the research . . . everyone knows where, how and why they are joining together on a particular journey' (Everitt et al., 1992: 63). A fluid approach to methods also opens up opportunities for women to come together in groups and collectivities to generate new knowledge (Maguire, 1987).

Direct action

Collective organization is always a key ingredient of participatory research (Freire, 1972: 40–41), including that conducted from a feminist perspective. People without power develop 'structures over which they have control' (Rahman, 1990: 45) which help them come to understand their experience of marginalization and believe in their ability to change it.

What began for Mies as research into the effects of the market economy on rural women, for example, ended up supporting and enhancing existing women's organizations in the area as well as giving 'women so much courage and strength that they could tackle a taboo topic like violence against women' (Mies, 1991: 73). The transformation began when Mies and her co-researchers chose to live in an Indian village, sharing everyday activities such as work in the fields and washing clothes in the stream, until they became participants 'with' women rather than researchers 'of' women. The local women, in their turn, appreciating that the visitors wanted to learn from them in this respectful way, agreed to come together in weekend camps to tell and compare stories from across the region, to connect as women, and then to organize around their common needs (1991: 70–71). This encompassing of direct action as a stage in the research process differentiates partici-patory feminist research from the more generalized commitment to influencing personal and/or social change (Kelly et al., 1994; Maynard, 1994) which is characteristic of all feminist research.

New challenges to participatory and feminist research

A diversity of experience

A central challenge to feminist research is the question of which women become involved, whether as researchers or participants (Kelly et al., 1994). An equivalent challenge faces participatory research. It is crucial for feminism to find appropriate ways to hear the voice of black (Afshar and Maynard, 1994; Phoenix, 1994), disabled (Begum, 1992), older (MacDonald and Rich, 1984; The Hen Co-op, 1993, 1995) and lesbian women. Interestingly, there has been important recent research about social work attitudes towards lesbians (Hardman, 1997). It was because it was conducted within lesbian feminist research design that this study was equipped to reveal that a rather woolly liberalism prevails, with some oppressive attitudes still to be found and little understanding of the potential for a distinctive lesbian response in social work practice.

As well as listening to a range of voices – including those which have traditionally been silenced by power relations or ideological conflict (Pottier, 1997; Unnithan and Srivastava, 1997) – we can learn from interrogating the silences within our own work (Maynard, 1994) and being reflective regarding our own biases (Pottier, 1997). For instance, being white encompasses both a multiplicity of ethnicities and of insights into racism (Dyer, 1997), while a straight lifestyle is a source of information about sexuality as well as about heterosexism and homo-phobia (Maynard, 1994). It is equally possible to theorize from normative omissions as from challenges to them, and equally fruitful to study the life of both oppressor and oppressed as long as these are subjected to a committed theorizing. There is increasing activity by feminist and male pro-feminist researchers in questioning men within a feminist paradigm, for example, in order to understand more about the operation of men's abuse of power and control (Hearn, 1994; Kelly et al., 1994).

Emancipatory research

Once oppressed groups have found a voice, they are able to use it to seek to exercise control themselves, including over the research process. When black researchers undertake their own evaluations, for example, they arrive at some extremely challenging conclusions for social work services (Butt and Mirza, 1996; Ince 1998) – services which are seen as so inappropriate, inaccessible, socially controlling and damaging that black projects have often developed to fill the gaps and to deliver help without further harming black service users (Francis, 1997; Jones et al., 1992; Sia, n.d.). It is an indictment of the traditional measures and values applied in mainstream evaluatory practice that too often they let such damage pass without comment. Theoretically, this means moving black perspectives into central focus (see, for example, Graham, forthcoming), with all else now in the position of deviating from a new set of norms. This is a more fundamental change than anti-racism alone proposes and requires a more radical rethinking than the equity model pursued by the Commission for Racial Equality. It may also, arguably, transcend the joint action ideals of participatory research, since the latter, though flowing from local people's own perspectives, has had more to say about reawakening those perspectives from the internalization of economic rather than racial oppression.

In the same way, each oppression is coming to formulate its own theory and sometimes its own methodology. Child-centred research is generating a new ethics and new ways of listening to children (Alderson, 1995; *Children and Society*, 1996). Part of this development rests on a new theorizing of children as hitherto disempowered social actors and it calls for a 'generational' approach to analysing the specific impact upon them of social issues (Qvortrup, 1997). This would be as far reaching as taking a gendered approach to re-examining the lives of women and men. At the other end of the chronological spectrum, adjustment models of ageing are challenged by the narratives of women 'growing old disgracefully' (The Hen Co-op, 1993, 1995), while the social model of disability is now firmly incorporated into social work, having grown out of the challenges of disabled people to the prevailing view of them as deviant and devalued.

The social model of disability can similarly underpin effective re-evaluations of services. A community researcher in Massachusetts came together with a group of people with disabilities to learn about access problems (Brydon-Miller, 1993). The group took on the neighbourhood shopping mall as a target for promoting accessibility. They collected their own data to prove that entrances, elevators, doorways and so on were not wheelchair accessible, and that there were additional needs for people with other mobility and sensory impairments. Over six separate court hearings, they increased in persistence and legal literacy until the case was finally won in the Supreme Court. Believing in access as a human right, they followed all the classic steps of investigation, education and action, and showed, above all, that services can only be properly evaluated by fully involving the people who use them, even against the most basic criteria of fitness for purpose.

Reconceptualizations of ageing, too, can be integrated into research and evaluation. In a town in northern France, a groupworker encouraged older people to survey the area in which they lived and to determine their own priorities for a new sheltered housing scheme (Coirier, 1988). Top of the list was that the supported housing should be integrated with that for other age groups and handy for all local services. Older citizens did not want to be segregated from a community to which they felt they continued to make an important contribution. There were clear lessons in this for social welfare professionals, not least because public and voluntary sector agencies had already been meeting to design the new provision before the older people's group came on the scene, and had proposed a scheme which the group rejected out of hand.

These examples stand as proof that, though a poststructural analysis can make it seem as if each individual will have to struggle in his or her own subjective solitude, groups in society persist in using their combined strengths to work for change and to take control of their own lives (Williams, forthcoming, writing about anti-racism). They persist in arguing from a common standpoint of disempowerment to pursue active social change rather than sterile deconstruction (Maynard, 1994, on feminism), while also recognizing that they encompass diversity and difference.

Evaluation research

Participatory research that builds upon strength in diversity can inform evaluatory practice by placing into a wider range of hands the right to say what count as effective, successful and desirable outcomes. Too often, evaluation is regarded as an exercise of outsiders being brought in to measure the work of practitioners against 'value for money' and efficiency criteria instead of as a debate about measures which might be valued by users or practitioners (Everitt and Hardiker, 1996).

Managerialist evaluatory approaches do not find a natural home in social work practice, let alone in empowerment or social action, not because they emphasize numbers but because they do so in a way which can tend to discount people. When this is challenged, quantitative data can as soon support people's struggles to make their needs understood by the power elite, provided there is a collective, grassroots verification of the meaning of the knowledge produced (Hick, 1997), as be used to impose service standards on people. It is also recognized within feminist research that political ends may be served by being able, for example, to quantify sexual violence, the feminization of poverty and gender inequalities in the labour market (Maynard, 1994). The same could be said of uneven access to services or inequitable expectations of informal caring, which could be exposed by an exercise of straightforward counting along gendered lines.

Crucially, though, social situations can never be satisfactorily explained in quantifiable terms alone. There are simply too many contributing factors which fashion human meaning and priorities, and through which we understand social reality. These include the 'internalized assumptions, ideologies, and belief systems which make up the consciousness of each individual' (Maclure, 1990: 3) as well as all the issues which have been used as reasons to silence people and which now need to be brought into the research process, including gender, ethnicity, disability, sexuality, age and socio-economic status. Furthermore, accountancy-dominated evaluation that is performed by external evaluators from 'outside' the historical and cultural context frequently fails to seek 'inside' experience and knowledge (Derricourt, 1988: 33). Top down evaluations can do more harm than good. They not infrequently put at risk the funding of worthwhile projects while maintaining the status quo which retains knowledge in the hands of 'experts' and leaves the consulted group of local people or service users mystified.

Dangers of co-opting participatory approaches to evaluation

Feuerstein (1988) alludes to a shift that is happening internationally as funders become disenchanted with conventional forms of evaluation and begin to seek less costly, more usable alternatives. In the longer term, however, if non-conventional, i.e. participative approaches are deemed cheaper, or become fashionable, there may be a danger of co-optation (Rahman and Fals-Borda, 1991). 'While many people in development activities may be ready to share responsibility, there are few who are genuinely ready to share power' (Feuerstein, 1988: 16).

The same danger will undoubtedly exist in social work agencies if they decide to jump on the bandwagon and attach 'participatory' claims to undemocratic evaluation procedures (Everitt and Hardiker, 1996). It is not unknown for so-called participation in social work evaluation (Hick, 1997) to consist of a few representatives of the community being assembled in the ubiquitous 'focus group', which has no roots in actual community groupings and derives its *modus operandi* from consumerist market research, not from social work practice or values (Cohen and Garrett, forthcoming).

Authenticity

Rahman and Fals-Borda (1991) encourage commitment to authentic participatory action research and suggest that the best people to verify it are the participants themselves, ensuring that the local community continues to act as the reference group. Similarly, empowerment practice in social work talks about transforming power and about groups of service users always setting their own goals and direction (Mullender and Ward, 1991). The equivalent in evaluation might be for collective self-advocacy user organizations or well established community groups, including women's groups and black groups, to set the terms of the debate or to conduct, or at least strongly influence, the evaluative process.

Hick suggests two criteria for evaluating authentic participatory research: who makes the decisions, and who actually conducts the research. Participants need to be satisfied with every aspect of the process (1997: 76), including the questions asked, the gathering and interpreting of answers, and the manner of disseminating the results. For example, are these made equally available to all participants in a form that reflects their own words and ideas? All these questions apply equally well to evaluation, where funders and programme planners need to be held accountable to the people, not vice versa (Maclure, 1990).

New learning

If people are to believe they have the right to question and complain, and the ability critically to analyse and come up with suggestions and plans for change, then practitioners will have to undertake new learning so as to move away from a professional socialization that leaves them more preoccupied with individual pathology than with structural injustice.

This will inevitably involve re-examining the old ways: 'Most professional health workers are ill-prepared for participatory research. They are taught to consider themselves and the western medical knowledge they have learnt as superior' (Cornwall and Jewkes, 1995: 1674). Similarly, social work is very much concerned with protecting its professional turf as well as with claiming 'ownership' of service users (Everitt et al., 1992: 120). This is not a mindset within which participatory research will work.

It would be exciting to see student social workers on Diploma in Social Work programmes routinely learning how to share ownership through participatory evaluation and just as routinely sharing their knowledge with local people while on practice placement.

Embedded in practice

Evaluation is a part of practice. It needs to be built into every project rather than undertaken as a 'one-off' event alien to the continuity and life of community members and their dialogue about how best to meet local needs. Evaluation should be holistic rather than fragmented, presenting a complete picture which emphasizes qualitative data to reveal the politics of power relationships and the nature of change, supplemented by hard statistics wherever applicable to demonstrate what programmes have delivered in terms that funders and managers will

understand but according to measures that local people control
(Marsden and Oakley, 1990).

Such a stance would suggest a more participatory, equalized relationship between social workers and service users in assessing service design
and delivery. This is not a bland concept. A more critical approach to
evaluation can make spaces for 'oppositional needs-talk' (Everitt and
Hardiker, 1996: 116), in order to hear those who are typically silenced by
the more dominant and therefore societally upheld social need 'discourses', including women, children in the public care, disabled and
older people. For this to happen, professionals and practitioners will
need to recognize that '[t]o be in a position to understand and name the
needs and problems that others experience is to be powerful' (Everitt et
al., 1992: 17), and to go about opening up and sharing that power both in
delivering and in evaluating services. Indeed, one opportunity for this
may have arrived in the form of recent calls from the Labour government
in Britain to determine 'Best Value' criteria – which are required to draw
on service user views – in place of lowest-cost, compulsorily tendered
contracting.

Conclusion

There is no excuse for not seeing people as the experts in their own lives.
We can certainly build on the strengths of local people to plan value-
based action for change. Professionals who are seen to place credence in
that strength will give people new confidence in their own views and
abilities. Owning service evaluation is a key part of empowerment
because it means that those who fund and manage services will be
required to hear the voice of those who have been traditionally
silenced.

The literatures on empowerment practice, community development
and community action, participatory education along Freirian lines, and
participatory action research can be used virtually interchangeably to
inform a democratic approach to working with people to resolve their
own problems through a critical awareness of wider social issues and
through a personally and collectively transforming action for change.
Participatory approaches grew out of a predominant concern with
economic (including global economic) status. A universally empowering
model of evaluation also needs to draw upon

- feminist theory and methodology;
- lesbian and queer theorizing;
- postcolonial and African-centred theorizing;
- the social model of disability;
- 'people first' and 'equal people' challenges to concepts of learning
  difficulties;

- child-centred research and theories of children's rights and perspectives;
- the challenges of the psychiatric survivors' movement;
- 'growing old disgracefully' ideas on ageing.

Putting all these together suggests that every marginalized group (including groups within groups) is nowadays asking its own questions in its own terms and that all practitioners need to interrogate their practice to determine whether it is sufficiently informed by that process. This form of evaluation lies at the heart of anti-oppressive practice – it cannot be added as an afterthought.

References

Afshar, H. and Maynard, M. (1994) *The Dynamics of 'Race' and Gender: Some Feminist Interventions*. London: Taylor & Francis.

Alderson, P. (1995) *Listening to Children: Children, Ethics and Social Research*. Barkingside: Barnardo's.

Anderson, J. (1996) 'Yes, but *is it* empowerment? Initiation, implementation and outcomes of community action', in B. Humphries (ed.), *Critical Perspectives on Empowerment*. Birmingham: Venture Press.

Anyanwu, C.N. (1988) 'The technique of participatory research in community development', *Community Development Journal*, 23 (1): 11–15.

Begum, N. (1992) 'Disabled women and the feminist agenda', in H. Hinds, A. Phoenix and J. Stacey (eds), *Working Out: New Directions for Women's Studies*. London: Falmer Press.

Brydon-Miller, M. (1993) 'Breaking down barriers: accessibility self-advocacy in the disabled community', in P. Park, M. Brydon-Miller, B. Hall and T. Jackson (eds), *Voices of Change: Participatory Research in the United States and Canada*. Toronto: Ontario Institute for Studies in Education.

Butt, J. and Mirza, K. (1996) *Social Care and Black Communities: A Review of Recent Research Studies*. London: HMSO.

Carr, W. and Kemmis, S. (1986) *Becoming Critical: Education, Knowledge and Action Research*. London: Falmer Press.

Central Council for Education and Training in Social Work (1995) *Assuring Quality in the Diploma in Social Work – I: Rules and Requirements for the DipSW*. London: CCETSW.

Children and Society (1996) 10 (2): whole issue on ethical and methodological issues in undertaking research with children.

Cohen, M.B. and Garrett, K.J. (forthcoming in 1999) 'Breaking the rules: a group work perspective on focus group research', *British Journal of Social Work*, 29 (3).

Coirier, M. (1998) 'Du groupe aux groupes: mobilisation pour la qualité de vie des personnes âgées', *Journées d'Etudes* ANTSG, 22–23 January, Association Nationale des Travailleurs Sociaux pour le Développement du Travail Social avec les Groupes.

Cornwall, A. and Jewkes, R. (1995) 'What is participatory research?', *Social Science and Medicine*, 41 (12): 1667–1676.

Coyle, G.L. (1980) 'Education for social action', in A.S. Alissi (ed.), *Perspectives on Social Group Work Practice: A Book of Readings*. New York: Free Press. (Originally published in 1939.)

De Roux, G.I. (1991) 'Together against the computer: PAR and the struggle of Afro-Colombians for public service', in O. Fals-Borda and M.A. Rahman (eds), *Action and Knowledge: Breaking the Monopoly with Participatory Action-Research*. New York: Apex Press.

Derricourt, N. (1988) 'Evaluating the process of community work: some issues of accountability and procedure', *Community Development Journal*, 23 (1): 33–39.

Dullea, K. (1992) 'Genealogy, Indian child welfare, healing lives and taking control: a participatory research practicum in Carrier and Sekani communities of Central-Interior British Columbia. Practicum report'. Regina, Saskatchewan: University of Regina (unpublished).

Dyer, R. (1997) *White*. London: Routledge.

Everitt, A. and Hardiker, P. (1996) *Evaluating for Good Practice*. Basingstoke: Macmillan.

Everitt, A., Hardiker, P., Littlewood, J. and Mullender, A. (1992) *Applied Research for Better Practice*. Basingstoke: Macmillan.

Feuerstein, M.-T. (1986) *Partners in Evaluation: Evaluating Development and Community Programmes with Participants*. London: Macmillan.

Feuerstein, M.-T. (1988) 'Finding the methods to fit the people: training for participatory evaluation', *Community Development Journal*, 23 (1): 16–25.

Francis, J. (1997) 'Why are we failing?' *Community Care*, 13–19 November: 20–21.

Freire, P. (1972) *Pedagogy of the Oppressed*. Harmondsworth: Penguin.

Gaventa, J. (1993) 'The powerful, the powerless and the experts: knowledge struggles in an information age', in P. Park, M. Brydon-Miller, B. Hall and T. Jackson (eds), *Voices of Change: Participatory Research in the United States and Canada*. Toronto: Ontario Institute for Studies in Education.

Graham, M.J. (forthcoming in 1999) 'The African centred worldview: developing a paradigm for social work', *British Journal of Social Work*, 29 (2).

Hall, B. (1993) 'Introduction', in P. Park, M. Brydon-Miller, B. Hall and T. Jackson (eds), *Voices of Change: Participatory Research in the United States and Canada*. Toronto: Ontario Institute for Studies in Education.

Hardman, K.L.J. (1997) 'Social workers' attitudes to lesbian clients', *British Journal of Social Work*, 27 (4): 545–563.

Hart, E. and Bond, M. (1995) *Action Research for Health and Social Care: A Guide to Practice*. Buckingham: Open University Press.

Hearn, J. (1994) 'Men's violence to women', in B. Featherstone, B. Fawcett and C. Toft (eds), *Violence, Gender and Social Work*. Bradford: University of Bradford, Department of Applied Social Studies.

Hen Co-op, The (1993) *Growing Old Disgracefully*. London: Piatkus.

Hen Co-op, The (1995) *Disgracefully Yours*. London: Piatkus.

Hick, S. (1997) 'Participatory research: an approach for structural social workers', *Journal of Progressive Human Services*, 8 (2): 63–78.

Hope, A. and Timmel, S. (1984) *Training for Transformation: A Handbook for Community Workers*, Books I, II and III. Gweru, Zimbabwe: Mambo Press.

Ince, L. (1998) *Making It Alone: A Study of the Care Experiences of Young Black People*. London: British Agencies for Adoption and Fostering.

Jones, A., Phillips, M. and Maynard, C. (1992) *A Home from Home: The Experience of Black Residential Projects as a Focus of Good Practice*. London: National Institute for Social Work.

Kelly, L., Burton, S. and Regan, L. (1994) 'Researching women's lives or studying women's oppression? Reflections on what constitutes feminist research', in M. Maynard and J. Purvis (eds), *Researching Women's Lives from a Feminist Perspective*. London: Taylor & Francis.

Lee, H. (1990) *Critical Social Research: Contemporary Social Research*. London: Unwin Hyman.

Lee, J.A.B. (1994) *The Empowerment Approach to Social Work Practice*. New York: Columbia University Press.

Lees, R. and Smith, G. (eds) (1975) *Action Research in Community Development*. London: Routledge & Kegan Paul.

Lewin, K. (1948) 'Action research and minority problems', in G.W. Lewin (ed.), *Resolving Social Conflicts: Selected Papers on Group Dynamics by Kurt Lewin*. New York: Harper.

MacDonald, B. and Rich, C. (1984) *Look Me in the Eye: Old Women, Aging and Ageism*. London: Women's Press.

Maclure, R. (1990) 'The challenge of participatory research and its implications for funding agencies', *International Journal of Sociology and Social Policy*, 10 (3): 1–21.

Maguire, P. (1987) *Doing Participatory Research: A Feminist Approach*. Amherst, MA: University of Massachusetts, Center for International Education, School of Education.

Maguire, P. (1993) 'Challenges, contradictions, and celebrations: attempting participatory research as a doctoral student', in P. Park, M. Brydon-Miller, B. Hall and T. Jackson (eds), *Voices of Change: Participatory Research in the United States and Canada*. Toronto: Ontario Institute for Studies in Education.

Marsden, D. and Oakley, P. (1990) *Evaluating Social Development Projects: Development Guidelines No. 5*. Oxford: Oxfam.

Martin, M. (1994) 'Developing a feminist participative research framework: evaluating the process', in B. Humphries and C. Truman (eds), *Re-thinking Social Research*. Aldershot: Avebury.

Match International Centre (1990) *Linking Women's Global Struggles to End Violence*. Ottawa: Match International Centre.

May, T. (1993) 'Feelings matter: inverting the hidden equation', in D. Hobbs and T. May (eds), *Interpreting the Field: Accounts of Ethnography*. Oxford: Oxford University Press.

Maynard, M. (1994) 'Methods, practice and epistemology: the debate about feminism and research', in M. Maynard and J. Purvis (eds), *Researching Women's Lives from a Feminist Perspective*. London: Taylor & Francis.

McCarl-Nielson, J. (ed.) (1990) *Research Methods: Exemplary Readings in the Social Sciences*. Boulder, CO: Westview Press.

Mies, M. (1991) 'Women's research or feminist research? The debate surrounding feminist science and methodology', in M.M. Fonow and J.A. Cook (eds), *Beyond Methodology: Feminist Scholarship as Lived Research*. Bloomington and Indianapolis: Indiana University Press.

Mullender, A. and Ward, D. (1991) *Self-Directed Groupwork: Users Take Action for Empowerment*. London: Whiting and Birch.

Park, P. (1993) 'What is participatory research? A theoretical and methodological perspective', in P. Park, M. Brydon-Miller, B. Hall and T. Jackson (eds), *Voices of Change: Participatory Research in the United States and Canada.* Toronto: Ontario Institute for Studies in Education.

Phoenix, A. (1994) 'Practising feminist research: the intersection of gender and "race" in the research process', in M. Maynard and J. Purvis (eds), *Researching Women's Lives from a Feminist Perspective.* London: Taylor & Francis.

Pottier, J. (1997) 'Towards an ethnography of participatory appraisal and research', in R.D. Grillo and R.L. Stirrat (eds), *Discourses of Development: Anthropological Perspectives.* Oxford: Berg.

Qvortrup, J. (1997) 'Childhood and societal macrostructures'. Paper presented at the second programme meeting of the Economic and Social Research Council Research Programme, 'Children 5–16: Growing into the 21st Century', 17 March, Keele University.

Rahman, M.A. (1990) 'Thematic paper' on 'Qualitative dimensions of social development', in D. Marsden and P. Oakley, *Evaluating Social Development Projects: Development Guidelines No. 5.* Oxford: Oxfam.

Rahman, M.A. (1991) 'The theoretical standpoint of PAR', in O. Fals-Borda and M.A. Rahman (eds), *Action and Knowledge: Breaking the Monopoly with Participatory Action-Research.* New York: Apex Press.

Rahman, M.A. and Fals-Borda, O. (1991) 'A self-review of PAR', in O. Fals-Borda and M.A. Rahman (eds), *Action and Knowledge: Breaking the Monopoly with Participatory Action-Research.* New York: Apex Press.

Ribbens, J. (1998) 'Hearing my feeling voice? An autobiographical discussion of motherhood', in J. Ribbens and R. Edwards (eds), *Feminist Dilemmas in Qualitative Research: Public Knowledge and Private Lives.* London: Sage.

Sia (n.d.) *The Black Manifesto: Highlighting the Needs of the Black Voluntary Sector.* London: Sia (The National Development Agency for the Black Voluntary Sector). Leaflet.

Standing, K. (1998) 'Writing the voices of the less powerful: research on lone mothers', in J. Ribbens and R. Edwards (eds), *Feminist Dilemmas in Qualitative Research: Public Knowledge and Private Lives.* London: Sage.

Unnithan, M. and Srivastava, K. (1997) 'Gender, politics, development and women's agency in Rajasthan', in R.D. Grillo and R.L. Stirrat (eds), *Discourses of Development: Anthropological Perspectives.* Oxford: Berg.

Vargas Vargas, L. (1991) 'Reflections on methodology of evaluation', *Community Development Journal,* 26 (4): 267–270.

Wadsworth, Y. (1984) *Do It Yourself Social Research.* Melbourne: Victoria Council of Social Services and MFCO.

Wadsworth, Y. (1991) *Everyday Evaluation on the Run.* Melbourne: Action Research Issues Association.

Ward, D. and Mullender, A. (1991) 'Facilitation in self-directed groupwork', *Groupwork,* 4 (2): 141–151.

Whitmore, E. (1994) 'To tell the truth: working with oppressed groups in participatory approaches to inquiry', in P. Reason (ed.), *Participation in Human Inquiry.* London: Sage.

Williams, C. (forthcoming in 1999) 'Connecting anti-racist and anti-oppressive theory and practice: retrenchment or reappraisal?' *British Journal of Social Work,* 29 (2).

Wolf, D.L. (1996) 'Situating feminist dilemmas in fieldwork', in D.L. Wolf (ed.), *Feminist Dilemmas in Fieldwork.* Boulder, CO: Westview Press.

6

COLLABORATIVE EVALUATION WITH SERVICE USERS
Moving towards user-controlled research

Clare Evans and Mike Fisher

Much of this book is about encouraging practitioners to undertake research: this chapter suggests that social workers should also consider their role in assisting users to carry out their own research and consider how to ensure their practice evaluation is user led. The NHS and Community Care Act 1990 gave service users and their carers an opportunity to participate both individually and collectively in the assessment of needs and in the delivery and evaluation of services. Users' views of the quality of services and their participation in providing regular feedback on all aspects of social work are therefore an essential part of good practice. However, as users have become more empowered and experienced in participation, there is a growing understanding of how they can themselves design and undertake such evaluation exercises. This chapter gives an account of examples of user-led and user-controlled research and examines the implications for practitioners.

First we examine examples of power sharing in research and relate this to the wider empowerment of service users. The next two sections concern users' experiences of research, partly in order to outline the rationale for increasing their power over research processes, but also to demonstrate successful user-led and user-controlled research. Finally, we outline the skills and commitment required of social workers if they are to assist service users in their research. In this chapter, we more often use the term *research* than *evaluation*. 'Research' has wide currency within user movements, and conveys the capacity of user inquiry to engage in conceptual exploration and theory development. We see 'evaluation' as in greater use amongst professional staff seeking to monitor the effectiveness of specific services in meeting their prescribed goals: this would be seen as one element in user research, but not its exclusive function. We also concentrate more on users than carers, principally because much of the development of user participation in research has been undertaken by service users, particularly by disabled people. We draw attention, however, to key points where practitioners must distinguish the different interests of users and carers.

User empowerment is critical to social research

What counts as knowledge is a key issue for service users, whose experiences may be defined by research 'experts' in ways which are neither recognizable to users themselves nor conducive to improvements in their lives. Research on disability is a key example where, as Oliver shows, the thinking behind research questions may be so far removed from the way disabled people see their lives that the questions no longer make sense. Thus Census questions, imbued with the individual model of disability, ask 'what is wrong with you', instead of pursuing the issues that arise from the social model of disability which would focus on 'what is wrong with society' (Oliver, 1992: 104). Lindow and Morris's review of studies of user involvement points out that even in this field the agenda has been largely set by non-user researchers (Lindow and Morris, 1995: 87).

Until very recently, however, there have been few examples of evaluation directly under user control. In their review of empowerment-oriented research in mental health, Rapp, Shera and Kisthardt suggest that service users should be involved in determining the scope of research, the measures used and in gathering data and disseminating the findings, but stop short of prescribing a role for service users in analysing and presenting the data (Rapp et al., 1993). Many of the studies of users' views of social welfare start from the viewpoint of professionals (e.g. Barnes, 1993; Marsh and Fisher, 1992). Studies which start from this viewpoint and then try to transfer ownership to service users encounter difficulties precisely because the thinking behind them is not that of service users and because organizations find it difficult to relinquish control (Bewley and Glendinning, 1994; Whittaker et al., 1993). A study by Whitmore, which was more successful than most in transferring power over the research to the single mothers whose services were being investigated, nevertheless failed to include the users in writing the final report, because the author felt that the funding body required the use of technical language and saw this as outside the competence of the user researchers (Whitmore, 1994: 96). In contrast, the Citizens' Commission study was undertaken with user involvement throughout all the research processes (Beresford and Turner, 1997). Similarly, the report by Roberts (1998) shows how young disabled people previously pupils at a Barnardo's school 'co-researched and co-wrote' a report about innovative practice and were involved in interviewing disabled children through their research and development programme.

The scientific rationale for employing participatory models is to improve the quality of the data: it is argued that good data on human experience require a reciprocal exchange between user and researcher (Reason, 1994: 41–49). This may be true, and an exchange may be preferable as a research experience to exploitation, yet it remains a long way from research controlled by users. It is the difference between engaging in a self-generated activity and being invited, with whatever degree of humanity, to join an activity already under way. Participatory models also retain a distinction between those who do research and those who are 'researched', a distinction Oliver argues is artificial, and which leads to what he terms the 'social relations of research production', or a replication within research of the power structures in wider society (Oliver, 1992).

The challenge to create new 'social relations of research production' has been taken up by feminist disabled people (Keith, 1992; Morris, 1992), by deaf people (Jones and Pullen, 1992), by psychiatric system survivors (Beresford and Wallcroft, 1997), and on behalf of people with learning difficulties (Booth and Booth, 1996). The debate addresses core methodological questions (which will surface again later in this chapter) about the national data sets on disabled people (Abberley, 1992), the role of qualitative methods (Barnes, 1992), the nature of objectivity (Barnes, 1996) and the key role of funding bodies (Ward, 1997; Ward and Flynn, 1994). The edited collection on disability research (Barnes and Mercer, 1997) contains substantial reviews of the body of user-led and user-controlled research, some of which has hitherto had limited recognition outside the user movement. While the disability movement has made considerable progress in redefining research, it would be wrong to assume unanimity: as Bury points out, it is important to recognize different views of the nature of oppression within the disability movement and the different implications for research (Bury, 1996).

This new research is intended to follow the emancipatory, rather than the participatory, model: that is, it is designed primarily to enhance the power of service users (Zarb, 1992). A key question with this model, however, concerns how far research can be emancipatory if it is not originated by service users and conducted under their control. These issues are critical to research involving users and to the role of the social worker, as is the further question of the different interests of users and carers in research.

Important questions are already emerging within the emancipatory approach about the group of people who are both service users (or survivors) and academic researchers. If emancipatory research is supposed to enhance the power of service users, does its conduct by 'professional' user-researchers guarantee this, or should such researchers also be accountable to 'ordinary' users? Given that academic researchers usually refer to their independence in reaching their conclusions, is this compromised by the kind of accountability to service users we are proposing? Shakespeare refers to these tensions within the emancipatory research model, when he argues that although researchers must see their work within the social model of disability, they must also resist the notion that there is a single 'right' way to do research, and must reserve the right to independent judgement (Shakespeare, 1996, 1997).

The emancipatory model recognizes the need for research to benefit users. The user-controlled model, however, requires researchers, whether disabled or not, to be accountable to the users of the service under review. We define user-controlled research in the following terms. It must bring service users greater power to define their needs and the outcomes that matter to them. Service users must select the issues for research and acquire control over the funds to conduct it. We think that service users should wherever possible become researchers, so that their influence pervades the research: this includes responsibility for data analysis and for dissemination.

User-led and user-controlled research

User participation is a key element in community care and user groups are increasingly involved in evaluation of services. In this section, a number of examples are drawn from the experience of Wiltshire and Swindon Users' Network, established by one of the authors (Clare Evans) in 1991 to promote collective advocacy among users of health and social services in Wiltshire (Evans, 1996, 1997). The management group for the organization had a majority of service users, and substantial funding was obtained to establish offices and to employ staff. The funding permitted the development of a network of support to service users in Wiltshire and direct links between service users and the social services. The Network also managed a number of service delivery projects in the field of advocacy, information and independent living. The infrastructure established in the Network enabled users to empower themselves to participate.

Network members have had various experiences of research. Many had been 'researched', and assessed by social services, processes in which their primary role was passive: they were uninvolved in design or implementation. The Network had become a means by which researchers in higher education institutions could contact large numbers of service users: this research gave credit and recognition to the researchers but had little benefit for service users. In particular, some individuals had given up considerable time to be interviewed by academic researchers whose standards of practice were such that they did not even respect the service users enough to contact them afterwards with the results of their research.

The Network had recent experience of externally commissioned evaluation of a Network-managed advocacy project which did not gather the views of the users of that service, despite an invitation to do so. The researcher appeared unable to draw the distinction between the views of service users and of user workers who were providing the service. Data collection had been limited to the views of the user-manager, user-worker and external professionals. The Network's view was that in any service, whoever was providing it – social services, independent sector, or user organizations – the only valid way of conducting research was by collecting the views of end users – those receiving the service.

The Network had also had more positive experiences, leading to a growing understanding and recognition of user expertise in research. The Network had collaborated with a user-led organization in the county undertaking research into disabled people's views of employment, in which disabled people had been employed as interviewers and in writing up the research. The Network also had experience of service users interviewing other service users in a clinical audit by health and social services into discharge from hospital. As a result we knew the difficulty that professionals had in understanding what were the important issues for service users and in knowing how to frame questions which would be meaningful for users to answer. At the same time, the participating users indicated that they felt safe being interviewed by other service users and able to give more reliable and thoughtful views. Employing user-interviewers is a useful way for practitioners to obtain more reliable research evidence.

We had also learned much from a longer-term piece of work with the Home Care service. A group of service users and quality managers on the commissioning side of social services was set up to look at ways of improving the quality of home care provision. Users both identified the need to seek views from a wider group of users by means of a survey, and were also involved in making the questionnaire accessible to service users. Distribution of the questionnaire to all users with their home care bill led to a very high response rate. The results were accepted by the home care managers and taken back to the users involved and the Network to discuss dissemination and implementation of the findings. As a direct outcome of this discussion, an integral role for users in evaluating the service was negotiated – local quality groups involving users were to meet regularly with managers, and users acting as trainers were to introduce monitoring of a service which effectively reflected the views and interests of service users. What was critical, was users' involvement from the start and a sense of accountability to the users who initiated the evaluation, accompanied by the development of an action plan which recognized the need for the research to be employed for the benefit of service users (cf. Zarb, 1992). User expertise informed all aspects of the evaluation and professionals' attitudes remained user

focused throughout. The systems designed jointly by users and professionals ensured that the views of users would be central in informing
new service developments, and that the interests of service users would
be furthered.

The way to ensure evaluation is user led from the outset is to arrange
that service users and allies in statutory organizations learn to work
together. But joint working also involves risks. There are dilemmas for
the user-controlled organization co-operating in this user-led evaluation.
On the one hand the emphasis on users' views to inform purchasing is
important, and the user workers' and user organizations' involvement
can make the evaluation more effective. On the other hand, the user
organization may be seen to be colluding with decisions about reduction
in services: the findings of the research and their use are out of the
control of users.

These risks were apparent in a further piece of joint work. A social
service commissioning manager, the users' network and the local council
voluntary service undertook pilot work on good practice in user-led
evaluation of services to inform the annual grant aid cycle. Users of
services were to be interviewed by a disabled worker from the independent user-controlled organization in order to ensure a safe environment
where users could speak freely. A number of issues had to be addressed
before an effective user-led model could be developed, including anxi-
eties felt by the voluntary sector management committee and staff that
the research was a token gesture to prepare the organization for cuts in
funding. On a committee where carers outnumber users the provision of
day care was seen as a resource for carers, and there was a fear that the
views of only the vociferous few would be heard. Staff too saw their
relationship with the centre's users as one where users confide in them
any concerns, so an independent facilitated piece of research was seen as
a threat. On the other hand, commissioners gave weight to the independence and professionalism of research, and any perceived lack in these
areas might have counted against the grant application. A further issue
for commissioners was what weight to attach to the views of current as
distinct from potential users, who might be in the same high need
category but who were excluded from the provision because they found
it unacceptable.

In this example, the Network was acting as a user-controlled development agency, and its position demonstrates the uneasy relationship
between service users' organizations and the state. The danger of colon-
ization and a silencing of the independent, challenging user voice is ever
present. Experience in Wiltshire showed that close, joint working was
possible only after several years developing relationships of trust
between practitioners and users. Other prerequisites were social services'
recognition of users and the Network as key stakeholders in community
care, and explicit messages about valuing the independence of the
Network and the likely ongoing tensions about this.

Voluntary organizations have often lacked similar opportunities and resources to develop user participation (Evans, 1996). However, within Leonard Cheshire, a large, national, independent voluntary organization providing social care, users have developed a good practice project called the Disabled People's Forum. One way in which participation has been developed within the project is by users acting as an advisory committee to the organization's research unit. Users on this group will have the opportunity to influence the research unit's work according to their agenda. This work was initiated by an open invitation to users to join a user meeting facilitated by the Forum's disabled co-ordinator and the research unit officer. Starting the meeting with an invitation to share their experience of research to date enabled the users to identify bad practice such as not receiving feedback, as well as their experience of planning short questionnaires to collect residents' views to present at management committees. The group's first task was to design a satisfaction questionnaire for all Leonard Cheshire users. Members were able to use their expertise to identify areas of users' experience it was important to explore, and ways in which users would like to be asked about them. For example, users' experience of living in rural areas led them to emphasize questions about transport, including views on such detailed issues as the fact that transport had to be booked six weeks in advance, that an accompanying carer had to be identified and that the vehicle was visibly labelled an ambulance. In this way, users were able to advise the professional researchers on evaluation methods and issues which should enhance the validity of the findings.

Users are also leading an evaluation of the Disabled People's Forum mentioned above. This evaluation is a three-year independent project, undertaken by Peter Beresford, a member of the psychiatric system survivor movement, from the Centre for Citizen Participation at Brunel University. A disabled person will be employed to carry out the research, working with other disabled people as interviewers and in other roles, and with an advisory committee controlled by service users. People who use Cheshire services have been interviewed to inform the design of the research project, and the research worker's brief, and the framework of the evaluation will be based on users' views about the effectiveness of the project in enabling them to be more empowered and about the impact it has on the provider organization.

Those commissioning research must also be wary of professionals' propensity to neglect distinctions between users and carers, and their need to participate separately. Carers are in our view another group of stakeholders in services with their own needs, quite distinct from those of users. In particular, commissioners and researchers need to guard against permitting carers to speak on behalf of users, when they have not been given that mandate by users (for example, by accepting research designs which do not distinguish the information to be gathered from users and from carers, or which do not distinguish different methods for seeking the views of each). In part, the potential for confusing the needs and roles of users and carers arises from the way that the traditional care system constructs disabled people as dependent. For example, the presence of family carers has often been taken as removing the case for disabled people to be placed in the high need category for access to services, and in this way disabled people are discriminated against by society and the care system. It remains true, of course, that carers may be taken for granted and not seen as legitimate stakeholders, and this may have serious effects on their well-being and sense of empowerment, but the operation of this discrimination is quite different from that affecting disabled people and their participation.

In formulating plans for its own research, the Network drew on broad principles which underpin the whole of its work (see Figure 6.1).

COLLECTIVE EXAMPLES		INDIVIDUAL EXAMPLES
User-controlled service provision	**CONTROL**	Own-care managers
Involvement on users' terms, not tokenism	**VETO**	Refusal to use services offered; going elsewhere
Developing policy; training professionals	**PARTICIPATION**	Involvement in assessment and care plan
Draft policies; Community Care Plan	**CONSULATION**	Involvement in choices offered
Publicity re provision and rights to service	**INFORMATION PROVISION**	Leading to choice of service offered

Figure 6.1   *Continuum of user involvement*

Our approach was to move user involvement away from mere information provision and towards user control. We sought to empower service users through collective advocacy, recognizing that members need support to make their voices heard. As the Network developed, we had learned to value ourselves and our expertise as service users. In terms of empowerment, we wanted to be in control of our lives and to be able to influence others, so that in addition to being able to live as we wanted we were also able to change the way services are designed and delivered. We had found that influencing social services was best achieved by a policy of 'riddling the system' with as many perspectives of service users in as many different pieces of work as possible. Over time, this had the effect of reducing invitations to participate in projects that had already been defined by professionals, and of increasing the invitations to become involved at the initial stage, developing policy proposals ourselves and in collaboration with professionals. What was critical about this process was that when we as users participated, it was increasingly on our own terms and in activities over which we exercised some control. Small successes bred confidence, and expectations of further influence. We were seen as a safe organization in which funders could invest. We felt we could take the risks of moving into new areas of work where our role as service users needed to be challenged. Critically, we were able to do this because collectively we took risks, which would not have been possible as individuals.

Understood in terms of Figure 6.1 much traditional research falls at the 'Information Provision' and 'Consultation end' of the continuum. The examples of research with social services and with Leonard Cheshire described earlier demonstrate involvement at the 'Participation' level, while the study we are about to describe, where the Network undertook research into one of its own services, is an example of user-controlled research.

An example of user-controlled research

We have given examples of the range of experiences of users *participating* in evaluation: now we want to move on to give a detailed account of research under *user control*. As a result of their previous experiences of research, members of the Wiltshire and Swindon Users' Network formed the view that user expertise was a key resource in evaluation, and that 'professional' involvement was no guarantee of appropriate research. We therefore decided to maintain user control of the research evaluation of Wiltshire Independent Living Fund (WILF), a third party cash payment scheme. Applicants were entitled to receive assistance from the WILF Support Service, which was developed and managed by the Network. Help was provided with both practical issues (employment, advertising, insurance) and the range of personal issues involved in setting up arrangements for assistance. In view of the national interest in direct payments, and of the need to explore the value of assistance provided by disabled people's organizations, the Network decided to evaluate WILF (Wiltshire and Swindon Users' Network, 1996).

In setting up this study, control of the funding was the first, essential step. Because of our credibility in user involvement among allies within social services, we were able to put the case for control of the research budget, and for sufficient funds to underpin the relatively high costs of bringing disabled people together. A wide invitation to participate aroused interest in a core group of users of the WILF service and other members of the Network, and this became the research advisory group, where key decisions about the use of funds were made. Following usual

Network policy, users were paid a fee of £5 an hour to attend the advisory committee. Where additional activities were required, such as interviewing, analysis or writing up, a higher rate was paid in recognition of the greater skills involved. The research meetings were facilitated, in the normal manner of work within the Network, by making assistance available, by providing a note-taker, and by ensuring that participants were paid at the time whenever possible. This format followed Network philosophy of empowering users by enabling them to participate with the support required, at a pace dictated by their needs. At an early stage, we secured the assistance of an academic ally (Mike Fisher) who was an associate member of the Network. His input was carefully negotiated and subject to a formal contract so that control would remain with the Network.

Work in a user-controlled group such as this involved recognizing the role of experience as much as specific research expertise. Few members had undertaken research, but most had received services, and it was difficult at times for members to move on from recounting their experience to using it to inform decisions about research detail, such as what the areas of questioning should cover. Others point to days when they 'accomplished very little of the "task" but a lot of process' of the research (Whitmore, 1994: 90).

Research normally involves careful attention to issues of confidentiality. In our case, this was complicated by the fact that the researchers were also users of the service and might know others receiving it. Some members also felt that records about any individual user of WILF were 'owned' by that user, and no data from these records, even if anonymized, should be used without user consent. Lengthy steps were required to obtain this consent from all who had ever made an application. As the background data about WILF users were accumulated, we next encountered the problem of assessing their representativeness in relation to the population of all those eligible for the service. Census data on those with 'limiting long term illness' were unacceptable because the group rejected the applicability of this concept to disability. Another avenue was to employ the criterion used to determine initial eligibility for WILF (receipt of Disability Living Allowance at the middle or higher rate), but data on DLA recipients were not available in geographical subdivisions corresponding to the county where the research was undertaken. No appropriate data could be located, pointing to a general difficulty for user-controlled research in assessing the generalizability of its findings against national data sets, which may be based on inappropriate assumptions.

The research group decided to gather information directly from WILF users about their experiences. The members had little formal experience of designing or undertaking qualitative interviewing, and so the interview schedule was drawn up over a two-day workshop, during which all members of the group had the chance to ensure the questions they thought important were included. A further two-day workshop was devoted to training four people as interviewers: as some had not been members of the advisory group up to this point, this was an opportunity to refine the work in the light of their experiences (three were WILF users). This workshop was jointly facilitated by the non-user academic ally and a user member of the Network with research experience, in order to ensure that users' knowledge was brought to bear on the learning.

The process of making contact with interviewees required careful thought. First, great care was taken to ensure that the invitation was to be made to service users, and not to their carers. The presence of carers during the interview would not be required, unless the user wanted this. Secondly, the Network operated with the philosophy that users were entitled to assistance from known and trusted people in order to make an informed decision about participation. This assistance would normally come from the WILF support workers whose work was being evaluated and whose influence over research participation would normally be minimized. We arrived at a compromise, where the sample was selected entirely independently but where members of the support service invited users to participate according to a carefully planned protocol designed to minimize variation in response which might be attributable to their influence.

We were determined that user control should extend to all research activities, even those such as analysis and dissemination which are often seen as requiring specialist skills. One member of the research group had statistical analysis skills from his previous work, but there was little experience of qualitative analysis. We set up a process which involved two people reading all the interviews (which had been taped and transcribed), and four combing through the interviews for particular themes. This mirrored a common practice in qualitative analysis based on grounded theory, of coding themes or categories in the context of a strong grasp of the overall stories of the people interviewed. The knowledge of the interviewers was thus brought directly to bear on the analysis of the interviews. In one case, a member of the group was both interviewer and interviewee, since her name had arisen during sampling and she had given permission to be identified to her research colleagues. The group also took responsibility for dissemination, allocating writing, design and production roles to members. The draft report was the subject of a full day's review by the group, who then took on roles for a presentation to the forthcoming Network AGM.

This detailed account illuminates some of the differences between traditional research (even that within the framework of empowerment) and user-controlled research, and suggests some of the roles professional allies might adopt in order to facilitate user-controlled research.

The implications for practitioners

Throughout this chapter we have tried to portray a different vision of social work research, one that goes beyond ensuring that professionals possess the techniques and the ability to undertake research to include attention to the role of research in the changing relationship between service users and professionals. If the purpose of research is to enhance the lives of service users, the principles which apply generally to empowerment-oriented practice apply with all the more force where the activity is one normally associated with exclusive expertise. We have shown, for example, that expertise must be conceptualized as belonging with service users as much as with professionals, and that professional skills lie as much in facilitating user-led and user-controlled research as in technical skills traditionally reserved to the 'researcher'. Some of these developments in the relationship between service users and professionals are portrayed graphically by Jones (see Figure 6.2).

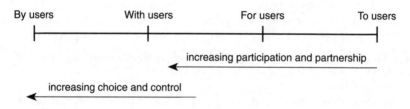

Figure 6.2 *Continuum of relations between service users and providers (Jones, 1995: 112)*

What we have tried to show in this chapter is that the more the principles underpinning practice progress towards choice and control, the more likely it is that services – including research – will be undertaken *by* service users, rather than *to, for* or *with* service users.

We are not arguing that professionals should stop doing research or that they do not need research skills. Indeed, we would argue that professionals have an increasing duty to acquire the ability to conceptualize and undertake research as services move further towards coherent examination of their outcomes and methods. The difference is that we see a growing need for professionals to recognize the potential research expertise of service users, and to work with service users in developing and conducting research. As an integral part of these developments, professionals must learn to place their skills in the hands of service users and to regard their work as accountable to users. In other words, it is not enough to know how to practise research: what is required is the ability to assist service users to participate in the research enterprise in an empowering way.

Such a shift of power and in patterns of working requires a change in both the attitudes and skills of professional social workers. In particular, we need to re-examine the traditional status accorded to professional researchers, which in our view has often depended on the exclusion of service users from an active role in knowledge creation. Instead of prizing collaboration, we have elevated individual research skills and the 'mystique' of research to the point where it is seen as beyond both ordinary people and basic grade practitioners. As front-line practice has explored the notions of partnership and empowerment, social work research has largely remained a non-participative activity, more empowering for its practitioners than for service users.

The first step is to recognize user expertise as valid alongside professional expertise. As several of the leading social work qualifying programmes have discovered, involving service users in teaching social work brings not only immediacy to the learning but a reshaping of the notion of expertise. Instead of expertise in knowing best, professional expertise can be recast as enabling service users to assess the issues they face and assisting them in making their own plans. Certainly, research calls for specific skills, but the examples of users and professionals working together on home care issues and the Leonard Cheshire research unit user advisory group show how the commitment to joint working and facilitation can reveal skills and experience among service users, which a traditional research approach would regard as immaterial. Of course, some skills are more difficult to acquire than others, and the example of WILF research highlighted areas such as sampling and data analysis where users had relatively little experience. Since all skills are learned, however, the issue becomes how to impart such skills to users, or, if service users prefer, how to place professional skills at the users' disposal, ensuring that users have the knowledge to make informed decisions about the research.

Professionals frequently use 'demystification' skills in order to ensure that service users have the information they need in a complex welfare state. Sometimes this is as basic as giving information which is difficult to obtain, but there are as many circumstances where users may feel they do not have the experience or technical ability to decipher the information available (benefit entitlement being a prime example). Sometimes, users may additionally feel they do not have the right to question decisions made by those perceived as powerful. Demystification therefore may involve not only giving information, but also reinforcing the right of service users to participate in decisions affecting their lives. Social work practice in research is thus no different from other forms of practice, where power, accountability, information and entitlement are key issues.

Social workers are familiar with service users ascribing to them rather greater power than they actually possess, and exploring with service users what they can and cannot do, and what knowledge they do and do not have, requires a degree of professional humility and a willingness to work with service users as colleagues. This is a difficult path to tread, and fraught with pitfalls. We have argued, for instance, that social workers may assist the more widespread development of user involvement in service organizations, so that user involvement in research is routine rather than novel. Social workers usually have less power to alter the organizational environment than service users assume, and it is important to be clear about the limits of any single worker's influence. It is equally important, however, not to avoid responsibility by portraying social workers as powerless (since there is little solace for service users in sharing professionals' sense of disempowerment). What is required is a strategic alliance between service users and professionals to develop organizational openness to service user involvement. Our experience of teaching social workers within a user-involvement philosophy suggests that they may experience their own sense of empowerment as the agenda shifts towards user participation, a shift which neither the professionals nor the service users can achieve alone.

As user involvement develops, social workers may fear that their role is diminishing, especially in adult community care, where there have been other attacks on the notion of professional expertise. The danger is that research is seen as one of the few remaining areas where expertise is respected. Social workers need to be aware that their skills are accorded greater respect by service users if they are facilitative and empowering than when they lead to an exclusive practice, and that this applies with equal force to research skills. They also need to be wary of the ascription of expertise, when it is accompanied by an uncritical approach to power and control. The current debate within social care about evidence-based practice, for example, suggests that the term 'evidence' be restricted to certain kinds of knowledge, often excluding the knowledge of service users. Similarly, the concern with measuring outcomes in adult community care needs to reflect more coherently the importance of outcomes defined by service users. In the WILF research, there were times when the users perceived a decision as requiring research expertise and referred it unnecessarily to the 'professional' researcher. In other words, in addition to a willingness to engage in inclusive, demystifying practice, social workers also need the ability to analyse the power and control implications of their research role.

Facilitation is a key skill for social workers, and user-led and user-controlled research flourishes when resources are provided to enable user-controlled organizations to develop a sound infrastructure and to commission research in line with their agenda. The WILF research was resourced and carried out within the framework of a confident and properly resourced user organization. The principles of good practice underpinning all user participation (such as accessible venues, payment of costs and a fee, appropriate timing of meetings and an acceptable structure) apply to this aspect of working as well.

It may be argued that this role for social workers is too demanding. Given the relatively undeveloped nature of social work research, we are now pointing to the need to go beyond conventional practice. If we have not attained the first step, how can we argue for the second? This implies, of course, a natural evolution for professional research, as though we must progress through exclusive, specialist expertise before we can engage in the participatory and emancipatory research agenda. Empowerment thinking is the key to dismantling these assumptions, since it provides the opportunity to re-examine the role of 'traditional' social research in reinforcing a passive role for service users (Evans and Fisher, 1997), and it provides the rationale for a different approach aimed at participative, empowering practice.

Developing such an agenda is a tough assignment in a social welfare context where health-service-derived models threaten to overwhelm social models of research development, and where a social work parallel to 'clinical' expertise may be seen as the goal. The empowerment research agenda can only be pursued effectively through collaboration, and through strategic alliances between professionals and service users. Professionals and users describe such joint working as starting on a journey together, recognizing the power imbalances and being open about where the journey will take them. Above all, this agenda requires a commitment from professionals to share the users' vision of the role of user-led and user-controlled research to bring about change – change in the services we receive to improve the quality of our own lives, and change in the discriminatory attitudes and systems of society.

References

Abberley, P. (1992) 'Counting us out: a discussion of the OPCS disability surveys', *Disability, Handicap and Society*, 7 (2): 139–155.

Barnes, C. (1992) 'Qualitative research: valuable or irrelevant?' *Disability, Handicap and Society*, 7 (2): 115–123.

Barnes, C. (1996) 'Disability and the myth of the independent researcher', *Disability and Society*, 11 (1): 107–110.

Barnes, C. and Mercer, G. (eds) (1997) *Doing Disability Research*. Leeds: Disability Press.

Barnes, M. (1993) 'Introducing new stakeholders – user and researcher interests in evaluative research', *Policy and Politics*, 21 (1): 47–58.

Beresford, P. and Turner, M. (1997) *It's Our Welfare: Report of the Citizen Commission on the Future of the Welfare State*. London: NISW.

Beresford, P. and Wallcroft, J. (1997) 'Psychiatric system survivors and emancipatory research: issues, overlaps and differences', in C. Barnes and G. Mercer (eds), *Doing Disability Research*. Leeds: Disability Press. pp. 67–87.

Bewley, C. and Glendinning, C. (1994) *Involving Disabled People in Community Care Planning*. York: Joseph Rowntree Foundation.

Booth, T. and Booth, W. (1996) 'Sounds of silence: narrative research with inarticulate subjects', *Disability and Society*, 11 (1): 55–69.

Bury, M. (1996) 'Disability and the myth of the independent researcher: a reply', *Disability and Society*, 11 (1): 111–113.

Evans, C. (1996) 'From those who know: the role of service users', in C. Hanvey and T. Philpott (eds), *Sweet Charity: The Role and Workings of Voluntary Organizations*. London: Routledge. pp. 69–81.

Evans, C. (1997) *From Bobble Hats to Red Jackets*. Devizes: Wiltshire and Swindon Users' Network.

Evans, C. and Fisher, M. (1997) 'User controlled research and empowerment'. Conference paper, Empowerment Practice in Social Work: Developing Richer Conceptual Foundations, Faculty of Social Work, University of Toronto.

Jones, L. and Pullen, G. (1992) 'Cultural differences: deaf and hearing researchers working together', *Disability, Handicap and Society*, 7 (2): 189–196.

Jones, R. (1995) 'Disability, discrimination and the local authority social services: the social services context', in G. Zarb (ed.), *Removing Disabling Barriers*. London: PSI. pp. 108–115.

Keith, L. (1992) 'Who care wins? Women, caring and disability', *Disability, Handicap and Society*, 7 (2): 167–175.

Lindow, V. and Morris, J. (1995) *Service User Involvement: Synthesis of Findings and Experience in the Field of Community Care*. York: Joseph Rowntree Foundation.

Marsh, P. and Fisher, M. (1992) *Good Intentions: Developing Partnership in Social Services*. York: Joseph Rowntree Foundation.

Morris, J. (1992) 'Personal and political: a feminist perspective on researching physical disability', *Disability, Handicap and Society*, 7 (2): 157–166.

Oliver, M. (1992) 'Changing the social relations of research production', *Disability, Handicap and Society*, 7 (2): 101–114.

Rapp, C., Shera, W. and Kisthardt, W. (1993) 'Research strategies for consumer empowerment', *Social Work*, 38 (6): 727–735.

Reason, P. (1994) 'Human inquiry as discipline and practice', in P. Reason (ed.), *Participation in Human Inquiry*. London: Sage. pp. 40–56.

Roberts, H. (1998) 'Look who's talking', *Community Care*, 29 January–4 February: 22–23.

Shakespeare, T. (1996) 'Rules of engagement: doing disability research', *Disability and Society*, 11 (1): 115–119.

Shakespeare, T. (1997) 'Researching disabled sexuality', in C. Barnes and G. Mercer (eds), *Doing Disability Research*. Leeds: Disability Press. pp. 177–189.

Ward, L. (1997) 'Funding for change: translating emancipatory disability research from theory to practice', in C. Barnes and G. Mercer (eds), *Doing Disability Research*. Leeds: Disability Press. pp. 32–48.

Ward, L. and Flynn, M. (1994) 'What matters most: disability, research and empowerment', in M. Rioux and M. Bach (eds), *Disability is not Measles: New Paradigms in Disability*. North York, Ontario: Roehrer Institute. pp. 29–48.

Whitmore, E. (1994) 'To tell the truth: working with oppressed groups in participatory approaches to inquiry', in P. Reason (ed.), *Participation in Human Inquiry*. London: Sage. pp. 82–98.

Whittaker, A., Kershaw, J. and Spargo, J. (1993) 'Service evaluation by people with learning difficulties', in P. Beresford and T. Harding (eds), *A Challenge to Change: Practical Experiences of Building User-Led Services*. London: National Institute for Social Work. pp. 109–125.

7

FEMINIST EVALUATION

Beth Humphries

In a book on evaluation, a chapter headed 'Feminist Evaluation' carries a danger that feminist evaluation may come to be viewed as yet another in a wide possible range of methods. The result might be that readers are implicitly offered a choice among say, 'action research', 'observation', 'case histories' and 'feminist evaluation', risking marginalizing feminist approaches, which in fact encompass almost the full spectrum of methods. Feminists agree generally that there is no distinctive feminist method, but that what is key to feminist approaches is what Stanley and Wise call 'feminist consciousness' (1990: 22). What is required is not adherence to one or other dichotomized model ('quantitative/ qualitative', 'deductive/inductive'), but detailed descriptions of actual research processes sited around an explication of feminist consciousness. Moreover, feminist consciousness suggests that the focus of research need not be exclusively women's experiences. Morgan (1981), in his research on masculinity, regarded his work as informed by a feminist consciousness. Nor need it be exclusively qualitative research. Survey research is one way of expanding understanding of the dimensions of the issues that concern us. A large scale survey in the USA of women alumni confirmed sexual harassment on campuses as not infrequent, but widespread across universities (Reinharz, 1992). West's (1996) analysis of official statistics on women's employment reveals the extent of women's subordination in economic activity, part-time work and sex segregation. Kelly et al. (1995) used self-report questionnaires to elicit experiences of sexual abuse from women and men college students, which helped in the development of feminist theory and practice on child abuse. Statistical data offer the wider picture which is not available to solely qualitative methods. Feminist consciousness can inform both topics and methods. Bell hooks makes the picture wider still:

> patriarchal domination shares an ideological foundation with racism and other forms of group oppression, and there is no hope that it can be eradicated while

Wiltshire and Swindon Users' Network (1996) *I Am in Control: Research into Users' Views of the Wiltshire Independent Living Fund*. Devizes: WCCUIN.

Zarb, G. (1992) 'On the road to Damascus: first steps towards changing the relations of disability research production', *Disability, Handicap and Society*, 7 (2): 125–139.

those systems remain intact. This knowledge should consistently inform the direction of feminist theory and practice. (1989: 22)

'Feminist consciousness', then, has the potential to offer insights into inequality and oppression in all their forms, and in this sense is compatible with the declared aims of contemporary social work practice. From this starting point, this chapter examines the theoretical perspectives which constitute the basis of knowledge within feminism, and looks at some examples of their impact on the evaluation of practice in social work and welfare.

Feminist consciousness and feminist theory

In the 1970s feminists raised concerns about the sexist bias of social science research, in which women's knowledge and experience were disregarded. Feminist research was defined as explicitly political work to give women a voice – research *on* women, *by* women and *for* women. The defining assumption was that 'woman' is a necessary category of analysis because all women share common experiences by virtue of being women. Little attention was given to problematizing the notions of 'woman', 'gender' or 'patriarchy'. The category 'woman' tended to reflect the experiences of white, middle-class, heterosexual, Western women, yet treated these as universally applicable (Mohanty, 1991).

A variety of epistemological influences underpinned feminist research and evaluation. On the political left, some women felt that gender issues were being ignored at the expense of class. They looked for the cause of gender inequality beyond simple economic explanations, but still within a Marxist framework (Firestone, 1970; Millett, 1969; Mitchell, 1971). Mono-causal theories of patriarchy were substituted for mono-causal theories of capitalism, or attempts were made to make the two work together. This tended to elide complex lived relationships, and it also threatened to reinscribe women in a position of powerlessness against men as all powerful oppressors. This made it difficult to theorize how women are to gain the means to overthrow their oppressors.

Liberal feminists argue that benefits such as property, work and positions of power are unequally distributed between men and women, and their aim is formal equality with men (Richards, 1982; Wollstonecraft, 1988). Compatible with this is *feminist empiricism* which, in the tradition of positivism, believes that the methods used in research in the natural sciences are appropriate to the social sciences. It holds that only those phenomena that are observable, amenable to the senses, can be warranted as knowledge. 'Feelings' or 'subjective experience' cannot be admitted unless they can be rendered observable. Feminist empiricism claims that gender/patriarchy is a missing element in the explanation of social phenomena. It points to the androcentric bias of traditional research and argues that prejudice enters social science research at the design stage and carries through to the conclusions, because it is based on the interests and view of the world of men. The main argument of feminist empiricism is the need for a stricter adherence to existing methodological norms of scientific inquiry, by taking account of the insights emerging from the women's liberation movement. It focuses on the *incompleteness* of existing research, without necessarily challenging the norms of empiricism (Eichler, 1987 is an example of feminist empiricism).

Feminist standpoint theory starts from the position that knowledge is based on experience. Women's experiences, informed by feminist theory, are seen as potentially more complete and less distorted than those of men. Knowledge is achieved through engagement in intellectual and political struggle which challenges taken for granted or dominant views of the world, and brings insights unique to the oppressed group, which are unavailable to dominant groups:

> it is through feminist struggles against male domination that women's experi-
> ence can be made to yield up a truer (or less false) image of social reality than
> that available only from the perspective of the social experience of men of the
> ruling classes and races. (Harding, 1987: 185)

This raises questions: what is female experience? Is there an essential differentness about women? Can we identify a universal female experi-ence, common to women? This is no easy task, since women exist in all classes, 'races', ethnicities, sexualities, abilities. This privileging and essentializing of a stereotypical 'female knowledge' contains a

> danger of romanticizing and/or appropriating the vision of the less powerful
> . . . to see from below is neither easily learned nor unproblematic . . . the
> standpoints of the subjugated are not innocent positions. (Haraway, 1988:
> 584)

Feminists have found aspects of *poststructuralism* to be compatible with feminist theory. Here our sense of ourselves – our subjectivity – is neither unified nor fixed. Unlike humanism, which implies a conscious knowing, unified, rational subject, poststructuralism theorizes subjectivity as a 'site of disunity and conflict, central to the process of political change and to preserving the status quo' (Weedon, 1987: 21). The focus shifts to *language*, where meanings compete and as a result construct subjects in different and contradictory ways. Language, far from reflecting an already given social reality, constitutes social reality for us. Foucauldian theory has been of particular interest to feminists. Foucault's notion of discourse and discursive fields is an attempt to understand the relation-ship between language, social institutions, subjectivity and power (Foucault, 1991). Discursive fields consist of competing ways of giving

meaning to the world, and of organizing social institutions and processes. Within the discursive field of the family, for example, not all
discourses will carry equal power, with consequences for women. Feminist discourse analysis can be used as a way of organizing historically
specific discourses analytically in discursive fields. Gail Lewis provides
an example of this in her interviews with black women social workers
(Lewis, 1996).

So, within the framework of 'feminist consciousness', there are complex and sometimes contradictory debates about what constitutes such a
consciousness. These have implications for what might constitute feminist evaluation. Conventional evaluation tends towards the reduction of
programme activity to measurable indicators. Effectiveness is thus statistically determined by a measurement of how well the system has created
change in individuals through the manipulation of a socially problematic
environment. Feminist empiricism is compatible with this approach, and
seeks to ensure that gender is included in the variables considered,
ensuring a more 'accurate' understanding. Evaluation from a feminist
standpoint perspective is derived from 'a committed feminist exploration of women's experiences of oppression' (Stanley and Wise, 1990: 27).
This is not without its problems, particularly a tendency to create a
hierarchy of 'standpoints', and the exclusion of some voices. Poststructuralist evaluation would construct a narrative of all possible view-
points on the programme and the 'social problem' on which it is
targeted. Haraway advocates the notion of 'situated knowledges' –
'partial, locatable, critical knowledges sustaining the possibility of webs
of connections called solidarity in politics and shared conversations in
epistemology' (1988: 584).

Towards feminist evaluation

As a framework for discussion, I have adapted the methodological
postulates set out by Maria Mies (1993), within which I shall pursue
some of the debates raised above, using examples of feminist evaluation
as illustration. Mies sets out principles which she sees as essential
elements in a feminist approach to research and evaluation.

The first is *conscious partiality*. A principle of conventional research is
neutrality towards the objects of research – a position of being value free.
Mies insists that this has to be replaced by conscious partiality which is
achieved through partial identification with the research subjects. The
sharing of the experience of being women, and therefore knowing a
common oppression, leads to empathy, connection and concern, which
are held to be women's special strengths. These imply the need for
appropriate intersubjective methods, emphasizing the experiential, and
being attentive to the concrete realm of everyday reality and human

agency. Oakley rejected the hierarchical, objectifying and falsely 'objective' stance of the impersonal interviewer as neither possible nor desirable, arguing that meaningful feminist research depends on empathy
and mutuality (Oakley, 1981). This position has strongly influenced
feminist evaluation and research over 20 years. However, Judith Stacey
wonders whether this appearance of greater respect and equality 'masks
a deeper, more dangerous form of exploitation' (Stacey, 1991: 113),
referring here to the identification of interviewer and interviewee which
can lead to intimate revelations which can then be used by the evaluator
to meet her own agenda – her interpretations, her voice. Stacey also sees
any published report as, of itself, an intrusion into the lives of the women
interviewed.

Within the mainstream academic community, 'partiality' has not been
welcomed because it is thought to be 'unscientific' or politically moti-
vated, and therefore overtly biased (Hammersley, 1995). The result is a
polarized debate which, crudely put, equates objectivity with quantitative methods and subjectivity with qualitative methods. But as Jayaratne
and Stewart (1995: 228) say, 'there is increasing recognition that the use
of particular methods and procedures does not automatically confer
objectivity, just as inclusion of analysis of one's personal subjective
experience does not preclude it'. A feminist consciousness does not
imply the renunciation of objectivity, and feminists have a responsibility
to seek procedures which guard against biased results. At the same time,
feminists 'reject the distinction between knowing subject and known
object – the division between subjective and objective postures'
(MacKinnon, 1989: 121). The notion of partiality questions the idea that
science can be value free, but does not dismiss the need for rigorous
methods.

Jayaratne and Stewart (1995: 230–232) offer strategies for making
explicit the meaning of 'partiality' in feminist methodology. In selecting a
topic, we should ask how the evaluation will help women's lives, and
what information is necessary to have such impact; and in interpreting
results, we should ask what different interpretations, consistent with the
findings, imply for change in women's lives.

Illustrative of 'conscious partiality' as an evaluative aspect of the social
work role is the example of the Johnsons, a white, working-class family
of wife, husband and three children, one of whom, Jessica, is physically
disabled and needs daily care. When Jessica was eight, her mother Joy
'came out' as a lesbian, left her husband and moved in with her lover.
She wanted to have her children with her, but she was regarded as an
unfit mother and custody was awarded to her husband. Home help
support was arranged for him in caring for Jessica. It soon became clear
that he was unable to cope with the demands of Jessica's condition. It
was concluded that Joy could after all look after Jessica, but that home
help support was not necessary.

A feminist evaluation of the handling of this situation would ask a number of questions:

- What is the basis of the assumption that 'normally' mothers are the best carers for children?
- What is the basis of the assumption that a lesbian is unfit to care for a child?
- What assumptions underpinned the decision to offer home help support to the man and not the woman?
- Did the social workers have any unspoken worries about a man giving intimate care to a female child? What was the basis of such worries?
- What were the imperatives which led to a redefinition of the situation, so that Joy was allowed to care for Jessica after all?
- Are there similar assumptions/patterns across other cases?

A feminist evaluation of intervention has at its heart a concern for – a conscious partiality towards – the most vulnerable, in this case Jessica. It does not place Joy's needs above that of her child, but it does ask whether sexist and heterosexist assumptions are being made about Joy's actions which result in prejudiced decisions that punish both the mother and the child, and indeed cause distress for the father and the other children. Failure to ask such questions leads to poor practice. But the evaluation needs to go further than single cases. There needs to be an examination of *patterns* of practice, so that genuinely anti-discriminatory work can be achieved.

The second of Mies's principles is *the view from below*. The vertical relationship between researcher and researched, the view from above, must be replaced by the view from below (Mies, 1993: 38). This is a rejection of the binary knower/non-knower division, which assumes that the researcher (or social worker) discovers knowledge and the non-knower supplies the data. It argues that women as subjects can be knowers, that their experience constitutes the basis of knowledge, and that their voice should be heard above that of the researcher. Usually this is best achieved by qualitative methods such as semi-structured interviewing or focus groups, or diaries, which can give direct access to the verbatim voices of women themselves.

In an attempt to make women's experiences – so long undervalued and invisible – a basis for legitimate knowledge, feminists coined the phrase, 'the personal is political'. This referred to an understanding that (1) women's experiences at a micro and domestic level reflected and interacted with their subordination at a macro level of society; (2) their individual experiences were grounded in the collective social and cultural experiences of other women; and (3) by politicizing these experiences change could be brought about in women's situation, personally and socially. This was an important development, for in 'creating a legitimacy to speak from experience, feminists (black and white) had made it possible to begin to undo established ideas about what it means to "know" ' (Lewis, 1996: 25).

It also led to a number of problems which are as much an issue for feminist social workers as for feminist researchers. The first concerns representation. Women's voices are always mediated through other women, usually those privileged within feminist discourses, namely white, Western and middle-class women. The question is how far such women can speak for women who are not white, Western and middle class, without imperially appropriating their voice. There is no universal feminist voice which can speak on behalf of all women. Disabled, lesbian, black and third world women have contested such representation, and drawn attention to the complexity of dialogue amongst women who understand themselves to be 'complexly like and different from each other' (Yeatman, 1993: 241). The global diversity of women's experiences demands that a multiplicity of voices be heard. Theory which developed as a result of these privileged representations of the 'other' was therefore narrow and centred on European and North American ideas. This totalizing view has been challenged by women from positions of difference, leading to a problematizing of the category 'woman' (Carby, 1982; hooks, 1982; Lorde, 1984; Riley, 1988).

Secondly, there was a tendency to privilege experience in the sense that experience *per se* became the criterion of knowledge, rather than the starting point from which to develop theory. 'I have experienced therefore I know' became the implied epistemological claim. The more experiences of oppression one had, the more authoritative the voice. Thus women who were black, disabled, lesbian and poor were endowed with the most authentic voice. This placed women contesting multiple oppressions in an invidious position. Rather than entering into a dialogue with other women about the complexities of experience, they were expected to speak on behalf of all 'others', all minorities, all difference, and often to educate other women about oppression. At the same time they were expected to choose one oppressed identity depending on the context in which they found themselves. 'I find I am constantly being encouraged to pluck out some one aspect of myself and present this as the meaningful whole, eclipsing or denying the other parts of myself' (Lorde, 1984: 120). The 'voice from below' was still the voice from outside.

Thirdly, the slogan 'the personal is political' became limited to the personal, and all conflicts among and within women are flattened (Mohanty, 1992: 82). The focus is on the psychological status of experience, and therefore on attitude and intention. The debate becomes ahistorical and individualistic, anchored firmly in European philosophical tenets.

Joan Scott calls for a problematizing of 'experience':

Experience . . . becomes not the origin of our explanation, not the authoritative (because seen or felt) evidence that grounds what is known, but rather that which we seek to explain, that about which knowledge is produced. To think about experience in this way is to historicize it as well as to historicize the identities it produces. (Scott, 1992: 26)

In other words, the category 'experience' needs to be interrogated within an historical context in order to interpret its meanings for different social groups at specific times. In feminist evaluation and research, listening to the 'voice from below' is an important principle, but it should not be treated as an unexamined category – where the experience of being female transforms us into feminists through osmosis (Mohanty, 1992: 77).

Gail Lewis grasped these complexities in her interviews with black women social workers, where she explored their use of the category 'experience' to make sense of their location as workers in social services departments (Lewis, 1996). By viewing what counts as experience as neither self-evident nor straightforward, but always contested, always political, Lewis opened up possibilities for thinking about the 'subject of experience' as 'at once shifting and multiple, because she stands at the intersections of complex webs of relations organized around numerous axes of power and differentiation' (1996: 50). Although all the women spoke of 'black women's experience', there was a realization that such an experience could not be unitary, since the institutional location of the women resulted in different 'experiences' from those with whom they had at one time constructed a community. Most of the black women workers were in subordinate roles in their jobs, but in relations of dominance over other women, black and white clients, and in a range of relationships with others: black men, white men, black women, white women.

black women in their multiple selves move within and across discourses as they communicate in modes of identification and differentiation with those who constitute an element of themselves. (Lewis, 1996: 53)

The complex experience which is spoken must be heard, but the circumstances of that speaking must be 'excavated and analyzed' (1996: 50). It is only then that the 'voice from below' is seen as constitutive of reality rather than descriptive of fixed 'experience'.

Social workers and social work managers use stereotypes all the time in their work. These are woven into unreflected-upon notions of 'carers', 'the elderly', 'the Irish', 'Asians', 'the disabled', which lead to decisions that often have profound effects on people's lives and careers. People's experiences may have commonalities with others, but also have radical differences. The view from below implies an attempt to understand those differences and commonalities, and to seek the views of those on whose behalf decisions are made and services offered. Lewis's point goes further in that a person's subjectivity is not fixed, but shifts according to context, and is therefore complex and changing. Evaluation of field and management practice will recognize and engage with this complexity.

Mies's notion of *praxis-orientation* is drawn from Marxism (Salamini, 1981), and implies active participation in struggles for emancipation. Knowledge and action are integrated and inseparable. Stanley argues that feminism is not just a 'perspective', a way of seeing; nor is it even this plus an epistemology, a way of knowing; it is also an ontology, or a way of being in the world:

> it is the experience of and acting against perceived oppression that gives rise to a distinctive feminist ontology; and it is the analytic exploration of the parameters of this in the research process that gives expression to a distinctive feminist epistemology. (Stanley, 1990: 14)

These elements are drawn together to create a feminist praxis. Evaluation and research become part of the struggle. Social work is well placed to work in praxis-oriented ways both on the job and in influencing policy. At the heart of praxis are methods which are collaborative, which search for theory and explanations that grow out of context-embedded data, and which treat subjects as active agents.

An example of praxis from the probation service is the Campaign against Double Punishment (GMIAU, 1997). This concerns the practice of imprisoning or otherwise punishing people who have committed offences, and then deporting them on completion of the punishment. The recipients of this unfair treatment are mostly black men, but partners and children are also punished by the break-up of families. By the systematic documentation of practice across several probation teams, the policy was recognized as both racist and sexist, by prisoners and ex-prisoners, partners of prisoners, probation officers, social workers, immigration aid workers and others, who initiated a campaign against it. The campaign made visible the practice, and educated probation and social workers to the extent that training is now offered to help them resist this unfair practice. This is the outcome of ongoing evaluation, informed by feminist and anti-racist consciousness. There are many opportunities for such praxis, if social workers have a mind to look for them.

Linked to praxis-orientation is *change of the status quo*. This implies that social change is the starting point for feminist evaluation. The aim is not only to understand the world, but to change it. Mies says that 'a scientific outlook is not the privilege of social scientists . . . the creativity of science depends on its being rooted in living social processes . . . of change' (1993: 41). Knowledge is conditioned by the historical context in which it develops, and is produced and legitimized from the perspective of dominant groups. Feminists and other critical theorists are concerned to construct knowledge from the perspectives of 'marginalized, deprived and oppressed groups of people and classes [in order to] . . . transform social realities' (de Koning and Martin, 1996: 14). Above I have pointed to some of the problems raised by such an enterprise. Feminists do not agree on what needs to be changed. There needs to be a recognition of the multiple differences between men and the multiple differences between women: 'we cannot do without some notion of what human beings have in common; we can and must do without a unitary standard against which they are judged' (Phillips, 1992: 20). This issue about 'difference' and 'universality' is at the centre of contemporary feminist debates about the construction of knowledge with the aim of changing the status quo.

The role of social work in this is a highly contested concept, and increasingly the task of social work is defined as one of control and surveillance. But social work is not a unitary activity and, as I have tried to illustrate, there are areas within the profession where, informed by a feminist consciousness, and by anti-racist and critical perspectives, changes can take place.

Mies's fifth principle, *conscientization*, is drawn from the work of Paolo Freire, the Brazilian educator (Freire, 1972). It refers to research and evaluation which aims to encourage participants to question relationships of dependency and exploitation, and to engage in social action for change. Education towards critical awareness is therefore an integral aspect of feminist evaluation. Martin, in her evaluation of a well woman centre, describes her experiences of conscientization (Martin, 1994, 1996). The negotiated purposes of the evaluation were to clarify the aims of the centre; examine the educational processes employed there; inquire into women's perceptions of their health education needs, the purpose of the centre and the extent to which it met users' health needs. It aimed to elicit workers' views of the style of leadership, and the views of local health professionals about the centre. The methods used were an examination of documents, semi-structured individual and group interviews, participant observation and mailed questionnaires. These are conventional methods, but informing them was a feminist consciousness which validated the women's experiences and attempted to share power. Martin describes the complexities of carrying through a feminist, participative design, and the educative process for the evaluator and the other women. The outcomes included an increase in confidence for the centre women in demystifying research and developing skill in evaluation techniques, in understanding decision-making in the centre, and a greater awareness of their right to services related to their own health. For the evaluator, the experience brought a vivid awareness of power amongst women and of class inequality, and the ways in which the evaluation process can give a voice to those without power (Martin, 1996). Social workers working with women's groups can take a similar approach with conscientization as one of their group goals.

Were data to be made available about the process of conscientization of social workers who are open to learn from service users, a picture would no doubt emerge of lifelong learning in unexpected ways. Martha was a black social worker allocated to a white single parent named Rachel, who had had four children. Behind Rachel was a childhood in care, fractious family relationships, a violent marriage, divorce. She suffered chronic ill health and lived on Disability Allowance. Two of her children were fostered, a third lived with her sister and the youngest was adopted at birth. Rachel was sustained by a religious belief, a strong longing for life, an adroitness in accessing state benefits, and eventually by a man who was devoted to her and who cared for her until she died aged 46. On the face of it a miserable life, a victim, an inadequate woman. Martha recognized in her a person of strength, insight and generosity, a survivor who refused the label of victim and who found a way through each crisis. Through this experience Martha was conscientized to gender, class and 'race' oppression, and was led to both anger and admiration. Through her evaluation of Rachel's case, she began to build up a broader picture of oppression and resistance in the lives of other women, leading her to see and work with their strengths rather than exclusively focusing on their inadequacies.

Conclusion

Evaluation research is sometimes viewed as a retrospective, purely technical activity which focuses on decisions already made and pro- grammes already in place. But as VanderPlaat (1995: 82) says, ' how the social problem is articulated and how one describes or measures what occurs within an interventionary site is shaped and constrained by the capacities of the evaluative discourse being used'. In other words, all evaluation is political, and even issues regarded as purely technical are influenced by ideology. The current dominance of managerialist and technicist approaches to welfare also influence evaluation practices. This can create problems for feminist consciousness and political agency in evaluation.

Moreover, computerized information systems do not capture the 'hid- den tasks' of social workers – moral reasoning, classification, categoriza- tion (Thorpe, 1994) *before* decisions are made about the service to be offered. The moral nature of the reasoning process is often transformed into technical and administrative descriptions which hide from view important processes in child protection and other forms of social work. The push towards the collection of quantitative data by central and local government need not be all negative, however. There is now enough evidence of domestic abuse of women, for example, for local authorities to be pressed to include it as a specific category in referral, assessment and monitoring activities. Mullender (1997: 65) argues that if economy is a goal of social services, early engagement with domestic abuse may prevent the need for resource-intensive statutory child care and/or mental health work at a later stage.

The evaluation of child protection carried out by Thorpe (1994) in Western Australia is an example of a useful statistical analysis which would have been enhanced by a feminist consciousness. Thorpe drew attention to the over-representation of poor and disadvantaged people – single female parent families and Aboriginal people – in child protection statistics. He pointed out that conventional child protection statistics fail to reveal 'the true nature of much child protection work – the observation of and categorization of parenting behaviours and the moral character of parents' (1994: 196), and he emphasized the importance of taking account of context. The analysis might have been taken further to expose the contradictions in the class, 'race' and gender subtext. The activities of social workers focused largely on the disciplining of poor and minority ethnic *women*. Any evaluation of services is distorted without a perspective of feminist consciousness.

Feminist consciousness and feminist evaluation are largely excluded from the culture of organizations, whether these are local government or social services oriented, or academic. Although I have said that feminism has the potential to influence the design and implementation of all evaluation and research, its insights remain largely marginal, and are seen as 'specialist'. Stanley (1997: 182) describes the 'gatekeepers, mechanisms for inclusion and exclusion, means of adjudicating knowledge-claims and canons of received ideas and "significant" literature' which guard the insiders against outsider knowledge, and reinforce the divide between theory and practice.

Mies (1993) calls for a collectivization of experiences, seeing as important the documentation and sharing of women's campaigns and struggles, the appropriation (making their own) of histories to which they have contributed but from which they have been excluded, and arguing for a continued praxis-oriented involvement in those struggles.

There are also alliances feminists can make with other critical social workers who find themselves in opposition to available evaluation criteria and strategies. This might involve redefining the purpose of intervention, judging it by

> the degree to which there has been movement to reduce oppressive conditions and whether the strategies employed are creating social processes and structures which provide the marginal person with greater access to goods and services and movement towards a psychological sense of community. (Bennett, 1987: 17)

VanderPlaat (1995) sees the continued adherence to the traditional discourse of social intervention as a limitation of conventional evaluation research. Following Habermas (1984, 1987), she formulates an alternative perspective which is entirely compatible with feminist aspirations.

First, social change requires an increase in the capacity of the dis-possessed to take action, and this ability is linked to the acquisition of specific skills. Secondly, actions are linked to the interests which govern them. Systemic interests informed by a scientific and technocratic ration-ality have come to dictate both the understanding of our discontent and the skills required to overcome it. Social workers could challenge such construction of social problems and their solutions, and use available resources in the interests of the dispossessed. People need to build communicative competence – the ability to discursively explore what their lived experiences mean – towards conscientization and action. This, not technical expertise, must be the starting point of meaningful social change. The evaluative strategy needs to take account of these dimen-sions, rather than to see an intervention programme as a set of activities designed to produce a certain outcome. VanderPlaat views evaluation as a 'narrative designed to increase subjective and intersubjective under-standing among all stakeholders', and as 'critique – a process by which we assess the non-instrumental social change potential inherent in a social program' (1995: 89). The lessons from a feminist consciousness for social work evaluation – taking sides with oppressed people, con-scientization for themselves and for service users, a redefinition of the aims of intervention and the development of skills – if worked out in social work practice, have the potential to make a difference to all those oppressed by social divisions.

References

Bennett, E.M. (1987) 'Social intervention: theory and practice', in E.M. Bennett (ed.), *Social Intervention: Theory and Practice*. Queenston, NY: Edwin Mellen Press. pp. 13–28.

Carby, H.V. (1982) 'White woman listen! Black feminism and the boundaries of sisterhood', in Centre for Contemporary Cultural Studies, *The Empire Strikes Back*. London: Hutchinson. pp. 212–235.

De Koning, K. and Martin, M. (1996) 'Participatory research in health: setting the context', in K. de Koning and M. Martin (eds), *Participatory Research in Health: Issues and Experiences*. London, Johannesburg and Atlantic Highlands, NJ: Zed Books. pp. 1–18.

Eichler, M. (1987) *Non Sexist Research Methods: A Practical Guide*. Boston: Allen & Unwin.

Firestone, S. (1970) *The Dialectic of Sex*. St Albans: Paladin.

Foucault, M. (1991) *Discipline and Punish: The Birth of the Prison*. London: Penguin.

Freire, P. (1972) *Pedagogy of the Oppressed*. London and New York: Penguin.

GMIAU (1997) *Information and Advice for Convicted Prisoners under Threat of Deportation*. Manchester: Greater Manchester Immigration Aid Unit.

Habermas, J. (1984) *The Theory of Communicative Action: Volume I*. Boston, MA: Beacon Press.

Habermas, J. (1987) *The Theory of Communicative Action: Volume II.* Boston, MA: Beacon Press.

Hammersley, M. (1995) *The Politics of Social Research.* London: Sage.

Haraway, D. (1988) 'Situated knowledges: the science question in feminism and the privilege of partial perspective', *Feminist Studies*, 14 (3): 575–599.

Harding, S. (ed.) (1987) *Feminism and Methodology.* Bloomington and Indianapolis: Indiana University Press; Milton Keynes: Open University Press.

hooks, b. (1982) *Ain't I a Woman? Black Women and Feminism.* London: Pluto Press.

hooks, b. (1989) *Talking Back: Thinking Feminist, Thinking Black.* London: Sheba.

Jayaratne, T.E. and Stewart, A.J. (1995) 'Quantitative and qualitative methods in the social sciences: feminist issues and practical strategies', in J. Holland and M. Blair with S. Sheldon (eds), *Debates and Issues in Feminist Research and Pedagogy.* Buckingham and Philadelphia: Open University Press.

Kelly L., Regan, L. and Burton, S. (1995) 'Defending the indefensible? Quantitative methods and feminist research', in J. Holland and M. Blair with S. Sheldon (eds), *Debates and Issues in Feminist Research and Pedagogy.* Buckingham and Philadelphia: Open University Press.

Lewis, G. (1996) 'Situated voices: black women's experience and social work', *Feminist Review*, 53 (Summer): 24–56.

Lorde, A. (1984) *Sister Outsider.* New York: Crossing Press.

MacKinnon, C. (1989) *Towards a Feminist Theory of the State.* Cambridge, MA: Harvard University Press.

Martin, M. (1994) 'Developing a feminist participative research framework: evaluating the process', in B. Humphries and C. Truman (eds), *Rethinking Social Research.* Aldershot: Avebury. pp. 123–145.

Martin, M. (1996) 'Issues of power in the participatory research process', in K. de Koning and M. Martin (eds), *Participatory Research in Health: Issues and Experiences.* London, Johannesburg and Atlantic Highlands, NJ: Zed Books. pp. 82–93.

Mies, M. (1993) 'Feminist research: science, violence and responsibility', in M. Mies and V. Shiva, *Ecofeminism.* London: Zed Books. pp. 36–54.

Millett, K. (1969) *Sexual Politics.* London: Abacus.

Mitchell, J. (1971) *Women's Estate.* Harmondsworth: Penguin.

Mohanty, C.T. (1991) 'Under western eyes: feminist scholarship and colonial discourses', in C.T. Mohanty, A. Russo and L. Torres (eds), *Third World Women and the Politics of Feminism.* Indianapolis: Indiana University Press.

Mohanty, C.T. (1992) 'Feminist encounters: locating the politics of experience', in M. Barrett and A. Phillips (eds), *Destabilising Theory.* Cambridge and Oxford: Polity/Blackwell. pp. 74–92.

Morgan, D. (1981) 'Men, masculinity and the process of sociological inquiry', in H. Roberts (ed.), *Doing Feminist Research.* London: Routledge & Kegan Paul. pp. 83–113.

Mullender, A. (1997) 'Domestic violence and social work: the challenge to change', *Critical Social Policy*, 17 (1): 53–78.

Oakley, A. (1981) 'Interviewing women: a contradiction in terms?' in H. Roberts (ed.), *Doing Feminist Research.* London: Routledge & Kegan Paul. pp. 30–61.

Phillips, A. (1992) 'Universal pretensions in political thought', in M. Barrett and A. Phillips (eds), *Destabilising Theory.* Cambridge and Oxford: Polity/Blackwell. pp. 10–30.

Reinharz, S. (1992) *Feminist Methods in Social Research*. New York and Oxford: Oxford University Press.

Richards, J.R. (1982) *The Sceptical Feminist: A Philosophical Inquiry*. Harmondsworth: Penguin.

Riley, D. (1988) *Am I That Name? Feminism and the Category 'Women' in History*. Basingstoke: Macmillan.

Salamini, L. (1981) *The Sociology of Political Praxis: An Introduction to Gramsci's Theory*. London: Routledge & Kegan Paul.

Scott, J. (1992) 'Experience', in J. Butler and J. Scott (eds), *Feminists Theorize the Political*. New York and London: Routledge. pp. 22–40.

Stacey, J. (1991) 'Can there be a feminist ethnography?' in S.B. Gluck and D. Patai (eds), *Women's Words: The Feminist Practice of Oral History*. New York and London: Routledge. pp. 111–120.

Stanley, L. (1990) 'Feminist praxis and the academic mode of production: an editorial introduction', in L. Stanley (ed.), *Feminist Praxis*. London and New York: Routledge. pp. 3–19.

Stanley, L. (1997) 'Writing the borders: episodic and theoretic thoughts on not/belonging', in L. Stanley (ed.), *Knowing Feminisms*. London: Sage. pp. 172–183.

Stanley, L. and Wise, S. (1990) 'Method, methodology and epistemology in feminist research processes', in L. Stanley (ed.), *Feminist Praxis*. London and New York: Routledge. pp. 20–62.

Thorpe, D. (1994) *Evaluating Child Protection*. Buckingham and Philadelphia: Open University Press.

VanderPlaat, M. (1995) 'Beyond technique: issues in evaluating for empowerment', *Evaluation*, 1 (1): 81–96.

Weedon, C. (1987) *Feminist Practice and Poststructuralist Theory*. Oxford: Basil Blackwell.

West, J. (1996) 'Figuring out working women', in R. Levitas and W. Guy (eds), *Interpreting Official Statistics*. London: Routledge, pp. 121–142.

Wollstonecraft, M. (1988) *A Vindication of the Rights of Women*, ed. C. Poston. New York: W.W. Norton. First published 1792.

Yeatman, A. (1993) 'Voice and representation in the politics of difference', in S. Gunew and A. Yeatman (eds), *Feminism and the Politics of Difference*. St Leonards, NSW: Allen & Unwin. pp. 228–245.

8

HISTORIES IN SOCIAL WORK

Ruth R. Martin

This chapter discusses the use of histories to evaluate practice in social work. The term 'histories' will be used as an umbrella to define life stories, family stories, oral histories, biographies, memories, narratives and the like. While many of these may appear to carry the same meaning, it is the centrality of histories that has meaning for this work. Social work is concerned with understanding the importance of history in the gathering of knowledge, and utilizing that information to make assessments and plan treatment approaches. Mary Richmond (1917), a pioneer in the field of social work, advocated the social worker gathering as much information as possible about the individual. She saw the usefulness of interviewing members of diverse systems, including both nuclear and extended families, and neighbours, as well as other institutions of society, including schools, hospitals and churches. This, she believed, would enable the social worker to make better assessments.

Histories are a form of qualitative research in line with the work of Becker (1963), Goffman (1961), Glaser and Strauss (1967), through to Atkinson (1998) – sociologists whose ethnographic, participant-observer works owe a debt to the tradition of the Chicago School – and its canonical works such as Robert Park's text on race and urban life, or Thomas and Znaniecki's *The Polish Peasant in Europe and America (1918–1920)*. The use of the term 'Chicago tradition' can be misleading because as Denzin (1995: 18) notes, 'There is no single Chicago school of sociology', but at least four distinct strands, including a statistical one. To engage in a genealogical discussion of the many different offshoots is not my intent here. However, Denzin also writes that the one strand often viewed as defining the Chicago School's approach is symbolic interactionism. While taking various forms, it adheres to three premises codified by Blumer.

The first premise is that human beings act towards things on the basis of the meaning the thing has for them. The second is that the meaning of such things is derived from, or arises out of, the social interaction one has with one's fellows. The third premise is that these meanings are handled and modified through an interpretive process used by the person in dealing with the things he or she encounters (Blumer, 1969: 2). I will use this concept of meaning throughout the chapter and will draw on some of the other works mentioned as I discuss their importance for social work education and evaluation.

Using histories in interpersonal direct practice

I believe a narrative is created through the gathering of data, whether these are generated by the telling of life stories/histories, fieldwork, storytelling, reminiscing, written biographies or autobiographies. However, in order to produce this narrative, a process must take place. This process begins with the questions: what do I want to produce, why, and how? To help you choose which of the methods you will use to tell your story, I will describe their similarities and differences and discuss their importance for social work practice and research. For the purpose of this chapter, I will divide history into two categories. The first category will include the gathering of data in which participants tell their story orally, thereby producing a written transcript as in oral history, life stories and life histories. I will include memoirs, biographies, autobiographies and reminiscence, and narratives which, like oral histories, have added to our understanding of their value for social work practice. Thus, 'oral histories, personal histories, and case histories, like autobiographies and biographies, and self stories and personal experience narratives, define one another only in terms of differences. The meaning of each spills over into the meaning of the other. The attempt to give a fixed meaning to each term is doomed to failure' (Denzin, 1989: 47). For the second category I will then draw on examples of various histories to show how they can be used for research, practice and evaluation.

Oral history, life stories and life history

A number of authors (Dunaway and Baum, 1984; Hoopes, 1979; Martin, 1995) have defined and discussed the importance of narrative. Their works describe the process and method of doing oral history, while Martin adds the evaluative quality for social work practice, assessment and research. Gluck and Patai (1991) describe the significance of oral history in *Women's Words: The Feminist Practice of Oral History*. They clarify the difference between the terms 'oral narratives' and 'oral history' which I will use throughout this chapter. Like Gluck and Patai, I am using 'oral narratives' to mean the material gathered in the oral history process, typically using a tape recorder. These narratives take a variety of forms, including life history, topical interviews, and testimonies. Oral history, in contrast, refers to the whole enterprise: recording, transcribing, editing, and making public the resulting product – usually but not always a written text. (Gluck and Patai, 1991: 4)

Clandinin and Connelly (1994) add to the extensive discussions surrounding the definition of narrative. They argue that 'narrative is both a phenomenon and method' in that it 'names the structured quality of experience, and it names the patterns of inquiry for its study'. The distinction is that 'People by nature lead storied lives and tell stories of those lives, whereas narrative researchers describe such lives, collect and tell stories of them, and write narratives of experiences' (1994: 416).

Shaw (1996: 141) in discussing the significance of life stories in social work evaluation and practice, writes: 'evaluating in practice will be enriched by thinking afresh of practice as entailing an understanding of history. The construction of life stories brings together the participatory aspect from observation methods and the interactive character of qualitative interviews.' Charlotte Linde (1993) has followed the same approach in her book on life stories. She discusses the creation of coherence as she teaches us that, 'In order to exist in the social world with a comfortable sense of being a good, socially proper, and stable person, an individual needs to have a coherent, acceptable, and constantly revised life story.' She writes of how 'such life stories are created, negotiated, and exchanged' (Linde, 1993: 3) and contends that individuals are confronted with a discontinuous, sometimes chaotic collection of events and decisions. She defines a life story thus:

A life story consists of all the stories and associated discourse units, such as explanations and chronicles, and the connections between them, told by an individual during the course of his/her lifetime that satisfy the following two criteria:

1. The stories and associated discourse units contained in the story have as their primary evaluation a point about the speaker, not a general point about the way the world is.
2. The stories and associated discourse units have extended 'reportability'; that is, they are 'tellable' and are told and retold many times over the course of a long period of time. (Linde, 1993: 21)

Oral tradition

'Oral tradition in the usual sense is the name given to verbal stories passed on from one generation to another as in the older back country villages of Africa' (Haley, 1976: 574). Hoopes draws on the work of Vansina to argue:

It is commonly accepted that in literate societies like the United States oral tradition is not as reliable as in illiterate societies, where people are well practiced in remembering stories, where story telling is highly ritualized, and where the teller may even be punished for changing the story's form or content. (Hoopes, 1979: 6)

Much of what black people learned about their history in the USA was handed down by word of mouth. That they were not permitted to read and write for nearly 300 years may have been part of the reason for this. Oral history can also refer to the collecting of an individual's account of his life or some occasion of which he has primary or secondary knowledge. Primary sources of data are individuals who have first-hand knowledge of the life events being reported. They are eyewitnesses of the events. Those who only heard about an event at that time or who received accounts at second hand are secondary sources.

Hoopes writes that 'history, like life, is a test of our ability imaginatively to place ourselves in the positions of other people, so that we can understand the reason for their actions'. Further, he suggests that 'because history is an act of our minds, historical knowledge can lead to self-knowledge' (1979: 3). He argues that 'to test or verify historical thought, we must check not only the data or facts but also our own thinking itself. We learn not only about history but [about] the quality of our minds' (1979: 3–4).

Oral history is necessarily a human challenge in that it involves direct contact with people. Wall and Arden, discussing their face to face encounters with Native American Wisdom Keepers, relate how they were changed, seized and shaken by the experience. They describe how as two journalists they went out to find a story and returned two 'runners' from another world waiting to tell their story (Wall and Arden, 1990: 10). Their close contact allowed them to hear the story, and to change their ways of looking at and understanding the Native American. In this work we also see the learning and teaching advantage for both the teller and the listener. Hoopes declares 'that research is a test of other people, of the accuracy of their memories, of their ability to assess their own lives realistically, and to profit from experience' (1979: 5). I see in the previous example the importance of people growing and having their self-worth affirmed. The challenge is even greater for social workers. 'It is a test of ourselves, of our ability to deserve and win the confidence of other people, of our ability to deal sympathetically but honestly and imaginatively with their memoirs, and of our ability to deal honestly with ourselves' (Hoopes, 1979: 5).

Morrissey (1984) provides us with some understanding of what is needed to be an oral historian. He argues that one must be able to master the art of building rapport, conducting interpersonal conversations about the past, and interpreting non-verbal communication. The oral historian should also understand language and its meaning, know autobiography, community and institutional studies and the skills folk artists apply to myths and intergenerational traditions (Morrissey, 1984: xx). I would take this further. One needs to know how to interview, and how to search for the meaning in the narrative. One must be able to discern not only what has been learned about the participant, but also what one has learned about oneself. This is necessary because of the 'interactions of experiences of participants in a field and researchers' experience as they come to that field' (Clandinin and Connelly, 1994: 419). One should now ask a series of questions about one's self, such as: am I a better interviewer, a keener listener, and more knowledgeable about another's culture? Can I now respect this culture? Have I found strength in this individual? Can I begin to view others through their lenses, if only partially? I mention this here briefly because I think it important for all who would attempt to use histories, whether oral or written, as a method of evaluation. I believe that if we as social workers are to use histories in social work to evaluate our clientele or ourselves it is imperative that we too, as Morrissey writes, are able to 'wrestle intellectually with philosophical questions about truth and meaning' (1984: xx). His suggestion that one might choose a course in how to interview calls to mind Reynolds, who wrote:

> The art, or skill, of professional social work consists of activities which cannot be standardized. One can no more train a person to be a good interviewer than to write good poems. One has to bring to bear what ability he has to see and hear and feel, and to perceive the meaning of what is before him. (1985: 52–53)

Rosengarten shares the meaning of oppression and human endurance in his oral history *All God's Dangers: The Life of Nate Shaw* (1974). His story of his first meeting with the 84-year-old farmer in 1969, and the eight hours he spent listening to the man tell his story, allows social workers to gain new knowledge, evaluate strengths, understand the need to see the world through others' lenses, and learn the techniques of interviewing and listening. These knowledge and skills were amplified in Rosengarten's second visit.

> I returned in June with a hundred pages of questions to ask Shaw. It became clear during our first session that I'd never get to a fraction of them. It would have taken years; moreover, my prepared questions distracted Shaw from his course. Since it was my aim to preserve his stories, I learned how to listen and not to resist his method of withholding facts for the sake of suspense. (Rosengarten,1974: xx)

While social workers may see as judgmental the statement that 'Nate held facts back for suspense', the lessons Rosengarten learned about listening demonstrate how one can improve interviewing skills. 'Everything comes out in time, everything' (1974: xx).

When discussing histories as a form of evaluative practice one must realize that when one is asking a person about something that happened historically, one is tapping into the person's recall, which may not be consistent or may appear inaccurate. One might ask, is this truth, and does it matter? The real question is whether this type of evidence meets the tests of reliability and validity. There is considerable debate over what constitutes good qualitative research. Denzin and Lincoln present for researchers four basic positions on this issue (Denzin and Lincoln, 1994: 479–483). For the purpose of this discussion, I will use the constructivists' view, and 'argue for quality criteria that translate into trustworthiness and authenticity' (1994: 480). Altheide and Johnson (1994) address some of these dilemmas. Refering to sociological thought during the 1960s and 1970s, they point to a reflexive turn in qualitative research. They argue that 'one meaning of reflexivity is that the scientific observer is part and parcel of the setting, context, and culture he or she is trying to understand and represent' (1994: 486). This period was followed by 'increasing numbers of qualitative researchers beginning to appreciate what this meant for the validity of ethnographic or qualitative research' (1994: 487). More recent writings have sensitized us to the fact that there is more to ethnography than what happens in the field. Another key part of it is what takes place back in the office when the observer or researcher is writing it up. What I see as important for social work knowledge, practice and evaluation is what Altheide and Johnson define as

> the nature of different kinds of experience in everyday affairs that is important for current debates about the knower and the known. The nexus between what we know and how we know it forges a critical linkage for the analytic realist seeking to fulfill the ethnographic ethic to turn his or her attention to the nature and criteria for assessing the adequacy of the research process itself. (1994: 493)

However, we cannot forget that some truths regarding the history of oppressed groups, such as African-Americans may be part-truths, untold truths, or there may be no empirically referenced truths available. The most plausible truth may lie in the oral accounts (Martin, 1995: 51–52). There will be occasions when an informant does not tell the story the same way each time. I advise researchers to question the informant about the inconsistency before they decide the informant is not telling the truth. The interviewee may have a logical explanation.[1] The value of this kind of research is that the researcher gets an opportunity to ask hard questions of the informant. There is also a subjective truth about life events that transcends the absolute facts of a situation. How one views an act will determine how one responds to the act. This is the level of veracity we seek most (Martin, 1995: 51–52). Rosengarten presents an excellent example of this:

We had come to study a union, and we had stumbled on a storyteller. Nate must have told his stories – at least the ones we heard – many times before. T.J. and Winnie, who listened as closely as we did, would stir whenever he digressed and remind him where his story was going. Nate would roll his tongue over the lone yellow spear-like tooth at the corner of his mouth and say, 'I'm coming to that, I just have to tell this first.' (Rosengarten, 1974: xvii)

This method of storytelling also teaches us the skill of patience, and the amount of time necessary to get a good story. Sharing a feeling that he and his partner expressed after a visit to Nate, Rosengarten writes, 'We could remember the details of Nate's stories but no reconstruction could capture the power of his performance. His stories built upon one another so that the sequence expressed the sense of a man "becoming." Nate had apparently put his whole life into stories and what he told us was just one chapter' (1974: xvii). He conveys lessons which social workers must learn if they are to make use of histories for practice and evaluation.

Karminsky (1984) demonstrates the power of reminiscing by giving us deeper insights into the meanings of the lives of the elderly. Matthews does this in her study, *The Social World of Old Women* (1979) as she describes how the women manage and give meaning to their lives. Allen used life histories of older women to study *Single Women/Family Ties: Life Histories of Older Women* (1989). Her work does much to confirm the importance of such inquiry methods for understanding the potential for diversity and adaptation, especially for a population whose life span is extending and who will have increasing need for the services of social workers.

Memoirs as history and evaluative tool

In touching on these 'reminiscences' we will briefly cast the net of 'life stories' wider to include the current boom in autobiographical, biographical and, particularly, memoir publishing in the USA, for these related genres have something to offer social workers looking to evaluate practice. 'No literary genre has become more popular and more hotly discussed in the past few years than the memoir' (Bing, 1998: 32). Whether we call the results memoirs or autobiographies, several authors have written narratives that touch the essence of practice knowledge and skills, ethical considerations and evaluations.

A memoir is a biography or biographical sketch, usually written by someone who knew the subject well. It can also be an autobiography, especially one that is eventful and anecdotal in emphasis rather than inward and subjective. It is sometimes used to report or record a significant event based on the writer's personal observation or knowledge, or is sometimes the report of a scholarly investigation or scientific study. For the purpose of this chapter I use 'memoirs' to describe the written works of authors who have elected to tell or to write about specific events or extended periods of their life. Many of these works have been published recently. Frank McCourt, in *Angela's Ashes* (1997), began with a story of pain and hard living, times of hunger and of little joy in Ireland and America. Yet I think that for social workers the survival depicted by writers of memoirs teaches the need to look for clients' strengths when making assessments. It may also remind social workers or alert them to some of the many oppressions and prejudices their clients may have received because of racism, sexism, religion, sexual orientation and political issues. This becomes clear when one reads about the experience of growing up in the racially segregated US South in *Coming of Age in Mississippi* (Moody, 1968). Such authors carry us back to a different time in history and show us through their lenses the difficulties and heartache they experienced, but also the strengths they used to survive. Social workers use positive examples such as these to reaffirm that although bad things happen, good can sometimes come out of them.

A recent work which closely corresponds to what life histories can add to evaluative practice in social work is Elisabeth Kubler-Ross's memoir, *The Wheel of Life: A Memoir of Living and Dying* (1997). Perhaps I am touched by the title because, after all, that is what all life stories are about. Kubler-Ross discusses her interaction with dying patients and with theology students who came to her for ideas on how they might gain practical experience in talking with the dying. She made contact with an elderly man on a ward. When she asked if she could bring four students in the next day, he suggested she bring them right away. She said she would bring them the next day, but when she and the four students came a day later the patient was too weak to say much. He recognized her and as tears rolled down his cheek said, 'Thank you for trying.' When she arrived back at her office with her students she learned the old man had died. She writes: 'I felt so lousy that I had put my own agenda ahead of the patient's. That old man had died without ever being able to share with another human what he was so eager to discuss the day before' (Kubler-Ross, 1997: 140–141). Kubler-Ross's experience exemplifies the importance of following through when you have found a topic and a participant to write about or to interview. Tomorrow for that participant may not come.

Kubler-Ross, who held many discussions with those who had not witnessed death, wrote, 'In those discussions, doctors, priests *and social workers* and students confronted their hostility and defensiveness. Their fears were analyzed and overcome' (italics added). Social workers doing life stories/histories, reviewing tapes, transcribing their own research, analysing their work, actively listening to their clients, learn 'what we should've done differently in the past and what we could do better in the future' (Kubler-Ross, 1997: 146).

Over the past years I have begun to collect data for my own memoirs. The first lesson I have learned is that I alone am not the sole author of my life story. Interviews with classmates with whom I attended a small, four-room elementary school, as well as an artefact like the ledger in which my mother recorded details of my father's sawmill business and other notes about family and church life, showed me that I stand on the shoulders of others. The organizational and entrepreneurial skills utilized by our grandparents and parents, their sacrifices and push for the education of their children, can be called forth to rejuvenate communities today.

Clandinin and Connelly (1994) touch on this form of inquiry as they write about personal experience. Drawing on Dewey (1916, 1934, 1938), they keep experience in the foreground. They make a compelling story, for the principal interest in experience is transformation in the telling and living of life stories. For them, as for Dewey, education, experience and life are inextricably intertwined. They argue that constructing a narrative underscores the reflexive relationship between 'living a life story, telling a life story, retelling a life story, and reliving a life story' (Clandinin and Connelly, 1994: 418).

Structural issues

Elliott (1988) points to the rise in the use of personal histories that he says help people make sense of their lives in light of accelerating modernization and attendant economic, technological and social change. He writes that such histories illuminate the ways in which ordinary people are linked to broader social and historical forces and ignite the sociological imagination. Elliott quotes the sociologist C. Wright Mills as being concerned with 'the difficulty that ordinary men and women found in making sense of their lives and overcoming feelings of entrapment, powerlessness, and meaninglessness'. Continuing, he writes that 'What was required was an ability to make connection between history and biography' and Mills believed that 'social scientists must accept the major responsibility for its development' (Elliott, 1988: 3). Further, he argues, to make the best use of biographical approaches and to persuade others of their value, we need to develop what we might call ' "forensic" potential', which he acknowledges conjures up the courtroom and denotes hard questioning: vigorous cross-examination (1988: 3–4). Elliott contends that such a process is unleashed when researchers using biographical techniques begin to interrogate received theories and generalizations. The utilization of histories can invigorate and challenge complacency in social work practice in much the same way.[2]

From story to interrogations

The need to go beyond mere story and use histories as a springboard for deep interrogations is also argued by John Kayser (1997). He gets to the heart of what histories are about as he responds to a writer's request that he review her narrative for a journal that publishes narratives of professional helping:

> As a reviewer for this journal, one of the things I encounter all too frequently are manuscript submissions in which authors set forth evocative accounts of their own particular personal and professional challenges, yet end without addressing what (to me) is the central point – how did this challenge or experience change their practice and/or teaching and/or their work with others? . . . because readers of narratives are looking for ways to apply what the author learned to their own practice and/or lives. (1997: 69)

One such narrative is that of Vanessa A. Brown (1997):

> The story of Martha is one that taught me strength and courage and to value my social work education. Martha was an 11 year old child who was sexually abused by her stepfather from age 6 to11. Martha's strength and courage to tell her story has been rewarding for both Martha and myself. Her courage allowed her to unlock years of pain and secrets. This was my first sexual abuse case as a Child Protective Services Investigator. I hope that her story will empower other practitioners to gain strength to fight for the rights of children and encourage parents to put their children first. (1997: 4)

As this worker took us through this narrative, I observed her professional growth and her ability to evaluate it at each new encounter, as she met first the mother, and later the stepfather, and finally saw them together as a couple.

The challenge I see for social work is to provide the big picture. In this chapter I use histories in social work to provide that big picture, to open a window to the world and show how social workers can use histories to evaluate their practice, teaching and interaction with others in this swirling universe. However, before we can make this leap we need to make a bridge from practice knowledge and skill to research skills.

Making the connections from practice to research to evaluation of others and ourselves

I have given examples of works of oral histories, life histories, life stories, memoirs, autobiographies, biographies, reminiscences, and fieldwork. I attempted to show how researching these histories can build knowledge and skills for social work practice, assessment and evaluation. I outlined what I see as good evaluative practice knowledge and skills that can inform us as practitioners about how well we are doing. The emphasis has not been only on clients, because many of the participants do not have client status. In fact, Kubler-Ross was the only person in her memoirs to speak of the doctor/patient relationship. Brown described what it felt like as a social worker to have her first case as a Child

Protective Service investigator. Throughout my own research projects I have reviewed many evaluative techniques used by professions other than social work, but I found that social workers use in practice many of the same techniques. What social workers must now do is to make the leap from practice to evaluation. As I read back through what I have written, I find I have identified more than 20 concepts in the histories which the authors described as they evaluated their experiences. The first concept is knowledge (including self-knowledge), and I have already discussed the significance of the knowledge one gains, and its role in deepening understanding.

A student in my research class designed an oral history project which her employing agency, a private school, approved. She plans to search for and interview as many African-American alumni as she can find. Early in the semester she informed me that she hoped to locate this group of alumni, which the school has lost track of. Many students have had no contact with the school since they graduated over the years. Aloud, she questioned: why am I having so much difficulty locating them? Why have they not kept in touch with the school or left no easy trail? Had their school experiences been such that they had no desire to maintain or renew their relationship? She saw an oral history project as an opportunity to ask and have students answer in their own words. This example of a student/employee's desire to know raises several questions about oral history. It shows how this student hopes to use histories to expand self-knowledge and skills as a practitioner. Moreover, the use of history can perform a critical role in the evaluation of her agency programmes and efficiency. This method of oral history might allow the school to evaluate how well it has done from the perspectives of this group of alumni.

Another class studied women who were being removed from the welfare rolls as a result of welfare reform in our state (and across the United States). Some of the mothers were still receiving some benefits as the law allowed a grace period before finally taking effect. Students were amazed to learn of the many difficulties the women faced as they search for work with little education, inconvenient modes of transportation, and poor child care facilities. Perhaps the student who was most devastated as a result of this study was the man who experienced so much difficulty finalizing his meeting with a mother. It took them more than three weeks to meet after failed appointments and missed telephone messages. Even though the class colleague who helped him to make contact kept assuring him that the woman wanted to meet with him, he began to feel and appear dejected. He began to question his method of approach, wondering if he had unknowingly offended her. Finally they met and he had a rewarding interview. He said of this experience: 'I am now able to place myself in a welfare client's position (or see through her lenses) and understand what it must feel like to keep trying to get an appointment to see your worker.' He vowed never to treat his clientele in such a shabby fashion. It is one level of understanding that social workers gain from doing histories as a research method.

Bloom, Fischer and Orme (1995) give guidelines for the accountable professional as part of a discussion of the single subject design method of evaluation:

> Because evaluation seems to imply research, statistics, mathematics, and computer science technology, it does raise ghosts that are fearful to some practitioners and students. But this misses the point because it is the logic of clear thinking and acting that is essential to evaluation, not a bunch of esoteric technologies. Good practitioners carefully observe and subjectively evaluate their own practice. This may be why they are good practitioners – they benefit from this precise observation and accurate feedback as they monitor the progress of their clients. (1995: 9)

What collecting histories permits that is different from, for example, single-subject design is that it allows the interviewers or social workers carefully to observe and evaluate themselves. The difference also has to do with purpose. Oral historians do not have as their main purpose the treatment of clients. The onus is on the interviewer to understand the meaning the participant makes of his life. The participant may or may not have client status. The social worker does, however, establish a trusting relationship and begins where the informant is. Such was the case with Rosengarten when he made his first trip to visit Nate Shaw. His purpose was to learn about a defunct union that was organized years ago. It was necessary for him to build a trusting relationship with Shaw and his family, and he was invited back again to finish the work.

Earlier I wrote that I had uncovered more than 20 concepts which could be described as evaluative examples. I believe it will be helpful to list them here. I will discuss these under two broad general headings and place them in the context of the chapter. The headings are, 'Knowledge of others' and 'Knowledge of self'. Kayser made a case for this when he reviewed a narrative submitted to a journal. He said 'Readers are looking for ways to apply what the authors have learned.' The two lists will provide a list of what the authors, including students, have learned. The lists may overlap because, as one gains knowledge, self-knowledge expands, and is applied in the next interview.

Knowledge of others
1 gaining knowledge of the life lived;
2 understanding diversity;
3 understanding the meaning of human behaviour;
4 understanding the meaning of human oppression;
5 understanding survival techniques;
6 listening to and hearing the story and understanding the strengths in the story;
7 understanding the reasons for people's actions;

8   understanding meaning;
9   learning how to affirm people's sense of self-worth, and how to make assessments, learn about their culture, and develop respect for it;
10 gaining education and experience;
11 understanding history.

Knowledge of self
1   gaining experience and education;
2   learning to interpret non-verbal communication and developing the ability to see, hear, feel and perceive meaning;
3   dealing sympathetically, honestly and imaginatively with others' memories;
4   dealing honestly with oneself;
5   winning the confidence of others;
6   establishing rapport;
7   developing keen listening skills;
8   developing excellent interviewing skills so that one can ask the hard questions when necessary;
9   gaining an understanding of history;
10 learning about and developing an appreciation for one's own culture, thereby being open to learning about others.

The types of history described, and I have touched upon only a few, should help a social worker to better understand survival techniques, diversity and the meaning of human oppression, and to discern the strengths in the story and learn what it means to conduct rigorous exchanges. To gather such data requires patience, good listening and interviewing skills. Good research skills are needed to learn what social, economic and political changes took place during the era in question and to find the meaning in the story. To understand the reason for others' actions, we must win their confidence, build rapport, and deal sympathetically but honestly with their accounts. It is this level of knowledge and the ability to apply it to practice that I am advocating, so that when a social worker says, 'I understand', it will mean, 'I understand both you and myself'. This is the level of self-knowledge and evaluation I hope the use of histories in social work will facilitate.

Notes

1 A helpful discussion of this problem from the standpoint of feminist research is given in Acker et al. (1983).

2 Social workers could benefit in this context from the sociological work on life course sociology (cf. Clapham et al., 1993; Morgan, 1985).

References

Acker, J., Barry, K. and Esseveld, J. (1983) 'Objectivity and truth: problems in doing feminist research', *Women's Studies International Forum*, 6 (4): 423–435.

Allen, K.R. (1989) *Single Women/Family Ties: Life Histories of Older Women*. Newbury Park, CA: Sage.

Altheide, D.L. and Johnson, J.M. (1994) 'Criteria for assessing interpretive validity in qualitative research', in N.K. Denzin and Y.S. Lincoln (eds), *Handbook of Qualitative Research*. Thousand Oaks, CA: Sage. pp. 485–499.

Atkinson, R. (1998) *The Life Story Interview*. Thousand Oaks, CA: Sage.

Becker, H.S. (1963) *Outsiders*. New York: Free Press.

Bing, J. (1998) 'Prairie wives, family trials and other tales of memoir mania', in *Writers' Yearbook*. Cincinnati: F. & W. Publications.

Bloom, M., Fischer, J. and Orme, J.G. (1995) *Evaluating Practice: Guidelines for the Professionals*. Boston: Allyn & Bacon.

Blumer, H. (1969) *Symbolic Interactionism*. Berkley, CA: University of California Press.

Brown, V.A. (1997) 'From one hand to another: the story of a sexually abused child's strength and courage', *Reflections: Journal for the Helping Professions*, 3 (2): 4–8.

Clandinin, D.J. and Connelly, F.M. (1994) 'Personal experience methods', in N.K. Denzin and Y.S. Lincoln (eds), *Handbook of Qualitative Research*. Thousand Oaks, CA: Sage. pp. 413–427.

Clapham, D., Means, R. and Munro, M. (1993) 'Housing, the life course and older people', in S. Arber (ed.), *Ageing, Independence and the Life Course*. London: Jessica Kingsley.

Denzin, N.K. (1989) *Interpretive Biography*. Newbury Park, CA: Sage.

Denzin, N.K. (1995) *Symbolic Interactionism and Cultural Studies: The Politics of Interpretation*. Oxford and Cambridge MA: Blackwell.

Denzin, N.K. and Lincoln, Y. (eds) (1994) *Handbook of Qualitative Research*. Thousand Oaks: Sage. pp. 479–483.

Dewey, J. (1916) *Democracy and Education*. New York: Macmillan.

Dewey, J. (1934) *Art as Experience*. New York: Capricorn.

Dewey, J. (1938) *Experience and Education*. New York: Collier.

Dunaway, D.K. and Baum, W.K. (eds) (1984) *Oral History: An Interdisciplinary Anthology*. Nashville, TN: Association of State and History.

Elliott, B. (1988) Editorial: 'Families and carers in history', *Journal of Life Stories/ Récits de vie*, 4: 3–4.

Glaser, B. and Strauss, A.L. (1967) *The Discovery of Grounded Theory*. New York: Aldine.

Gluck, S.B. and Patai, D. (1991) *Women's Words: The Feminist Practice of Oral History*. New York and London: Routledge.

Goffman, E. (1961) *Asylums*. New York: Doubleday.

Haley, A. (1976) *Roots: The Saga of an American Family*. New York: Doubleday.

Hoopes, J. (1979) *Oral History: An Introduction for Students*. Chapel Hill, NC: University of North Carolina Press.

Karminsky, M. (1984) 'The uses of reminiscence: new ways of working with older adults', special issue of *Journal of Gerontological Social Work*, 7 (1–2).

Kayser, J.A. (1997) ' "Dear narrator": the untold story of a manuscript reviewer', *Reflections: A Journal for the Helping Professions*, 3 (4): 67–71.

Kubler-Ross, E. (1997) *The Wheel of Life: A Memoir of Living and Dying*. New York: Scribner.

Linde, C. (1993) *Life Stories: The Creation of Coherence*. New York: Oxford University Press.

Martin, R.R. (1995) *Oral History: Research, Assessment and Intervention*. Thousand Oaks, CA: Sage.

Matthews, S.H. (1979) *The Social World of Old Women: Management of Self-identity*. Newbury Park, CA: Sage.

McCourt, F. (1997) *Angela's Ashes: A Memoir of a Childhood*. New York: Scribner.

Moody, A. (1968) *Coming of Age in Mississippi*. New York: Dell.

Morgan, D. (1985) *The Family: Politics and Social Theory*. London: Routledge.

Morrissey, C.T. (1984) 'Introduction', in D.K. Dunaway and W.K. Baum (eds), *Oral History: An Interdisciplinary Anthology*. Nashville, TN: American Association for State and Local History. pp. xix-xxiii.

Reynolds, B.C. (1985) *Learning and Teaching in Social Work*. Silver Springs, MD: National Association of Social Workers.

Richmond, M. (1917) *Social Diagnosis*. New York: Russell Sage Foundation.

Rosengarten, T. (1974) *All God's Dangers: The Life of Nate Shaw*. New York: Vintage Books.

Shaw, I. (1996) *Evaluating in Practice*. Aldershot: Ashgate.

Wall, S. and Arden, H. (1990) *Wisdomkeepers: Meetings with American Spiritual Elders*. Hillsboro, OR: Beyond Words.

9

WORK IN PROGRESS

The contribution of observation to the development of good practice and evaluation

Karen Tanner and Pat Le Riche

An observation narrative

Jenny picks up the toy pig and says, 'I'm not angry with you today', her face devoid of expression. She turns to her toy medical kit, takes out the stethoscope, puts it to her ears and holds the shiny disc against the pig's chest. Sarah lies on her side on the floor, head propped up against the palm of her hand. She watches Jenny intently. After a few moments Jenny picks up a plastic syringe, holds it against the pig and repeatedly pushes the plunger in and out, in and out. Next she takes a small round hammer and with great care gently rubs it up and down the pig's chest. As she does so Jenny's expression takes on a rather distant quality.

Suddenly Jenny discards the pig and with rapidity turns to the doll's house. Sarah sits up, looks to the observer and grins widely. She watches as Jenny scoops up the miniature dolls and thrusts them all into one room of the doll's house. As quickly as she puts the dolls into the room she pushes them all, higgledy-piggledy fashion through a connecting door into the next room. Jenny then moves all the dolls into a bedroom, shouting angrily that they must do as they are told. Suddenly with a gleeful expression she throws the dolls down the stairs. Sarah is by now sitting next to her sister, wriggling with excitement and shouting in a mocking tone at the dolls.

Jenny and Sarah are white and aged six and three respectively. Their life experience has been characterized by uncertainty, inconsistent attachments and loss. Sarah has a congenital health problem, which will severely limit her life expectancy. The sisters are the subject of full care orders and are placed with a short-term foster carer. The observer is a social worker who has been brought into the case to undertake a piece of direct work with the children which will inform the assessment of their needs and the planning process. The social worker has decided to begin the work with an observation of the children playing and going about their usual activities in the foster home. Following the introductions and questions about who she was, why she was visiting, and for how long, the social worker asks the children if she can get to know them a little bit by sitting as quiet as a mouse and watching them. The children think this sounds fun and so with their agreement she observes them quietly; occasionally the children turn to look at her and when they do so they place their fingers over their lips and whisper, 'Shush mousy'.

The above illustration is an example of a practitioner incorporating observation into her day to day social work. Whilst this example is located in work with children and families and with issues such as hearing the voice of the child and the attachment needs of young children, observation has a universal application and is transferable to work with other client groups (Le Riche and Tanner, 1998). However, observation as a method of practice is still unusual in mainstream social work. It is therefore not surprising that its evaluative dimension is recognized even less. It is our intention in this chapter to make connections between the advantages of using observation in different aspects of social work and the development of evaluation both on and in practice.

Why use observation?

Social work practice with children and families has been criticized for a failure which can be summarized as the child being lost from sight and dropped from mind (Blom Cooper, 1985; Bridge Consultancy, 1997). In the United Kingdom this theme is reflected in the Children Act 1989 where explicit reference is made to the recognition of children as individuals whose views should be elicited and taken seriously. In response the social work profession has placed a higher premium on direct work with children and prioritized training accordingly. Within mainstream organizations, at both qualifying and post-qualifying levels, this training has been characterized by the development of skills in communicating with children, especially in the development of play techniques. A small but significant voice has argued that this focus on technique needs to be complemented by a grounding in theory and a recognition of the value of observation for this area of practice. Briggs (1992, 1997), Trowell and Miles (1991), Wilson (1992) and others have developed important arguments about the use of observation in social work with children and families. Here we will concentrate on two or three points demonstrated by this particular case.

In the example above the social worker is using observation to find a way into the world of the children. In doing so she will obtain important content information and use the experience to reflect on some of the processes that occurred.

Let us look at the potential content information generated by the observation of Jenny and Sarah. The social worker will develop some sense of the relationship between the sisters; patterns of communication can be revealed and ideas about materials to facilitate communication considered. The observation will generate some preliminary thought about the children's knowledge of and preoccupation with their circumstances. In particular, the social worker can focus on the issue of being in care and what is known, understood, and possibly feared about Sarah's health. The social worker can prepare the work of assessment and planning as well as identify gaps in her knowledge base, for example relating to children's developmental understanding of death and research findings on the impact of chronic illness and death upon siblings.

In terms of process it is probably an uncontested argument that one of the aims of the above piece of work will be to hear the voice of the children. Truly seeing the children and hearing their voice is difficult. The social work practitioner is constantly exposed to the trauma and pain experienced by children like Jenny and Sarah. Such exposure carries the risk of developing a protective shield which stops the worker hearing and feeling the material being communicated. The inclusion of observation in the work with Jenny and Sarah will enable the practitioner temporarily to reshape the professional role with its characteristic participation and action, and, as an observer, to pay close attention and to absorb, with all the senses, the events taking place. Observation creates an emotional and mental engagement that can help to ensure that the practitioner is responding in an attuned and thinking way to Jenny and Sarah.

The relationship between observation and thinking is another significant part of the process of the practitioner's work. Developing a capacity to receive the range and intensity of a child's communications means the practitioner must be pervious to their emotional impact. It is not uncommon for feelings of anger, anxiety and confusion to be stirred up. The issue is what happens to these feelings? Do they become the basis of thinking which then informs a response or do the unprocessed feelings become the basis of 'jumping into action' precipitately (Hughes and Pengelly, 1997: 81). In the observer role the practitioner is forced to stay with the feelings being stirred up by the events unfolding in Jenny and Sarah's play. She is unable to relieve these feelings through intervention but does have the opportunity to think and critically reflect. These reflections can then be taken to supervision for further consideration of their meaning and use in the work with Jenny and Sarah.

Whilst the practitioner above used observation regularly as a means of informing and improving her practice it did not feature as a mechanism for explicitly evaluating the process and outcome of her intervention. Before moving on to explore the potential of observation as a tool in evaluation we will discuss its characteristics and briefly explore the knowledge base which underpins it.

What is observation?

Normative assumptions about observation mask both its complexity and the multidimensional nature of its characteristics. In everyday life observation is taken for granted since it is a pervasive aspect of social processes. This uncritical use of observation has been characterized as 'tacit' by Weade and Evertson (1991) in their discussion of classroom observations. In this chapter we will not focus on observation in this everyday context since Weade and Evertson argue that tacit observation is unintentional and informal. In carrying out professional roles in social work the process of tacit observation continues to take place since we make use of watching, listening and noting skills. However, in the professional role the worker will also make use of these skills as an essential part of more purposeful observations when undertaking a range of core tasks such as assessment, planning, supervision and service delivery. This is described by Weade and Evertson as 'intentional observation' and what distinguishes it from tacit observation is that it has a clear purpose and results in action. It is this formal and intentional observation which we will focus on in relation to the discussion of the place of observation within evaluation.

Intentional observation also differs from informal observation because of the power inherent in the role of the observer (Le Riche and Tanner, 1996, 1998). Whether the observation is used as part of the assessment process, as in the example of Jenny and Sarah, in social work education or in management, the power of the observer in role will always be a significant factor. This power dimension has been underemphasized in both the epistemological development of ideas about observation and also in discussion of how observation practice has developed within social work.

Underpinning these ideas is the extent to which the nature and purpose of observation are influenced by the epistemological traditions within which it is located. We will illustrate this point by briefly discussing two broad traditions, suggesting that ideas about the nature of knowledge and the function of observation have enhanced its development.

The first tradition we may call the *scientific model* and, as the name implies, this tradition has grown out of ideas about the development of knowledge in the natural sciences. This epistemological tradition has been influential in shaping the characteristics of quantitative, clinical and positivist approaches to the social sciences. These characteristics include an emphasis on objectivity, accuracy and validity where the ideal stance of the observer is to be as objective as possible: in other words, for her to be a 'fly on the wall'. The behaviour being observed is likely to be disaggregated to enable the observer to focus on specific and detailed material. Observers may structure the information they receive by noting the regularity with which it occurs or they may observe specific problem behaviour with a view to bringing about change. An example of this approach would be the frequency with which repetitive communication patterns are observed in the responses of an older person with dementia. Alternatively, the observer may focus on the ways in which these patterns are affected by the resulting behaviour of the carer. Observers working within this tradition are usually trained to provide data that are as detailed and accurate as possible. The resulting information is re-corded in charts, codes or symbols representing variables such as fre-quency, severity or stimulus. These records exclude the views of the observer in an attempt to produce material which is as 'scientific' as possible. In this model the observer strives for objectivity rather than involvement; the observer is external to the process.

In contrast, the *narrative model* recognizes and values the inevitable subjectivity of the observation process. It reflects a range of epistemo-logies that challenge positivist assumptions about the nature of know-ledge. These epistemologies include approaches from within qualitative sociology such as ethnography, feminist and poststructuralist and post-modern discourses. The model does not attempt to eliminate subjectivity but works with it and aims to understand its impact. The implications for the boundary position of the observer therefore can vary. One position is the physically detached but emotionally engaged stance described in the Tavistock Model (Reid, 1997), which has been highly influential in the practice of observation in social work and psycho-analysis in the United Kingdom and Europe. This contrasts with the more engaged participant-observer role which has been much empha-sized in social science research (Fairhurst, 1990; Guba, 1978; Hendricks, 1995; Tindale, 1993; Whitehead, 1993). Unlike the scientific position where knowledge is seen as neutral, within the narrative approach knowledge can never be neutral since it is the product of personal and contextual constructs. Theories are informed by experience rather than observational experience being theoretically predetermined.

Frequently, the model is characterized by a holistic approach. On one level holism refers to the model's focus on the broad picture in which all the complex events and processes occurring are receiving the attention of the observer. This approach may be adopted at the beginning of work with a family in order to obtain a broad picture of the family's function-ing in a family assessment centre and as illustrated earlier in this chapter. This is similar to the progressive focusing discussed by Parlett and Hamiliton (1981) in their research model of illuminative evaluation. In the social work context observation enables more detailed attention to be paid to particular themes and behaviours but still within the narrative approach: i.e. it does not dislocate behaviour from whatever else is going on. Returning to the family assessment example, the observer may choose to focus on the expression and management of conflict within the family. To use Briggs's metaphor, within the narrative model the observer operates with a 'moving' rather than a 'fixed' lens and has the potential for both a 'wide angle' and 'zoom' perspective (Briggs, 1997: 32).

Whether the observer is focusing on the broad picture or on specific issues the observation is usually recorded in narrative form, though audio or video material is increasingly being used. When a narrative form is used the material will be constructed as a text and not converted into charts or schedules. Factors such as what is included or excluded, level of detail and vocabulary used are all important issues to take into account.

It is our belief that observation within both these models can contribute to the development of good practice. The epistemological differences that we have outlined mean that the characteristics of observation, both its priorities and its processes, are completely different. We are aware that in this chapter we have primarily made use of approaches which are generally within the narrative model. At a later stage we will address the flexible nature of observation and the implications of this for evaluation in and on practice. It is our view that observation within both models is complementary and can be applied broadly. However, whatever approach is used needs to be clearly identified, owned and fit for purpose.

The connections between observation and evaluation

Observation and evaluation are about improving the quality of social work in terms of direct practice and service provision. We share Shaw's view that 'a reflexive practice, a concern with plausible evidence, a commitment to evaluate both for and with the service user, an anti discriminatory evaluating, and an ethical purposefulness are the hallmarks of evaluating in practice' (Shaw, 1996: 13). We believe that observation has a contribution to make to the development of this approach to evaluation in practice. Intentional observation has great potential as an evaluative tool since it builds upon the tacit observation skills inherent within social work, allowing them to become a continuous and accessible dimension of practice. We want to develop ideas about the ways in which observation can be a resource in evaluation. We will do this by looking at four key issues: the critical stance of the observer; observation's contribution to facilitating reflection and reflexivity; its

ability to access complex data at all levels; and its flexibility in com-
plementing a range of approaches to evaluation.

The critical stance of the observer

In observations which we have earlier described as intentional the
practitioner can use the observer role as a means of positioning herself
on the boundary of the work rather than in the midst of it. In this
position the observer is able to look critically at issues such as the use of
self and the worker's relationship to the personal/professional boundary. An illustration of how these characteristics of the observer role can
be valuable in practice is provided by the following example from the
field of social care.

> Mrs Jenkins is an 87-year-old resident of a voluntary care home. She has been there for
> nearly a year and her behaviour has deteriorated as a result of dementia. When she was
> first admitted to the home Mrs Jenkins was interested in talking to other residents and
> staff. She slept a lot during the day but her key worker could usually persuade her to
> join in conversation and some of the home's activities.
>   However, she has gradually become more verbally aggressive, particularly in her
> contact with two other female residents whom she 'blames' for her problems. She is
> also retreating from the world around her and becoming preoccupied with her own
> internal conversations. The effect of this has been to isolate her from other residents,
> some of whom are frightened by her behaviour. The staff have to make more effort to
> communicate with her as she becomes progressively 'harder to reach'. At the
> instigation of her key worker her medication has been changed but so far this appears
> to be having little effect. The care staff feel they need to evaluate the plans they have
> made for working with Mrs Jenkins in order to try to halt the progress of her isolation.
> This topic will be the focus of discussion in the forthcoming review.

Part of the planning process in the residential setting will involve
continuous assessment of Mrs Jenkins as a means of building up a
picture of her progress in social care. Ongoing, tacit observation is
a significant part of the skill base of workers in social care but building in
planned, intentional observations in relation to the situation described
here can add significantly to the depth and breadth of the evaluation
process.
   One of the most significant aspects of work with people with dementia
is to ensure that they retain their individuality and that assessment and
planning continue to value and enhance their remaining strengths
and capabilities (Marshall, 1997). In personal terms structured observations would enhance the key worker's ability to do this by generating
'rich' data for the review and providing a detailed picture of Mrs
Jenkins's behaviour at particular times. This could take place at different
points in the day, or when she is interacting with those residents with
whom she has the most difficulty. These 'snapshots' have the potential to
increase the understanding of all staff about Mrs Jenkins's daily experi-

ence. Over a period of time these narratives can map the progress of Mrs Jenkins in the residential setting, providing a key longitudinal perspective on her life.

This use of observation does not have to be lengthy or time consuming since relatively brief observations can be structured and recorded. Such purposeful observation enhances the quality of practice in a number of ways. For those working with Mrs Jenkins access to the 'richness' of observational data can minimize the risk of turning her into the stereotypical 'older woman with dementia'. This has much to do with the holistic nature of the resulting material. Anything that enables workers to remain creative and optimistic can only enhance the quality of the social work intervention with people with dementia. By taking advantage of the critical stance inherent in the role of the observer, workers can reflect on their emotional response to situations such as those illustrated by this example. Stereotypical and routinized practice can be the result of the fear and hopelessness engendered by responses to the ageing process. This sense of inevitable decline and powerlessness operates at both a personal and a professional level, and the development of institutional defences as a means of counteracting such feelings has been well documented (Menzies, 1970; Obholzer and Roberts, 1994). The use of intentional observation is one way in which workers can escape from the feelings of 'stuckness' that may result from being closely involved with people over a long period of time. The observer role provides the creative distance from which to review past and present practice and construct future plans.

Reflection and reflexivity

At the beginning of this chapter we argued for the connection between observation and reflection. The observer role, in which the practitioner is temporarily 'being' and not 'doing', creates a unique space for reflection, a space which usually is difficult to find in the action-oriented and defended culture of social work. Not only is it difficult to find but the language of reflective discourse can often be experienced as alien to busy practitioners and managers, particularly, and paradoxically, when considering effectiveness and outcomes. As a local authority training consultant stated: 'all people want is guidance telling them what to do and a checklist to tick off that it has been done'.

The resistance to reflective practices is linked in part to personal and organizational defences to the primary task already discussed. However, this resistance may also be linked to lack of clarity about the relationship between reflection and reflexivity, in which the dynamic, monitoring and change potential of the reflection–reflexive process is unrecognized. Any process of reflection, that is 'the intellectual, and affective activities in which individuals engage to explore their experiences in order to lead to new understandings' (Boud and Knights, 1996: 26), has the potential for reflexivity. By this we mean using these new understandings and appreciations for change, either of our own behaviour and practices or that of others. It is in this context that the contribution of observation to evaluation is located. Observation begins with looking, involves reflection and has the potential for reflexive monitoring and change. It is a thoughtful process whose dynamic possibilities are relevant to contemporary, evaluative social work.

In the same terms observation is applicable to a wide range of settings within different levels of an organization: at the level of practice and throughout the various tiers of management. While managers have specific responsibilities for managing effectiveness and quality of service, they also have a pivotal role in establishing the culture of an organization. How might observation assist a manager to evaluate the quality of service provided and inform whether and what development is required?

> The Management Group in a Children and Family Area Team are concerned about the standard of practice on duty. Specifically the concern is about the quality of initial assessments and their impact on the subsequent decision-making and planning processes. A range of views is expressed as to likely reasons for the difficulties, and possible solutions identified. A decision is taken to undertake a thorough review and evaluation of the duty system and use the information generated to inform any changes.

We would suggest in the first instance that evaluative observation is a means of balancing the tension between practice and management which is experienced by many social work and social care managers. Observation is a skill that managers bring with them from practice. It is also a traditional aspect of managing in many other organizations, for example in manufacturing industry, where managers look at what is happening on the shop floor by 'walking the job' (Kearney, 1998). By using observation managers have the opportunity to integrate practice, evaluation and management. In walking the job the manager can use observation in different ways – the wide angle and zoom lenses identified earlier. For instance an observation of the reception area would provide a broad picture of the quality of service offered to people when they walk through the front door: how long do people wait, what is the quality of information given to service users? This could be complemented by targeted observations of the duty team in action. Here the observation could focus on obtaining the following specific data: continuity of response to referrals, time given to planning initial assessment visits, and the process of formulating the assessment. This would allow a conclusion to be reached about the extent to which this reflects current research findings, professional protocols and a theoretical understanding of the issues.

In contemporary management, knowledge of the detail of practice may not be achievable or desirable. However, managing involves an understanding of the processes involved in the social work task and knowledge of how to empower practitioners to achieve their own and the organization's goals.

The advantage of managers incorporating evaluative observation into the process of measuring effectiveness, as above, is that the manager is observed observing. In modelling the value of observation to improving practice the manager can help develop an ethos of evaluation within the organization. Furthermore, this approach demonstrates that management and evaluation can be informed by the values of social work practice; that management does not have to be managerialist.

If the process of observation includes negotiation with staff prior to it taking place (essential from our perspective because of the emotional impact of being observed and the power dynamics involved) and a commitment to feedback, evaluation can become part of a dialogue. The opportunity for dialogue can help to diminish practitioners' sense that evaluation is an alien event done to them, and hopefully it can foster participation and ownership.

Finally, we would endorse Kearney's argument that evaluative observation 'can provide managers with what they often find lacking in their daily practice: the chance to step outside their administrative role, take time to reflect on what they see and begin to manage' (Kearney, 1998: 177).

Observational data

In our experience, the evaluation of service delivery described above and the exploration of possible change usually involve the area manager discussing the issues with other service managers. This is understandable in hierarchical bureaucracies. But we want to suggest an alternative approach to service evaluation, which is still relevant in such situations. The inclusion of intentional observation in this equation has the effect of transforming an approach which is potentially top down and consensual to one which accesses raw and immediate data and addresses complexity. To describe such observational data as raw and unprocessed does not imply that the material is unsophisticated, but that it provides opportunities to reflect in action and subsequently on action. Even in hierarchical organizations there will be times when managers need to find out for themselves, collecting data at first hand. Observation is one way in which managers can do this. Additionally, observation can access the interaction of the range of factors which impact on final outcomes. Some of these may be subjective and intangible and therefore not so easily accessed by other forms of evaluation. Frequently, these are dynamic issues which may not be easily quantifiable, for example accessing problems which duty teams are unable to manage, and processing the level of anxiety inherent in crisis intervention work. It is easy for duty managers to become part of such systems, which are action-oriented and devoid of any thinking dimension. Since the area manager is outside the system it is easier for her to access material which others inside the system might not find so easy to recognize and articulate.

The significance of validating a range of material of different orders has to be acknowledged if a holistic picture of process and outcomes is to be achieved. In the duty example the manager could make use of the quality of the experience derived from being part of the duty system in the observer role, which involves reflecting on this experience as an important strand of data. For example, does the system seem orderly or overwhelmed? Are the communication patterns effective for the primary tasks? Observation can also access more traditional data such as the availability and effectiveness of resources both personal and structural and how different parts of the system are connecting in order to work effectively. Critically, how far is practice conforming to recognized national agreed standards of good practice? Is the information obtained of good enough quality and informed by a theoretical framework which structures plans and subsequent actions? Such observational data have the potential to provide a wide range of options to achieve the goal of an improved service. These options might include more concrete changes such as the reformulation of referral and assessment information sheets, better-directed resources such as phone lines or support staff. Or they could involve more comprehensive changes, such as training in order to structure the information obtained in a more coherent way.

Another characteristic of observational data is that they enable competing discourses to be heard. By obtaining such data at first hand the manager not only accesses complex and holistic material but also engages with the range of voices of those involved in providing a duty service – voices which may not be directly heard when she limits her consultation to those closest to her in the hierarchy. In hierarchical organizations it is usually the views of the most powerful that are heard and are most likely to be accepted as the norm.

Observation has the potential to sustain the values which are central to social work by hearing and respecting the voices of those with less power.

Many of the advantages of using observational data in service evaluation are also relevant to the evaluation of direct practice. In the earlier example of Mrs Jenkins we suggested that intentional observation would enable the key worker to access material which builds up a holistic picture of Mrs Jenkins's experience. By keeping in touch with the whole person rather than merely responding to a diagnosis the key worker can both convey the meaning of Mrs Jenkins's experience to others and respond more sensitively to her needs. These ideas about 'personhood' and the development of quality care are similar to those of Kitwood and his colleagues, who have developed an approach to work with people with dementia which they describe as dementia care mapping (Kitwood, 1997; Kitwood and Bredin, 1992). This person-centred approach uses observation and the subsequent data both as a method of direct practice and as a means of evaluating practice.

> As the concern to provide good care has grown, it has been increasingly recognized that there is a need for quality standards and for sound methods of evaluation. Several observational methods for evaluating the actual process of care have now been developed. . . . It is now possible to devise integrated strategies for evaluation and quality improvement, giving staff clear and usable feedback on the progress of their work. (Kitwood, 1997: 57)

This comment highlights the significance of supervision for the provision of 'usable feedback' and emphasizes the need to develop the skills of reflection and reflexivity at all levels in practice. The development of observational data requires a critical context if their use is to be maximized, both in direct work with users and carers and in the parallel processes of evaluation.

Flexibility

In relation to evaluation, observation is a complementary tool, which can be used together with a number of other approaches and methods. This flexibility contributes to rigorous evaluation by facilitating triangulation, which involves using a number of different approaches to give greater validity to research or evaluation. In this situation observation can be combined with approaches stemming from either qualitative or quantitative methodologies, for example interviewing, self-completion questionnaires, measurement scales and statistical surveys. In Mrs Jenkins's situation, for example, the use of intentional observation in the planning process could complement interviewing and time sampling. All these approaches will need to be considered by the multidisciplinary team when planning effective interventions.

Another dimension of observation's flexibility is its application to a variety of aspects of social work and social care practice. The examples we have chosen illustrate observation's use in evaluation at different levels of the organization, including the individual (direct work with children), the collective (the care planning process), and the macro level (making a policy change). We have also suggested ways in which observation can illuminate the effectiveness of practice both in different parts of the organization and in relation to different aspects of its primary task. In some respects the development of intentional observation is ideally suited to work in the field of social care, where tacit observations are already widely used. We also envisage a place for intentional observation in the repertoire of supervision skills, particularly when workers need help with the feelings of hopelessness and powerlessness which can become a part of the process of crisis or long-term intervention.

In relation to the primary tasks of social work, observation can assist the quality of practice at points when key decisions have to be made. In the first example in this chapter, the social worker used her intentional observation to inform her approach to fundamental issues such as those of loss and change, and ideas about permanency planning. With Mrs Jenkins the observations have the potential to develop a greater awareness of the impact of ageism and stereotyping as well as helping with the management of challenging behaviour. We have also outlined the value of the use of observation at different points in the social work and management process including intake and assessment, planning and at times when more information is needed or when existing interventions are not working.

The observational perspective can be tailored to the needs of the evaluation: it can be as broad or as focused as the evaluation requires. The focus of attention can be either on improving the quality of direct practice or on improving the standard of service provision. Intentional observation can therefore contribute to both dimensions of the purpose of evaluation which Shaw describes (1996: 21).

Finally . . . the way forward

We recognize that in developing ideas about the practice of observation in social work we need to acknowledge the tensions that continue to exist. We identify the nature of these tensions as follows:

- In the current position of observation in social work and social care, observation is still perceived as a specialist activity relevant to particular areas of practice such as family therapy, psychotherapeutic work with children and social work education.
- The observer role entails an inevitable discomfort. The nature of the role in observation demands that workers pay close attention to the material in front of them rather than rushing in to act upon it and 'make things better' in some way. This close attention can be very revealing, and seeing what is going on can be distressing and can cause concern.
- Observation is frequently conceptualized as an activity that is 'done to' others and therefore has the potential to be oppressive.

These characteristics are similar to those Shaw identifies as relating to the place of evaluation in social work. 'Evaluators in practice operate at the boundaries. They are outsiders on the inside' (Shaw, 1996: 9).

Evaluative observation therefore creates a 'double dose' of these characteristics for those workers attempting to put it into practice. This raises ethical problems similar to those facing participant observers (Bulmer, 1982).

This discomfort of being on the margins is a recognizable, and arguably inevitable, experience in social work practice (Shaw, 1996). We should continue to recognize and work with these tensions rather than avoid them since the overall aim of evaluative observation is to improve the quality of practice. It is essential to continue working at moving evaluation and intentional observation from the margins to the mainstream. From our perspective the most significant tension is the issue of power relations. Contemporary social work practice is informed by the principles of partnership and empowerment. These principles are apparent in the theoretical basis, legislative framework and values of social work (Le Riche and Tanner, 1998). If evaluative observation is to be congruent with these principles it must address the experience of it as an alien and imposed exercise. We suggest the following points for consideration:

- It is critical that observer evaluators work to develop the role by recognizing its perceived oppressive nature. This will include acknowledgement of the status of the observer and the impact of her power and authority upon those being observed. On another level it requires an honest recognition by the observer of her powerful position in filtering and shaping what is seen. Attention needs to be paid to the complexity of ethical issues such as confidentiality, consent and the ownership of the recorded material (Le Riche and Tanner, 1998). By developing the observer role in empowering ways even when there is no choice or negotiation about evaluation taking place, the arguments about oppression can be alleviated.
- There are always differences in power in observation, and these are compounded when aspects of difference such as race, gender, class, sexuality and physical ability are part of the equation. Frequently these differences are complex and multifaceted, for example when in a duty team, a white male manager is evaluating a team of black and white women. In these circumstances it is important not only to acknowledge differences in perspective and experience but also to discuss how these issues will be valued and incorporated into the evaluation.
- Linked to the above, practitioners at all levels of the organization need to be aware of the significance of careful negotiation, which takes account of the emotional impact of the experience as well as of the need to provide appropriate information as to why the observation is taking place, its purpose, focus and how the resulting data will be used. This is crucial when the worker is moving between the practitioner and observer evaluator roles.

- Feedback must be available after the evaluation. The feedback process has to take account of all the voices involved, particularly those of the least powerful. It enables debriefing and checking out to take place as well as analysis of the material to take account of issues of distortion and inaccuracy.

A model of evaluative observation which is characterized by an understanding of the complexities of the role and the centrality of power relations is more likely to move evaluative observation from the margins to the mainstream and thus help to improve the quality of practice.

References

Blom Cooper, L. (1985) *A Child in Trust*. London: Borough of Brent.

Boud, D. and Knights, S. (1996) 'Course design for reflective practice', in N. Gould and I. Taylor (eds), *Reflective Learning for Social Work*. Aldershot: Ashgate.

Bridge Consultancy (1997) *Bridge Report for Cambridgeshire County Council Social Services Department on Professional Judgements and Accountability in Relation to Work with the Neave Family*. Cambridge: Cambridgeshire County Council.

Briggs, S. (1992) 'Child observation and social work training', *Journal of Social Work Practice*, 6 (1): 49–61.

Briggs, S. (1997) *Growth and Risk in Infancy*. London: Jessica Kingsley.

Bulmer, M. (1982) *Social Research Ethics*. London: Macmillan.

Fairhurst, E. (1990) 'Doing ethnography in a geriatric unit', in S. Peace (ed.), *Researching Social Gerontology: Concepts, Methods and Issues*. London: Sage.

Gould, N. and Taylor, I. (eds) (1996) *Reflective Learning for Social Work*. Aldershot: Ashgate.

Guba, E.G. (ed.) (1978) *Towards a Method of Naturalistic Inquiry in Educational Evaluation*. Los Angeles: UCLA.

Hendricks, J. (1995) 'Qualitative research: contribution and advances', in R.H. Binstock and L.K. George (eds), *Handbook of Ageing and the Social Sciences*. New York: Academic Press.

Hughes, L. and Pengelly, P. (1997) *Staff Supervision in a Turbulent Environment*. London: Jessica Kingsley.

Kearney, P. (1998) 'Observing management', in P. Le Riche and K. Tanner (eds), *Observation and its Application to Social Work: Rather Like Breathing*. London: Jessica Kingsley.

Kitwood, T. (1997) *Dementia Reconsidered: The Person Comes First*. Buckingham: Open University Press.

Kitwood, T. and Bredin, K. (1992) 'A new approach to the evaluation of dementia care', *Journal of Advances in Health and Nursing Care*, 1 (5): 41–60.

Le Riche, P. and Tanner, K. (1996) 'The way forward: developing an equality model of observation for social work practice and education', *Issues in Social Work Education*, 16 (2): 3–14.

Le Riche, P. and Tanner, K. (eds) (1998) *Observation and its Application to Social Work: Rather Like Breathing*. London: Jessica Kingsley.

Marshall, M. (ed.) (1997) *The State of Art in Dementia Care.* London: Centre for Policy on Ageing.

Menzies, I. (1970) *The Functioning of a Social System as a Defence against Anxiety.* Tavistock Pamphlet No. 3. London: Tavistock Institute of Human Relations.

Obholzer, A. and Roberts, V.Z. (1994) *The Unconscious at Work. Individual and Organisational Stress in the Human Services.* London: Routledge.

Parlett, M. and Hamilton, D. (1981) 'Evaluation as illumination', in M. Parlett and B. Dearden (eds), *Introduction to Illuminative Evaluation.* Studies in Higher Education. Guildford: Society for Research into Higher Education, University of Surrey.

Reid, S. (1997) *Developments in Infant Observation: The Tavistock Model.* London: Routledge.

Shaw, I. (1996) *Evaluating in Practice.* Aldershot: Arena.

Tindale, J.A. (1993) 'Participant observation as an evaluative method', *Canadian Journal on Ageing,* 12 (2): 200–215.

Trowell, J. and Miles, G. (1991) 'The contribution of observation training to professional development in social work', *Journal of Social Practice,* 5 (1): 51–60.

Weade, G. and Evertson, C.M. (1991) 'On what can be learned by observing teaching', *Theory into Practice,* 30 (1): 37–45.

Whitehead, J. (1993) 'From field to faculty club: framing the face of universal hu(man)ity', *Resources for Feminist Research,* 22 (3–4): 19–22.

Wilson, K. (1992) 'The place of child observation in social work training', *Journal of Social Work Practice,* 6 (1): 37–47.

10

INTERVIEWING AND EVALUATING

Jan Fook, Robyn Munford and Jackie Sanders

Interviewing is probably one of the most commonly used sets of skills within social work practice and in its broad totality of settings – interpersonal, group and family work, community-based practice, administration, research and policy work. Yet one of the ironies of current social work practice is that it is most often associated primarily with direct service work, so is seen as having less relevance to the practice of research, and vice versa.

It is the main purpose of this chapter to illustrate how the practice of research, particularly evaluative research, and the practice of interviewing, are, and can be, integrated. After a brief discussion of the concepts of evaluation and interviewing, the chapter will demonstrate how evaluation is in fact a dimension of interviewing practice, by outlining how particular research methods can be used for evaluative purposes, as an integral part of interviewing. Selected research techniques will be reviewed and discussed regarding their evaluative potential in interview practice. Some specific examples from the fields of practice with children and disabilities will also be considered.

Evaluation and interviewing

The concept and meaning of evaluation will differ, of course, according to the different contexts in which it is enacted, the different purposes which are intended, and the various political expectations which come into play. These are statements of the almost obvious, but at the same time they indicate that evaluation can be viewed either in relation to its more public purposes (for example programme development, planning, funding accountability: Owen, 1993), or in relation to its more private uses (for example self-evaluation and learning: Cooper, 1994a). Sometimes evaluative studies have been categorized according to whether their focus is on outcomes or process (Cheetham et al., 1992: 48). Often the purposes may seem mutually exclusive or conflictual, and sometimes they are, as Belenky and others have shown in their study of women students, who found that the process and act of assessment often militated against learning outcomes (Belenky et al., 1986: 208).

In this chapter we will focus on the ways in which particular evaluative methods may be used to meet a number of different purposes. What is of equal importance, although we do not have the space to discuss it in detail here, is awareness of the purposes for which the evaluative methods are being used, since this will influence their effectiveness and relevance in any given situation. We will assume that evaluative research can be used to measure, document and record interviewing practice, for the purposes of ensuring accountability, for assessment, or for improving and developing practice. Evaluation can be multi-purpose and multi-focused.

Much the same argument applies to our approach to the concept of interviewing, which has been defined, most pragmatically, as a 'conversation with a purpose' (Kadushin, 1983: 13; Rodwell, 1995: 204). The type of interview will thus differ depending on setting, purpose and political dimensions. Social work practice education has tended to focus on the teaching of interviewing as an interpersonal direct practice tool, used for information collection, diagnostic or therapeutic reasons (Zastrow, 1992). This implies that the one-to-one interview is the mainstream form, and that the main purpose is enabling. However, interviews take place in a variety of settings much broader than direct practice contexts (with groups and families, and for research purposes), and often are used to impart information, and/or to perform monitoring, supervisory or controlling functions. Interviews can also be more or less informal. From this point of view, an interview can be seen as any type of extended interaction, dialogue or exchange which incorporates a significant verbal component, since it should not be forgotten that communication takes place in a variety of ways, including through physical structure and non-verbal behaviour.

As with the concept of evaluation, what is important about an interview is awareness of the purpose or purposes for which it is intended. An interview cannot be understood, and therefore effectively evaluated, without an appreciation of its function within a particular context.

The practice of interviewing is one particular set of skills in the repertoire of the practising social worker, which cannot be evaluated separately from the broader context in which it is practised, or indeed, separately from the broader holistic process (be it counselling, research, job selection, relationship formation) in which it is practised and experienced. Any evaluation of an interview needs to take into account the specific purposes, functions and effects of it within the whole process of which it is a part.

It is also important, in developing the evaluative and research dimensions of the interview, that the many components of interview practice and experience are appreciated. For instance, Cheetham and others make the basic point that processes (as well as outcomes) of social work practice are legitimate focuses for evaluation (Cheetham et al., 1992: 48). The interview process thus involves a range of components: the establishment of initial contact and rapport; communication skills; and the structure, form and stages of the interview. If the interview is a counselling one, it may also involve (depending on the model adhered to) dimensions of relationship building, information gathering, assessment, problem solving, microcounselling skills (for example listening, questioning, reflection, reframing, confrontation) and strategy formulation. All interviews are influenced by organizational, policy and physical setting, and involve different roles for interviewers and interviewees, which may be more or less egalitarian, depending on the purpose and approach of the interview. Obviously there may be more people present than in the standard 'one-to-one' interview – interviews can take place with co-interviewers, and with couples, small family groups, or larger group sessions.

Practice and research

It is difficult, and sometimes artificial, to separate the functions of practice and research. In fact, it is the more positivist paradigm, which has been dominant in constructing our approach to social work research, which has led us to separate practice and research aspects of everyday experience (for example Piele, 1988). With the questioning of a purist positivist paradigm, from theoretical perspectives such as feminism, critical theory, constructivism and postmodernism, and reflective and participatory action research models, comes a recognition that practice, theory and research are inevitably intertwined (Fook, 1996). The pathway is thus opened for a legitimate research focus on practice experience as both data and process, and on the practitioner as both researcher and researched, knower and known. The field of social work practice becomes an integrated site at which research is conducted, and where changes indicated by the research process are enacted.

This view is essentially an enabling one for practitioners, in that it locates the responsibility for, and source of, research, squarely in the field of practice experience. This is the line that we support.

Methods and processes for evaluating interview practice

In this section we will describe some selected methods and processes which may assist in recording and analysing interview practice experience.

Critical incident analysis

Critical incident analysis first began life as a research tool and is attributed to Flanagan (1954). A critical incident was an observable human activity, sufficiently complete to permit conclusions and predictions to be made about the person performing the act (1954: 327). It has been used in a variety of research ways subsequently, especially as a method of studying the specific experience of practitioners, grounded in context. The researcher may choose to focus on incidents which are critical (important or significant) to the experiencing person for a variety of reasons, depending on the purpose of the research. For instance, if studying professional expertise, practitioners may be asked to describe incidents critical to them because they felt they demonstrated a particular skill. If studying learning, practitioners may focus on an incident that was critical to them because it changed their thinking in some way. The list of possibilities is limited only by imagination – incidents may be critical because of their mundanity, because of the emotions they elicit, because they were unpredictable, because they were demanding, or because they are remembered pleasantly. The critical incident, in this sense, is simply a description of a concrete piece of practice, which provides the material for analysis of this practice. How this material is analysed, and the associated functions this analysis serves, is another matter, and will obviously be influenced by the purposes for which the research is undertaken, and the theoretical perspectives from which the analysis is approached. For example, records such as critical incidents can be analysed as documents, interview transcripts or narratives. They might be analysed through content analysis, thematic analysis or semiotic analysis (Kellehear, 1993).

Critical incident analysis, in more recent times, has become well developed as an educational tool, especially in self-evaluation and self-learning, most notably within the educational field (Brookfield, 1995; Tripp, 1993), but also to some extent within social work (Cooper, 1994b; Fook et al., 1994). Critical incident technique is a perfect example of a research tool which can perform evaluative functions of concrete practice, and can assist in the evaluation of concrete interviewing practice, at many different levels.

Let us imagine that an interviewer wishes to evaluate the process of an interview. Did it go according to plan? Could it have been handled more smoothly? How were unpredicted events handled, and how could they have been handled differently or better? She or he could record the interview as a critical incident, preferably in writing. This would involve writing their memory of what happened in the interview, taking care to record the detail as faithfully as possible. This might include not just observable events (who said and did what and when), but also thoughts and feelings. How did the interview open? What did I say, and what skills did I think I was using? How did the person respond? What were my impressions at the time? Why did I respond in that way?

This record can then be analysed for the degree to which it fits with what the interviewer consciously intended. What skills did I demonstrate? Were they used appropriately? What patterns emerged about my practice? What themes or ideas are evident?

Different aspects of interview practice may be evaluated in a similar way, but by varying the focus of the critical incident record and the analytical questions. For example, the record could focus on the practice of a specific skill such as reframing. The critical incident record might concentrate on several interchanges where the interviewer thought they were using this skill, and may record exact words, and phrasings, and responses. The analysis might focus on the patterns and assumptions inherent in the framing used, and what types of choice (frames) were posed to the person being interviewed. If the evaluator is particularly interested in how choices were received by the person, she or he might focus on the content and patterns of responses. If the evaluator wants to develop new ways of reframing arising out of the evaluation, she or he might focus on asking what other ways there might have been of reframing the person's experience.

Recording concrete practice experience, and analysing it in this way, is similar to the reflective process, which enjoys growing popularity as an educational approach, particularly in the professions (Gould and Taylor, 1996).

The reflective and critical reflective approaches

The theory of these approaches is covered elsewhere in this volume by Gould and Ruckdeschel. However, the process of describing and reflecting upon practice can clearly perform combined functions of research and learning. The critical incident method, already described, can be used in a multitude of ways to assist in this reflective process.

A more detailed set of questions to guide analysis of the critical incident, based to some extent upon poststructural theorizing and semiotic analysis, is included in Fook (1996). This process can also be used to assist the practitioner to develop further theorizing about practice. We can summarize the guiding reflective questions as follows:

- What main themes/patterns emerge?
- What different thoughts, feelings, interpretations, intentions, assumptions are evident? Whose are they?
- How do these influence the situation?
- What is missing?
- What language is used and what frameworks does it imply?
- What was unexpected and why? What does this imply about my assumptions?

- What patterns emerge to connect my experience in this incident with others? How do I explain this?
- What current theories exist to give meaning to my experience?
- How do I need to modify current thinking to take account of my experience?
- What further questions arise?

Important elements of reflectivity are the ability to connect personal experience – assumptions, interpretations, emotions – with social situations and actions; and the ability to use the knowledge so generated in developing and improving practice.

Critical reflectivity goes a step further. Reflectivity is a broad approach which can assist in 'hunting assumptions' (as Brookfield, 1995: 2 terms it). The process only becomes critical if the assumptions uncovered assist in understanding how considerations of power influence situations and relations, and how these very considerations can work against our best interests (Brookfield, 1995: 8). In other words, in order to perform *critical* functions, the reflective process must contribute to an emancipatory project of more egalitarian social relations, by assisting us to uncover self-defeating assumptions (Fook, forthcoming).

Critical reflection on interview practice should assist in evaluating the power dimensions of that practice, and should uncover, challenge and question the ways in which interview practice might participate in perpetuating improper uses of power. In this way it should contribute to developing interviewing practices which empower all participants.

Personal, interpersonal and group applications

Critical incident analysis, and reflective and critical reflective processes, can be used in a variety of ways within the workplace, to evaluate interview practice. The examples used in the foregoing discussion were primarily framed for personal use, that is, for the individual worker seeking to self-evaluate their interview practice, either for a one-off case, or as a pattern of practices over a given length of time. However, it is also a model that can be used by a practitioner-researcher to evaluate the interview practice of a number of workers within an agency, or across agencies. For example, a number of workers might be asked to record critical incidents from their interview practice, and patterns might be analysed across all records. This could also be a useful design for managers wishing to identify the extent to which stated agency philosophy is embodied in worker practice, or for those wishing to elicit and develop agency policy from existing practice. It can be a fruitful design for the development of best practice models, and can function to validate and legitimize the practice of workers.

Brookfield outlines a useful design for critical incident analysis and evaluation of classroom teaching practice (1995: 114–123), which could easily be applied as a design for evaluating an interview or a series of interviews. He asks students, at the end of each class, to write down answers to specific questions about moments in which they felt most engaged or distanced, actions which they found helpful or confusing, and aspects which surprised them. Responses are then analysed for common themes, and are discussed with students the following week. Interviewees could be asked similar questions about interviews, and feedback used as a basis for negotiating changes in interview practice.

At an interpersonal level, the critical incident and reflective models can be used in a supervisory relationship to evaluate and improve practice. This is a well-used model within field education, between supervisor and student, but the model can also be used between peers. It often provides a more focused and structured way to research, analyse and develop practice, than perhaps a more traditional supervisory relationship.

The same model can be used in group situations, and can again perform supervisory, research, evaluative or learning functions, or a combination of these. Indeed, there is argument to suggest that group or collective methods might be preferable in some instances.

An example of a group research method, which can be applied in the evaluation of interview practice, is collective memory work (Koutroulis, 1996; Martin, Chapter 8 in this volume; Schratz and Walker, 1995). Collective memory work was developed by feminist researcher, Haug (1987), as a way of accessing elements of identity formation through memory of past events, feelings and acts. It rests upon the argument that identity is socially constructed, and that early memories may therefore hold the key to uncovering some of the ways in which this has occurred. Once an awareness of how identity is constructed and constrained is attained, the possibility of change is created. An emancipatory element is integral to the method. The work must occur collectively, since the goal is to facilitate a different awareness to that already developed by the individual person in isolation (Schratz and Walker, 1995: 44).

Similar principles can apply in the analysis of memories of social work practice, particularly in examining what were formative experiences for practitioners in their notions of what constitutes appropriate behaviour and assistance in a social work setting, and how these notions have translated into current interviewing practice. It is possible that we have paid too little attention to popular social and cultural notions, and the ways in which these inform workers' practice – these notions may remain, no matter what professional social work learning is grafted on to them (Fook et al., 1994: 15). A method like memory work might be helpful in uncovering socially constructed assumptions or prejudices, which might undermine effective and empowering interview practice.

Focus groups are another method of data collection which are gaining rapidly in popularity. Although developed by sociologist Robert Merton, they are probably most commonly used as a market research tool (Thomas et al., 1992). There is a rapidly growing literature on qualitative research uses of focus groups (Barbour and Kitzinger, 1998; Kreuger, 1994; Morgan and Kreuger, 1997; Shaw, 1996a). A focus group is primarily a group interview, a major advantage of which is to maximize the number of responses. Responses arising from group interaction are a further source of information. They are commonly used when the researcher wishes to elicit a range of experiences or views, and wishes to gain information that is then enriched through debate and interaction between group members. A major difficulty is in facilitating and recording the focus group interview – co-facilitators may be needed.

Focus groups, as a research tool, may be of use in the development of agency policy or programmes around interview practice. They may also be an appropriate tool in assisting with a critical reflective process in analysing interview transcripts or critical incident records. It is especially useful to be able to elicit a range of interpretations of one particular situation – this helps to illustrate that interpretations are just that, rather than 'fact'; and it allows for critical debate between perspectives, and for comparison of formative experiences. Since knowledge is at least partly formed through dialogue and interaction, as critical theorists argue (Habermas in Agger, 1991), then a research process which models this should be created.

Other forms of recording for interview evaluation

Critical incident recording is only one form of documentation and analysis relevant to the evaluation of interviewing practice. Critical incidents may be recorded in other forms – either audio- or videotaped – although it is sometimes harder to see patterns of language in these forms. However other cues may be picked up – non-verbal indications of particular emotions, for example.

Audio-visual records and process records of entire interviews are of course not new to students of social work (see Kagle, 1991). What does perhaps need closer attention in the use of these methods, is how, and for what purpose, the recorded material is analysed. It is often less threatening, and learning potential is maximized, when these are used as methods of self-evaluation, for ongoing learning, rather than as one-off, often decontextualized examples of practice. Their value as research and evaluation tools is maximized when they are used to reflect upon and further develop practice.

The reflective journal is another, not new, example of a tool which can be used for both learning and evaluative research. If used to record changes in thinking and practice, the journal can trace progress, as a type of processual evaluation tool.

Examples relating to disability and children's research

Interviewing in evaluative research is a core component of social work practice. In our previous research (Munford, 1989; Munford et al., 1996, 1998) we have demonstrated that practice research, including evaluative research, can be integrated into the daily tasks of social workers and social service organizations. Critical reflectivity (Fook, 1996), and an acknowledgement of the potential of the emancipatory elements of practice research, can be incorporated into frameworks for evaluative research. Having said this, it is important to be specific about what it is we mean when we cite such terms as 'critical reflectivity' and 'the emancipatory potential for research' as discussed earlier in this chapter. The following represent a number of core principles developed out of our previous and ongoing research with families and disabled people. These principles can be posed as a series of statements to be taken into account when designing evaluative research that has the potential to bring about change for clients, social workers and social service organizations. We will begin with research with disabled people and then move on to a discussion about children and their involvement in research.

Principles for carrying out evaluative research in the disability field

THE PURPOSE OF THE RESEARCH   One of the dangers of evaluative research, and, hence, the difficulties that can be encountered when interviewing within social service organizations, is the lack of clarity as to the purpose of and outcomes expected from the research. In our reflection with clients who were part of ongoing family research we often explored the differences in expectations of the research from the perspective of the participants and the researchers. If one is to be successful in carrying out evaluative research one must be explicit about the purpose of the research and the purpose of the interviews and the use to which the data will be put. This includes being explicit about who will ultimately benefit from the research findings and who has the authority to bring about the required change in practice identified by evaluative research findings.

ACKNOWLEDGEMENT OF POWER   Munford (1994a), Bennie (1996) and Boyles (1997) identify the importance of naming the relations of power present in the research relationship and acknowledging the difficulties this may present in the interviewing process. Bennie, in his research on supported employment for disabled people, notes from Zarb's work that it is 'crucial that power relations that have traditionally favoured the researcher be countered throughout the research process' (Bennie, 1996: 22). In the disability field research has traditionally been carried out without consultation with disabled people themselves (Boyles, 1997; Oliver, 1992). Disabled people have often found themselves powerless within the research process. This has been particularly so in evaluative situations where research has been carried out in order to meet the needs of service providers and as a result has often meant that disabled people were excluded from input into how the research would be interpreted. As Munford (1994b) has pointed out, a deficit model of disability which views disabled people as dependent and not able to contribute to the development of research questions and design has often meant that they have been excluded from full participation and inclusion in all aspects of the research process.

RECIPROCITY One of the key observations we have made in our ongoing agency research is to note the conflict about the interpretation of research reciprocity. Lunn (1997) in her research with disabled women canvasses the debates around feminist research and the notion of reciprocity. She argues that one of the key elements of reciprocity 'lies in the potential it holds in terms of empowering the research participants and searching for new ways to legitimate and make audible previously silenced voices' (Lunn, 1997: 98). Reciprocity involves giving something back to research participants, such as returning transcripts. Lunn argues that reciprocity must be specific to the requirements of the participant and, given this, may at times require the researcher to change the direction of the research process. For example, some participants are not interested in receiving copies of transcripts to edit and others require no feedback other than what is provided at the end of the interview process.

We have found in our research that there are a number of levels at which reciprocity can operate and it is imperative that the researchers honestly adhere to procedures that they have laid down at the beginning of the research process. For example, participants may not want to assist in devising research questions and providing feedback on interviews, or to attend focus groups and subsequent meetings to hear feedback on the research. Involvement in reciprocity can become an additional stress factor for participants involved in evaluative research in that (in the case of our research on families) trying to find baby-sitters so that they can attend feedback interviews, or simply trying to find the time, can place already stretched families under additional burdens. It is our experience that practical assistance is often more helpful and that the very process of listening within the interviewing setting can be more beneficial than asking participants to be involved in extended research processes. Reciprocity must be carefully matched to the situation in which the research takes place, it should ideally be defined by participants, be of direct benefit to them and require no ongoing obligations on their part. In research with disabled people, the researchers' desire to be involved in bringing about social change can place additional burdens upon individuals whose current concerns may not be with large scale social change, but rather with achieving important daily goals such as gaining access to quality educational opportunities.

Chapter 6 on collaborative research with service users in this volume (by Evans and Fisher) carries the notion of reciprocity further by exploring how social work researchers might develop collaborative relationships with service users so that research is more user led and controlled.

NON-DISABLED RESEARCHERS   One of the key issues in the disability field currently is the commitment that non-disabled researchers have to working alongside disabled people to carry out evaluative research. Whittaker (1994) demonstrates how disabled people can be fully involved in evaluation of social services. In particular, non-disabled and disabled people can work with service users to develop effective procedures for evaluation and service development. Munford (1994b) discusses how research collaboration between disabled and non-disabled people can assist in moving disabled people from passive to active research roles in designing the research and carrying out interviews. One of the key elements here is to provide ongoing training for new interviewers so that they have opportunities to reflect critically on the interview process and develop new skills. Storytelling is a key method in evaluation and has considerable potential to generate data and to provide alternative ways of developing effective involvement in the research process.

INTERPRETATION AND RESEARCH EXPECTATIONS   Becoming involved in research implies a commitment on the part of the researcher to make explicit how interviews will be interpreted and what the expectations of the research will be. For example, attending 20 hours of interviews could raise the expectations of the participants that the researcher will be able to create some change in service delivery. Clear identification of expectations is an integral part of the whole research process. They relate not only to expectations of the entire research process, but also to practical details such as the length, focus and locations of interviews and to the expectations of research participants and researchers.

LANGUAGE   In disability research language has been a key element which has required deconstruction. For example, Bennie (1996) utilizes Rees's framework to explore the possibilities of carrying out emancipatory research with disabled people. Bennie (1996) and Rees (1991) have argued that language has been used to exclude disabled and other marginalized groups and that certain concepts such as empowerment have been misinterpreted by those who have the power to determine their meaning in practice. In our research, we take care to define words such as empowerment, emancipation, choice, flexibility and so on with research participants so that there is clarity as to the meaning of these. Much current social policy literature in New Zealand uses these words in ways that function to *exclude* disabled people, while at the same time raising expectations that cannot be met by services. Other words such as partnership, participants and ownership of research results can be problematic in evaluative research. It is important to explain to participants the nature of their involvement and whether or not they do in fact have a role as partners, or as participants. Researchers should avoid the temptation to appear to be inclusive if this is not possible or realistic.

A MOSAIC OF INTERVIEW STYLES   Having a commitment to a mosaic of research methodologies and interview styles can enhance the information which comes out of the evaluative process. First, be clear about what it is you are asking people to do in the interview and for what reason. The parameters of the interview must be clarified and one of the key things that we have found in our research is that interview instruments that parallel the instruments used in clinical work such as checklists and assessment tools may create difficulties for research participants. Assessment tools have often been used to exclude people from services. If these are then used in evaluative interviews they may create substantial issues for participants which have no direct relationship to the evaluation itself but instead connect directly with the experience of being 'assessed'. A number of alternative methods can be used. These include guided storytelling, life histories, open-ended interviews, critical incident techniques, scenario writing, constructing vision galleries and visual tools such as web charts. These have all been useful in the research process and have potential for development as effective evaluative interview techniques.

Principles for carrying out evaluative research with children

PURPOSE OF THE INTERVIEW   Shaw (1996b) talks about interviewing children in qualitative research and argues that qualitative work with children can be regarded as a process of narrative inquiry. Research in this sense is directed not only at understanding certain patterns or facts, but also at what it is like to 'be a child'. Shaw discusses the interpretation of children's stories in terms of whether they are 'objective' accounts of the world or interpretations of the world through the eyes of children. It is essential when involving children in research that the issues around the purpose of the research, the scope of the interview and the use of the material gained is clear. This must be made explicit to both the children and their legally defined caretakers.

IMPACT OF THE INTERVIEW   Interviewing children is a powerful strategy for eliciting the meanings about the way they view the world. As Shaw (1996b) points out, the interview is not only a method for gaining information, but can be a key moment in the child's life. For example, the child may use the interview to tell a story in order to work through some current difficulties they are facing at school or within their family. As when interviewing adults, the significance of the interview must be underlined, and the researcher must understand the impact their entry into the child's life can create. As with having clarity about the purpose of the research, the child must be reassured that they are not being judged in the interview and that the purpose of the interview is not to measure them against some ideal or correct interpretation of an event or situation.

PRACTICAL ISSUES – A MOSAIC OF TECHNIQUES   In interviewing children a number of practical issues emerge. These relate to factors such as the location of the interview, the interview length and style, how the interview will relate to wider issues in the child's life, interviewer style and the impact of the interview on the child. The interview must take account of what stage in the developmental process the child has reached and also recognize other activities or learning processes in which the child is involved. For example, when setting up research on family well-being and interviews with children, it was important that we located this within the current learning tasks of children, such as 'keeping-ourselves-safe' programmes run within school settings. A range of interview techniques and styles can be adopted. A key method is storytelling and allowing the child to direct the interview process. The skills required in social work interviewing apply here, such as active and reflective listening. The use of games, drawing of pictures, and working alongside children in activities such as listening to music are also effective mechanisms. A fundamental principle in this endeavour is to value the child and, as occurs in strengths-based family work (Munford and Sanders, 1999), to elevate the child to the position of 'expert' with a real and valid contribution to make.

ETHICAL ISSUES   Research involving children is ethically challenging. In addition to the usual concerns about the potential to cause harm and the need to obtain informed consent, there are matters relating to obtaining consent from legally defined caretakers. Here, issues around how much significant others are involved in the interview process and issues of confidentiality in the interview setting can be problematic. For example, will consenting adults expect to receive information from the interview, and how does the researcher mediate this and balance it against the separate interests of the child? How will the researcher deal with issues of disclosure of abuse? If the child wishes to have another person present at the interview, there must be clarity regarding who will answer the questions and whether or not this person has rights additional to the child participant. Confidentiality issues must be addressed with any individuals who are acting in a support role. Another key ethical dilemma relates to the role of the researcher's relationship with the child. Children's expectations of adults who display an interest in them are clearly different to those of adults, who may be expected to be able understand the fleeting nature of research encounters. Finally, the way that feedback will be provided to child participants also needs to be explored, bearing in mind that a return visit from an interviewer might be interpreted as an indication of ongoing interest by the researcher in the child as an individual separate from the interview process. The potential of interviews to connect with past experiences of children and to cause a reinterpretation of events that might otherwise have been closed for the child also needs to be borne in mind. Researchers must develop procedures for addressing such issues, should they arise. It is here that the ability of research to have negative consequences for the well-being of children lies. For this reason, considerable thought must be given to the way in which these sorts of issues will be dealt with.

Conclusion

One of the issues we have encountered in our current research is the 'obsession' with measuring the outcomes of social service delivery through the use of quantitative methods. While we do not deny the contribution that quantitative methods can make, the qualitative techniques outlined in this chapter provide valuable additional methods of building richly textured understandings of the nature of social service activity. The development of the contract culture has brought with it a heavy emphasis upon the quantitative measurement of 'deliverables' by social service agencies as the only way of demonstrating that funds have been spent appropriately. The contract mechanism has become the motif around which many aspects of service delivery are organized, from the provision of funding to the measurement of agency and individual performance. Munford and Sanders (1999) canvass some of the issues this raises for those involved in the delivery and evaluation of social services. These include factors such as the specificity and fragmentation of purchase and reporting wherein accountability is tightened and focused to such an extent that this may create a distorted picture of the actual services being purchased and provided. Another key issue is that of reductionism, where evaluation is reduced to the measurement of tightly defined outputs but where the understanding of how the service is provided is missing.

In their current use within social work, contracts basically seek to define precisely what will be provided, how often and at what cost. In accountability terms, this translates into providers furnishing information about what they did, how often and at what cost with clients or users. This may seem simple. However, the experience in both health and welfare over the past 15 years has been that collecting this informa-tion consistently within services has been difficult, and achieving this in comparable ways across services or organizations has proved to be notoriously elusive. A whole new industry has grown around service delivery systems concerned with developing, recording and analysing information generated within and across service groupings.

Wilson (1986) talks about the need for social service agencies to be measured in terms of responsibility rather than accountability and argues that the 'performance culture' and its associated emphasis upon the readily measurable has missed the point. In fact, according to Wilson, the 'outcomes' of such agencies are not reducible in all situations to a series of statistical pieces of information and both funders and providers gain an inaccurate picture of what is actually being done within services if this is all they focus on.

In this context, the ongoing development of qualitative methodologies is crucial. If Wilson (1986) is correct then the best defence against the misrepresentation which accountability (rather than responsibility) holds is the development of sound and replicable qualitative techniques for evaluating and monitoring social services. Additionally, critical reflective research techniques can be used, in a number of ways, to develop our understanding of the way in which the performance culture has devel-oped and how it has contributed to the erosion of the role of the state in service provision. The challenge is to develop strategies that enable us as researchers to critique purely measurement-focused evaluative proce-dures and to provide alternatives. In this sense, critical reflective tech-niques can function to document and improve practice (Fook, 1997), which ought also to be one of the ultimate goals of measurement.

As researchers, a valuable role we can play is to support providers in developing mechanisms that enable them to avoid being captured by a purchaser's orientation. Providers should concentrate on innovation and development in delivery, and on using current purchasing systems to the maximum. This includes requiring funders to meet the full extent of their responsibilities in terms of the contracts they produce, and using the fullest extent of the rights providers have under contract law and other legislative mechanisms to ensure that they receive the maximum that is possible for the delivery and the evaluation of social services. It also includes helping providers to harness their collective strength to exert force for changes which will both enhance their ability to provide services and to deliver maximum benefit to clients.

In this chapter our concern has been to discuss ways in which a variety of research techniques, such as critical incident analysis, collective mem-ory work and focus groups can be combined, with a critically reflective approach, to enable practitioners to integrate evaluative processes within the everyday practice of interviewing. By discussing how evaluative research might be integrated with practice in the disability field, and in work with children, we also raised some issues which arise directly out of practice, such as issues of empowerment and reciprocity, and the need to use a mosaic of interview techniques. Finally, we examined the implications of our suggestions for current work within the contract state, and the pressure towards quantitative measurement. The approach to integrating evaluation and interviewing practice that we have outlined should both contribute to more responsible practices and enable critical change.

References

Agger, B. (1991) 'Critical theory, poststructuralism, postmodernism: their sociological relevance', *Annual Review of Sociology*, 17: 105–131.
Barbour, R. and Kitzinger, J. (eds) (1998) *The Use of Focus Groups in Health Research*. London: Sage.
Belenky, M., Clinchy, B., Goldberger, N. and Tarule, J. (1986) *Women's Ways of Knowing*. New York: Basic Books.
Bennie, G. (1996) 'Supported employment and disabled people in New Zealand: from assimilation to transformation'. Unpublished PhD thesis, Department of Social Policy and Social Work, Massey University Palmerston North.
Boyles, P. (1997) 'Emancipatory research models and their role in the field of disability', in P. O'Brien and R. Murray (eds), *Human Services: Towards Partnership and Support*. Palmerston North: Dunmore Press. pp. 82–96.
Brookfield, S. (1995) *Becoming a Critically Reflective Teacher*. San Francisco: Jossey-Bass.
Cheetham J., Fuller, R., McIvor, G. and Petch, A. (1992) *Evaluating Social Work Effectiveness*. Buckingham: Open University Press.
Cooper, L. (1994a) 'Improved assessment practices in field education', in J. Ife, S. Leitman and P. Murphy (eds), *Advances in Social Work and Welfare Education*. Perth: Australian Association for Social Work and Welfare Education, University of Western Australia. pp. 110–124.
Cooper, L. (1994b) 'Critical storytelling in social work education', *Australian Journal of Adult and Community Education*, 33 (2): 131–141.
Flanagan, J. (1954) 'The critical incident technique', *Psychology Bulletin*, 51: 327–358.
Fook, J. (ed.) (1996) *The Reflective Researcher*. Sydney: Allen & Unwin.
Fook, J. (1997) 'Educating social workers in a changing cultural context. Response: an Australian perspective', *Social Work Review*, 9 (4): 9–11.
Fook, J. (forthcoming) 'Critically reflective practice', in B. Pease and J. Fook (eds), *Transforming Social Work Practice: Postmodern Critical Perspectives*. London: Routledge.
Fook, J., Ryan, M. and Hawkins, L. (1994) 'Becoming a social worker: educational implications from preliminary findings of a longitudinal study', *Social Work Education*, 13 (2): 5–26.
Gould, N. and Taylor, I. (eds) (1996) *Reflective Learning in Social Work*. Aldershot: Avebury.
Haug, F. (1987) *Female Sexualisation: A Collective Work of Memory*. London: Verso.
Kadushin, A. (1983) *The Social Work Interview*. New York: Columbia University Press.

Kagle, J. (1991) *Social Work Records*, 2nd edn. Belmont, CA: Wadsworth.

Kellehear, A. (1993) *The Unobtrusive Researcher: A Guide to Methods*. Sydney: Allen & Unwin.

Koutroulis, G. (1996) 'Memory work: process, practice and pitfalls', in D. Colquhuon and A. Kellehear (eds), *Health Research and Practice Vol. 2*. London: Chapman and Hall. pp. 95–113.

Kreuger, R.A. (1994) *Focus Groups: A Practical Guide for Applied Research*. Thousand Oaks, CA: Sage.

Lunn, M. (1997) 'What am I . . . for her? Feminism and disability with/in the postmodern'. PhD thesis, Department of Social Policy and Social Work, Massey University, New Zealand.

Morgan, D.L. and Kreuger, R.A. (1997) *The Focus Group Kit*, 6 vols. Thousand Oaks, CA: Sage.

Munford, R. (1989) 'The hidden costs of caring: women who care for people with intellectual disabilities'. PhD thesis, Department of Sociology, Massey University, New Zealand.

Munford, R. (1994a) 'The politics of caregiving' in M.H. Rioux and M. Bach (eds), *Disability is not Measles*. Toronto: L'Institut Roeher. pp. 265–284.

Munford, R. (1994b) 'Caregiving – a shared commitment', in K. Ballard (ed.), *Disability, Family/Whanau and Society*. Palmerston North, NZ: Dunmore Press. pp. 265–292.

Munford, R., Sanders, J., Tisdall, M., Mulder, J., Spoonley, P. and Jack, A. (1996) *Working Successfully with Families: Stage 1*. Wellington, NZ: Madison.

Munford, R., Sanders, J., Tisdall, M., Henare, A., Livingston, K. and Spoonley, P. (1998) *Working Successfully with Families: Stage 2*. Wellington, NZ: Madison.

Munford, R. and Sanders, J. (1999) *Supporting Families*. Palmerston North, NZ: Dunmore Press.

Oliver, M. (1992) 'Changing the social relations of research production?' *Disability, Handicap and Society*, 7 (2): 101–114.

Owen, J.M. (1993) *Program Evaluation: Forms and Approaches*. Sydney: Allen & Unwin.

Piele, C. (1988) 'Research paradigms in social work: from stalemate to creative synthesis', *Social Service Review*, 62 (1): 1–19.

Rees, S. (1991) *Achieving Power: Practice and Policy in Social Welfare*. Sydney: Allen & Unwin.

Rodwell, M.K. (1995) 'Constructivist research: a qualitative approach', in P.J. Pecora, M.W. Fraser, K.E. Nelson, J. McCrosky and W. Meezan (eds), *Evaluating Family-Based Services*. New York: Aldine de Gruyter. pp. 191–214.

Schratz, M. and Walker, R. (1995) *Research as Social Change*. New York: Routledge.

Shaw, I. (1996a) *Evaluating in Practice*. Aldershot: Ashgate.

Shaw, I. (1996b) 'Unbroken voices: children, young people and qualitative methods', in I. Butler and I. Shaw (eds), *A Case of Neglect? Children's Experiences and the Sociology of Methods*. Aldershot: Avebury. pp. 19–36.

Thomas, S., Steven, I., Browning, C., Dickens, E., Eckermann, E., Carey, L. and Pollard, S. (1992) 'Focus groups in health research: a methodological review', in J. Daly, A. Kellehear and E. Willis (eds), *Annual Review of Health Social Sciences*. Bundoora: La Trobe University. pp. 7–20.

Tripp, D. (1993) *Critical Incidents in Teaching: Developing Professional Judgement*. New York: Routledge.

Whittaker, A. (1994) 'Service evaluation by people with learning disabilities', in A. Connor and S. Black (eds), *Performance Review and Quality in Social Care*. London: Jessica Kingsley.

Wilson, J. (1986) *Bureaucracy: What Government Agencies Do and Why They Do It*. New York: Basic Books.

Zastrow, C. (1992) *The Practice of Social Work*. Belmont, CA: Wadsworth.

11

QUALITATIVE CLINICAL RESEARCH AND EVALUATION:
Obstacles, opportunities and issues

Roy Ruckdeschel

We are in a period when we are reassessing who we are as social workers and the direction in which the field is headed. An important part of that process is how we go about evaluating the various forms of practice. The primary focus of this chapter will be on the evaluation of various types of clinical practice. Quantitative methods have been the approach of choice for those undertaking the task. However, qualitative methods of evaluation have recently emerged as a viable choice or alternative for at least some social workers and for some forms of practice. This chapter will explore the current status of the latter methods and their potential as the profession heads into the millennium. It is a rapidly changing landscape, one of both obstacle and opportunity. In the 25-year timespan from 1975 until the year 2000, an admittedly somewhat arbitrary benchmark, qualitative methods have emerged from the shadows of what was once perceived as an exploratory methodology to approach the mainstream of general methodology and of methods of evaluation. As an aside, this period also marks the timespan in which the author has been involved in social work education.

Before engaging in this task in detail, it is necessary first to identify a number of assumptions that the author makes about evaluation. The first relates to the definition of evaluation. In much of the literature, evaluation is associated with outcomes and with instrumentation. That is, evaluation is seen as an activity that utilizes some form of measurement tool or instrument to assess the effectiveness of a programme or practice approach. While this may be in part true of summative forms of evaluation that focus on outcomes, it is an unnecessarily restrictive view of the task. Patton (1990) for example discusses formative and process-oriented types of evaluation where the primary purpose is to improve the programme or the practice approach. Bergin and Garfield (1994) note the surge of process-oriented research on clinical practice between 1986 and 1994. Above and beyond even this distinction, evaluators need to bring a critical perspective to the task. Elsewhere, I have argued that evaluation, and in particular qualitative evaluation, is about finding the value and the meaning of that which we are studying (Ruckdeschel et al., 1994). Thus evaluation is somewhat analogous to an act of deconstruction in that it is essentially reflective and interactive in nature. The key outcome is not a finding *per se* but rather the generation of useful information, utility in turn depending in large part on the perspective of the user of that information (Patton, 1990). Utility and value may involve outcomes, process and/or the political context of the evaluation. The qualitative researcher/evaluator of necessity brings a reflective, interactive and subjective perspective to the task. Underlining this point is the assertion that the researcher is the instrument! (Ruckdeschel et al., 1994).

Secondly, and consistent with the above and with the orientation of this book, evaluation must have a pragmatic relationship to practice. That is, evaluation must be framed in a way that it fits into and facilitates practice. This applies especially to clinical practice. Practitioners will not adopt techniques that are intrusive in terms of time, training and theory (Heineman-Pieper, 1994). Social workers historically have not viewed research as a vital component of practice. Although this has applied primarily to quantitative forms of research, it would be naïve of the qualitative research advocate to think that this applies any less to their methods. The twin potential sins are intrusiveness and irrelevance. This in spite of the view of some that a potential strength of the qualitative approach is its putative consonance with practice (Goldstein, 1991).

Given the above assumptions, I will examine obstacles, both real and perceived, to the further use of qualitative methods in the evaluation of social work practice. We will then explore some potential opportunities for growth and important, unresolved issues. The chapter will conclude with examples that hopefully illustrate some of the dynamics of the contemporary qualitative evaluative process.

Legitimacy: that which appears to be an obstacle but may not be

Legitimacy, or lack thereof, has been an issue historically associated with qualitative methods. Qualitative methodology has been viewed by many researchers as soft, suspect, lacking in rigour, and therefore lacking in legitimacy. This perception has existed in both the social sciences and in social work. The lowly status of qualitative methods was reflected in a variety of ways, some of which will be touched on here. Research and practice texts tend to reflect the conventional wisdom of the time in which they are written. Twenty-five years ago there was relatively little discussion of qualitative methods in such texts and in fact there was not even agreement on a common term to characterize such methods. Fairly typical of the treatment of the time was the tendency to devote only a single chapter to qualitative research and to frame its prime utility as exploratory. Both in the texts and in the literature, there was virtually no discussion of qualitative methods in the context of evaluation. In neither Fischer's influential review of social work effectiveness nor his later clarion call for a scientific revolution in social work was there any mention of qualitative methods (Fischer, 1973, 1981). Rather debate focused on how greater scientific rigour could be brought to the task of evaluation and how quantitative research needed to be better integrated into practice. (This came to be called the research utilization debate.)

A further indicator of the state of affairs of the times was the goings-on in the social work PhD programmes. The number of such programmes rapidly increased over this timespan. However, the emphasis was on programmes strong in quantitative research methods and on quantitative, empirical dissertations (Guzzetta, 1982). One suspects that few social work academicians would have identified themselves as qualitative methodologists.

The intent of the above abbreviated discussion is simply to set the stage. If we fast-forward to the present, much has changed and along with it the salience of the question of legitimacy of qualitative methods. We have witnessed protracted epistemological debates of the kind that Haworth has termed paradigm wars (1991). One hopes that much of this is behind us and that we can get on with the business of using qualitative research methods without having to justify that use.

A brief look at the current landscape and where we are today with qualitative methods and qualitative evaluative research in social work and social care supports the point. The murky world of the present could probably best be characterized as one in which mixed methodologies, or what Bergin and Garfield (1994) term methodological pluralism, dominates. While some might see positivist methods as obsolete (Heineman, 1981) they continue to be the dominant force in research and in evaluation. However, qualitative methods have become increasingly accepted. There also have been some significant attempts at *rapprochement* (Reid, 1994). Examples of change would include the ever-growing body of publications in qualitative methods. (Sage Publications, for example, has several whole series devoted to specific issues in qualitative evaluative research.) There are also various journals devoted entirely or in large part to the topic, such as *Qualitative Inquiry, Qualitative Sociology,* the *Journal of Narrative and Life History,* and *Qualitative Health Research.* An interesting example in social work is the journal *Reflections: Narratives of Professional Helping,* which publishes accounts of practitioner narratives.

Perhaps one of the most striking examples of change is shown by the different editions of the popular Rubin and Babbie social work research text. In the most current edition, the authors note that one of the most substantial changes is in the extensive addition of qualitative material. In the preface, they list the following significant changes, all of which relate to issues raised by qualitative methods:

- Expanded coverage of content on qualitative inquiry.
- New illustrations of how qualitative and quantitative methods can be integrated.
- Increased acknowledgment of epistemological approaches other than positivism and post-positivism.
- Demonstrations of connections between epistemology and research methods. (Rubin and Babbie, 1997: 6)

In a similar vein, the 1997 edition of the text by Grinnell is now entitled *Social Work Research and Evaluation: Quantitative and Qualitative Approaches* and includes five new chapters on qualitative research. In the general field of psychotherapy, the 1986 edition of the *Handbook of Psychotherapy and Behavior Change* (Garfield and Bergin) makes no mention of qualitative research while the 1994 edition has numerous references. Another barometer of the current state of affairs is the number of newly minted PhDs who identify with qualitative methods or did a qualitative dissertation. The author has been involved in faculty search efforts for the last several years and has been astounded by the number of would-be faculty who did qualitative dissertations. A review of the Council on Social Work Education *Teachers Registry* for March 1998 revealed that five of 36 candidates indicated that qualitative methods was one of their *primary* areas of interest (CSWE, 1998).

Yet another barometer of change is the growth of interest groups. A number of qualitative methods interest groups now exist in social work and related fields. The Study Group for Philosophical Issues in Social Work has as one of its focal points qualitative research. The Internet and the World Wide Web have made possible rapid communication among qualitative research interest groups. Examples of this trend are the qualitative software and the qualitative research listservs (*Qualrs-L* and *Qual Software* among others). These listservs facilitate ongoing discussion of current issues and techniques. The international flavour of this development is illustrated by the formation of the Asia Pacific Region Association of Qualitative Researchers, with its headquarters in Melbourne, Australia.

The point is not to suggest that qualitative methods have triumphed. Rather it is to claim that the situation has changed, is changing, and that legitimacy is not the major issue it once was.

Obstacles of the mundane but important variety

Qualitative research and evaluation is not for the faint of heart. Questions of epistemology and utility aside, qualitative methods are, generally speaking, time consuming and difficult to master. The task by its very nature is different from other forms of research. The implications of this difference will be discussed in this section.

Quantitative research and evaluation is primarily founded on the principle of measurement (Hudson, 1978). Measurement is in turn linked to outcomes as the major task of evaluation. Outcomes are operational measures of key programmatic and clinical variables. Outcome research has become more or less the method of choice in assessing programme and clinical effectiveness. One of the major tasks of quantitative research is the development of valid and reliable measures of outcomes; i.e. instrumentation. Thus, there is a continuing tendency to associate evaluation with specific tests and scales. Framed in this way, the clinical or programmatic evaluative task is to select the appropriate instrument(s) and to use it to assess the effectiveness of practice. Walter Hudson has developed numerous such measurement instruments for evaluation of clinical practice (1982). These can be in the form of paper and pencil tests or they can be accomplished with the use of a personal computer. Ease of use is the major appeal; it is also a handy-dandy way to do single-subject research. The use of such simple tests to conduct single-subject research becomes a way of linking research and practice. However, and as is true of all measurement, it presupposes an operational link between the instrument and that which it is intended to measure (a matter for more complete debate elsewhere in this book). This measurement-oriented approach is limited in its actual practice utility. The jury is still out on the matter, but there seems little evidence that single-subject design has been widely embraced by the practice community.

There have been some similar efforts to develop and promulgate the qualitative equivalent to instrumentation. As previously noted, this is not the author's view but is part of the continuing tendency to frame qualitative methods in ways analogous to quantitative methods. An article by Franklin and Jordan (1995) is instructive in this regard. This was a review of efforts to develop and utilize abbreviated forms of qualitative assessment and to apply them to practice evaluation. While such qualitative instruments have some utility and may make qualitative research more acceptable in traditional settings or those that favour multiple methods, the appeal of this form of evaluation is limited. It is in the extended, detailed forms of qualitative data, those of solid observation, of rich storytelling and of narrative that the real potential of qualitative methods lies. These are the real sources of appeal to clinical practitioners and ought to be the focus of qualitative evaluation.

However, there is no easy shortcut to narrative forms of evaluation and data gathering. It is precisely the mundane and detailed descriptive type of data which have the most potential for assessing and/or under-standing practice. It is the rich observational and interview detail that takes us into the worlds of others. While there have been numerous studies of homelessness and shelters, what better conveys the homeless experience for women than Liebow's *Tell Them Who I Am* (1993)? What better conveys life on the street for black inner city teens than Anderson's *Streetwise* (1990)? There is no substitute for density and detail. Qual-itative practice evaluation at its best must honour this tradition.

In the scheme of things, this means spending time in the field, taking extensive fieldnotes, and conducting in-depth interviews. This is a time-consuming and difficult process and one that requires specific training. In turn, the qualitative data gathered in this fashion must be turned into a form that is suitable for analysis. The data are essentially textual in nature, and therein lies one of the obstacles to their use in practice evaluation. Collecting, organizing and analysing textual material is tedious. If we are to be at all honest with ourselves, we must recognize that the adaptation of this form of data gathering and research to actual practice situations is indeed problematic.

The primary way in which such data are likely to be gathered in clinical practice is as a result of some form of unstructured or loosely structured interviewing. The interview situation is after all the centre-piece of most forms of clinical practice. The recording of interviews in audio and sometimes video form is quite common in both social work education and in practice. The recording process is relatively easily accomplished. While there may be concerns that recording may interfere with the naturalness of the situation, we live in a society in which we are getting accustomed to being recorded. It is the next steps in what might be termed the transformational process that become obstacles for the practitioner. Transformation in this case refers to the transformation of verbal and non-verbal information into usable qualitative data. However much a practitioner may value narrative data, the tapes are of limited use unless they are transcribed and turned into text. Personal experience and that of colleagues and students suggest that a good typist will need anywhere from 4 to 8 hours to transcribe one hour of audiotape. The 'coding' and transcribing of videotapes would be geometrically much higher. The same would be true if one were working with group interview or focus group data, forms of qualitative data gathering that have become increasingly popular. While there is considerable value in an interactive sense in the researcher-practitioner transcribing their own tapes, few would have the time or patience for this task. Searight (now Smith) in an early attempt at a qualitative self-evaluation of practice (1988) noted that while the taping of practice sessions went smoothly, the transcription of tapes was so time consuming as to be impractical. If tapes are to be farmed out to a commercial firm it will be costly, and the turnaround time may be lengthy. Most tapes also require considerable editing to be useful.

Two points flow from the discussion so far: one is the assumption that at present transcribed audiotapes are the single most vital and useful type of qualitative data. The second is that the transcription process is a mundane but significant barrier to the greater incorporation of qualitative research methods into practice evaluation.

Alas, the obstacles and difficulties do not stop there. Even if one has solid and well-transcribed data, how does one analyse them? Many qualitative researchers would probably agree that the analysis components of qualitative methods are among the most difficult and the least well developed. Perhaps the most conventional approach and actually the most useful is a form of thematic or content analysis (Patton, 1990). That is, one sorts the data into a number of recurrent themes or patterns. The more extensive the volume of the data, the more difficult the task. In the very recent past, most of this was done by hand. Typically data were put on to index cards and sorted into piles reflecting possible patterns. Over time, qualitative methodologists have come to rely on computer word-processing programs to facilitate the task. Such programs also have the advantage of having modest search and retrieval functions. Even so, the task remains a daunting one from both a time and a conceptual perspective.

The author firmly believes that the growth in qualitative forms of evaluation of practice will be stymied until problems of transcription and textual analysis can be solved. However, there is hope for change.

Opportunities of a technical type

While the time and costs of transcription and textual analysis are considerable, and thus continue to be issues, there is reason to believe this is in the process of change, and change occurring at an accelerating rate. The issue of transcriptions has been the topic of much discussion among qualitative methodologists on the various Internet listservs (see for example the Qualitative Research and Qualitative Software listservs). The existence of Internet listservs itself greatly expands the qualitative methods discussion process. Virtually any methodological topic can be and is debated. In the context of transcription issues, there has been a growing discussion of and interest in voice recognition computer software. Among these are such programs as Naturally Speaking and DragonDictate by Dragon Systems and ViaVoice Gold by IBM. These programs are relatively inexpensive and readily available commercially. They require the software to be vocally 'trained' by the user. That is, the software 'learns' to recognize the speech patterns and inflections of the user and to transcribe these patterns into word-processing-type documents. The learning curve at present is fairly steep in that much time must be spent on the training of the software. There are also continuing questions of accuracy and speed. Clearly, this software is still in its infancy and users tend to be divided on its current utility. As of this date there is no published research discussing the merits of such software. However, there is great future potential in this software to solve some of the difficulties of the transcription process. The author is confident that by the time this book is published, there will be substantial improvements in voice-activated software. Given the recent development of the digital tape recorder, we may shortly reach the point where a clear audiotape could be directly transcribed into a computer.

Once transcribed, data must be analysed. This too has been a significant obstacle. As noted, this has been done by hand or with the assistance of word processors. Today, there is growing availability and use of a number of qualitative analysis software packages. Of note are such packages as ATLAS/ti (1998), Ethnograph (1998) and NUD*IST (1997). The level of support for such packages is on the rise. There are also various Internet sites devoted to each particular program. The standardization of such programs facilitates training and the sharing of qualitative data. In an attempt to promote such standardization and cooperation amongst qualitative researchers in different disciplines, the interdisciplinary Qualitative Research Committee on the campus at which the author teaches recently adopted NUD*IST as the university-wide standard.

These software programs facilitate a form of thematic analysis, which can be simple or complex depending on the theoretical proclivities of the researcher. The analysis is both more powerful and more efficient than that possible using earlier techniques. While much further along than voice recognition software, it would be fair to say that these programs are still somewhat difficult to learn and use. Again, it is clear that there is a growing market for such programs and that over time they will get better and better.

All of this is not to suggest that computers have solved the drudgery problems associated with the collection and analysis of qualitative data. Rather, the claim is that we may be at the point where a technical breakthrough that will facilitate the democratization of qualitative data processing is possible. This, rather than the instrumental approach to qualitative research, is where much of the potential for growth in the application of qualitative evaluative method lies.

Opportunities of a non-technical type: the world of clinical practice

The opportunities for the further use of qualitative forms of evaluation are not simply a result of technological changes that facilitate the collection and analysis of qualitative data. There has also been a growing appreciation of practice approaches that have natural affinities with qualitative methods.

As previously noted, there has been an explosion of interest in narrative forms of practice. Also of significance is the growth of various new forms of family therapy. Family therapy has been closely associated with systems theory. Systems theory while not a qualitative approach *per se* has some degree of confluence with it: both share an emphasis on the complexities of interactions and the importance of context (Moon et al., 1990).

Some family practitioners question the utility of scientific method. Of particular interest is the growing importance of social construction approaches to family therapy, which clearly build on some of the same roots as qualitative methods (Atwood, 1996). The interdisciplinary American Association for Marriage and Family Therapy through its *Journal of Marital and Family Therapy* has encouraged the use of qualitative methods to complement the more traditional forms of research. Its editorial in October 1990 called for the greater use of qualitative evaluative methods to study complex interactions, discover theoretical propositions and to provide contextual data (Sprenkle, 1990). The *JMFT* continues to encourage the submission of qualitative-based articles and in its July 1994 issue had a special section on qualitative research. The influential text, *Research Methods in Family Therapy*, contains articles on such qualitative methods topics as ethnographic research, grounded theory methods, phenomenology, conversational analysis and focus groups (Sprenkle and Moon, 1996).

Some leading social work educators have raised questions about which voices are heard or not heard in research and practice. Hartman refers to the tendency for expert and scientific forms of knowledge building to subjugate other forms of knowledge. Borrowing from Foucault she refers to the former as 'global unitary knowledges' and claims that social workers must entertain the claims of local, discontinuous and illegitimate knowledge, the claims of those who have been silent (Hartman, 1992). This is consistent with the position of Sjoberg, who maintains that the task of qualitative methods and a case study approach is to give the poor a voice (Feagin et al., 1991).

Feminists and feminist forms of practice have been gaining a greater voice in practice. Feminists have long had a connection to qualitative forms of research. The classic work *Women's Ways of Knowing* challenged conventional academic wisdom about how women develop intellectually. The research was based on participatory, open-ended interviews that were consonant with the very model of knowledge building advocated by the authors (Belenky et al., 1986). In a similar vein Liane Davis (1994) has argued that that feminist research is inherently qualitative.

Thus on a philosophical and ideological level, qualitative methods have a new and potentially growing audience. There is increasing acceptance of a variety of methodologies. The cognitive psychologist, Jerome Bruner (1984), has discussed alternative ways that humans process information. In his view, the narrative mode is different from but as important as the scientific or paradigmatic mode. Hartman (1992) has suggested that there are many ways of knowing and that social work must honour these. Again the point is not that qualitative logic and methods are superior but that the dialogue of evaluation *must* include both qualitative and quantitative approaches.

Continuing issues

Clearly, in both social work and in related fields we are on the doorstep of a widespread use of qualitative data-gathering approaches and of their application in evaluation. This is a cause for some celebration and satisfaction.

However, there remain a number of significant issues that still need to be addressed. In a sense these issues are of an internal nature. That is, the debate is less that of qualitative vs. quantitative than about how and in what ways we will use qualitative evaluation approaches. The central issues relate to the role of theory and conceptualization and of training.

The role of theory and conceptualization

The potential exists for increased use of qualitative data and qualitative methods of evaluation. But perhaps analogous to Ogburn's (1964) theory of cultural lag, we are in danger that the technological will outpace and perhaps even overwhelm the conceptual. Computers, tape recorders and software may facilitate the collection of literally mounds of raw data, but what then do we do with them? Mishler (1995) reminds us that transcriptions are not facts *per se* but rather a form of selective reconstruction and transformation. The present author worries about what he terms 'narrativism'. This is the excessive use of extended quotes. Quotes are a necessary part of a qualitative report but they lose their effect when piled one on top of another with little conceptual purpose. Over the course of the years, I have read numerous student papers and have developed the dreadful habit of skimming through rather than reading extended quotes in research papers.

Bergin and Garfield (1994) lament what they see as the atheoretical nature of much contemporary clinical research. In a controversial piece, Kreuger (1997) has prophesized the death of social work at the hands of technology. Kreuger also views the old theoretical models as obsolete and unnecessary in his brave new world. While I may share some of Kreuger's views about the likely inroads of technology, I have difficulty with the argument that we are moving beyond the need for conceptual models. On the contrary, evaluation in the next millennia will remain both a political and conceptual task. There is no escape now nor will there be in the future from the essential political question: 'evaluation for whom and for what purposes?' Likewise, there is a need to engage with the transformational possibilities of qualitative methods. Well-done qualitative research has the potential to transform not only the data but also the researcher. To do this, we must meaningfully engage the researcher-practitioner, who in turn must fully engage his or her own data. The guiding questions of qualitative research must emerge from clinical experience and determine research design (see Miller and Crabtree, 1994).

At present, there is almost a dichotomous quality to the discussion and presentation of qualitative methods and qualitative forms of evaluation. Much of the discussion is pragmatic and even technical in nature. This is particularly true of the listservs. What are the best qualitative analysis programs, what are the best recording devices, what are the logistics of focus group interviews, what are the pros and cons of voice-activated software? Although I place some value on such discussions and believe that technical advances will lead to the greater use of qualitative methods, what may be lost is awareness of the continuing importance of the conceptual. At present, much of the conceptual discussion has become esoteric and arcane. One of the more important interdisciplinary qualitative journals, *Qualitative Inquiry* tends to highlight the more esoteric interests of some qualitative researchers. Thus we have seemingly endless discussions by deconstructionists, postmodernists, post-postmodernists, radical feminists, etc. We need to find a greater degree of balance between the theoretical and the esoteric both in social work and in wider arenas. There is much continuing value in such classic theoretical traditions as symbolic interactionism and conflict theory. Our discussion of evaluation must be both politically realistic and theoretically grounded if qualitative methods are to be meaningfully employed and used in ways other than the instrumental.

Training

While we can scan in vast amounts of information into computers we need to think through what information we need and why. The effective practitioner needs training in both qualitative method and theory. One does not simply do qualitative evaluation; one must think about and understand the pros and cons of the different data-gathering methods and how they might apply to the issue at hand. One must also be committed to research, both qualitative and quantitative, in social work education and practice. Only through knowledge of relevant theories and adequate training in methods will practitioners be able to integrate research in the field and in practice. The dilemma in social work education is how to do all of the above in an ever pressured curriculum.

Some illustrative examples

What follows is an attempt to illustrate the discussion of obstacles and opportunities via personal research experience and that of students and colleagues.

Starting with the latter, one of my colleagues, Dr Maria Bartlett, is a qualitative methodologist, a practitioner and a practice theory teacher. She also chairs the Health Concentration – one of three areas of social work practice specialization within the School. One of her interests is in working with and studying older people with dementia. A technique she uses to engage the elderly in conversation is the life review. The life review has gained in popularity among social workers in gerontology but has rarely been used with the demented. Bartlett believes that older people with mild to moderate impairment can still tell their story. Her life review is in essence a loosely structured qualitative interview. The interview is taped and transcribed and can be used for practice, teaching and research purposes. Her simple but effective life review consists of three basic questions: 'Tell me about your childhood . . . your middle age and now' (Bartlett, 1995).

In 1988 Priscilla Searight (now Smith) pioneered the use of qualitative methods to evaluate one's own practice. In her dissertation, Smith did a study of her family-therapy-type social work practice in a day treatment school. The research involved self-reflections on practice, and detailed observational descriptions of the practice context and sessions with clients. She saw herself as a participant-observer practitioner. Smith taped the practice sessions but found it was not feasible to transcribe all the data herself and too costly and time consuming to pay someone else do it. In spite of this, she developed a vast set of fieldnotes and self-reflective data. Her study showed that the line between research and practice is a thin one and to some extent arbitrary. In addition, one of her major conclusions, and one generally overlooked in much evaluative research, was that her practice could only be understood and evaluated in light of data gathered on the wider agency and institutional context (Searight, 1988).

A continuing source of feedback is my contact with students who take a master's course on qualitative research methods. In a previous article, two of these students demonstrated the value of the qualitative case study in revealing significant aspects of a social work practice setting (Ruckdeschel et al., 1994). Some of my more recent students have continued to explore evaluative applications of qualitative methods. Typically, these students take copious fieldnotes and conduct, audiotape and transcribe in-depth interviews using the interview guide approach. Much of the research is done in a team format with a final paper that is a team product. Many of the students are current or former practitioners. In correspondence, one such student, K. Mills observed the following:

Qualitative research has been an exciting discovery for me. My prior experience with research had been with the quantitative method, which I found to be very cumbersome, difficult, and an extremely unfulfilling approach for me to use. On the other hand, qualitative research has been like a breath of fresh air. I find this method to be stimulating and rewarding.

This method catches aspects of the key players and the setting, that are not easily measured and may perhaps otherwise go unnoticed. The process of data collection using in-depth, open-ended interviews, direct observation, and written documents is a very natural method of research for social work professionals to use. At the conclusion of my research, I feel as though I have gained a much deeper and more complete understanding of my subjects and their experiences, opinions, feelings, and knowledge.

Another student, E. Halterman, experimented with an early version of the voice recognition programs called Voice Pad by Kursweil. She made the attempt to use this program because of her previous experience with the difficulties of transcribing audiotapes. Whilst the experiment was unsuccessful for the kinds of reasons previously noted, the student firmly believes voice recognition software, when and if perfected, would allow the clinician to transcribe notes faster and to conduct more interviews and would thus facilitate research on practice. Interestingly, both students did their research projects at women's shelters.

In the summer of 1997, I was asked by a major university-wide committee to do an assessment of the status of the ethics curriculum at the university. The assessment was connected to strategic planning across the university. The evaluation was to be of a qualitative nature. Prior efforts using quantitative methods had not been notably successful. The request was illustrative in that it suggested that there were few if any lingering concerns in the minds of policy planners relative to the legitimacy of qualitative methods. It also suggested that qualitative methods could yield the kind of in-depth data that would facilitate a better understanding of the key issues. The context was political: results of the research would have far-ranging implications for the undergraduate and graduate curriculum of a Catholic Jesuit university.

The research involved the gathering of documents and the in-depth interviewing of key faculty informants who had expertise on the topic. An interview guide was used and all interviews were audiotaped. Extensive handwritten notes were taken at each interview. The interviews were to be transcribed and analysed using newly acquired NUD*IST 4 software, the latter being a key selling point in getting the research funded internally.

All of the above essentially suggests opportunities. There was also a variety of obstacles; a major issue was the transcription and analysis of the data. Due to insufficient support, the audiotapes piled up and were not transcribed in a timely fashion. For want of fully transcribed data, it was not possible to use the computer software analysis package. Transcribing remains an obstacle!

By mid-fall 1997 a report of some kind was due. I constructed what I termed a preliminary report based on handwritten notes of the interviews and my sense of what transpired in those interviews. Among the findings was the lack of faculty support for a university-wide centre to co-ordinate the teaching of ethics, in spite of administrative advocacy and support for such a centre. Instead the faculty interviewed favoured more localized, grassroots faculty development. The report was presented at a number of meetings and essentially carried the day, notwithstanding the fact that I noted and was well aware of the limitations of the data.

The majority of the tapes remain untransribed. There will probably be no further reports nor in a political sense is there a need for more complete reports. It is the overall context of the research that determined its value, rather than a particular set of outcomes or some instrument that could be validated.

We may be on the brink of an explosion in use of qualitative methods of data gathering and evaluation of social work practice. We need to put aside issues of legitimacy and focus instead on the practical uses of this method and the appropriate role of technology, theory and training.

Note

Study Group for Philosophical Issues in Social Work. 697 Bement Avenue, Staten Island: New York.

References

Anderson, E. (1990) *Streetwise*. Chicago: University of Chicago Press.

ATLAS/ti (1998) Scolari Sage Publications Software. Thousand Oaks, CA: Sage.

Atwood, J. (1996) *Family Scripts*. Washington, DC: Accelerated Development.

Bartlett, M. (1995) 'Looking back: the value of reminiscence', *Newsletter of the Alzheimer's Association St Louis Chapter*. January: 7.

Belenky, M., Clinchy B., Goldberger, N. and Tarule, J. (1986) *Women's Ways of Knowing*. New York: Basic Books.

Bergin, A. and Garfield, S. (1994) *Handbook of Psychotherapy and Behavior Change*. New York: Wiley.

Bruner, J. (1984) 'Narrative though neglected', *American Psychological Association Monitor*, 15 (11): 1.

Council on Social Work Education (1998) *Teachers Registry and Information Service*. March. Alexander, VA: CSWE.

Davis, L. (1994) 'Is feminist research inherently qualitative, and is it a fundamentally different approach to research?' in W. Hudson and P. Nurius (eds), *Controversial Issues in Social Work Research*. Boston: Allyn & Bacon. pp. 63–74.

Ethnograph (1998) Qualis Research Associates. Amherst, MA.

Feagin, J.R., Orum, J. and Sjoberg, G. (1991) *A Case for the Case Study*. Chapel Hill, NC: University of North Carolina Press.

Fischer, J. (1973) 'Is social work effective: a review', *Social Work*, 18 (1): 5–20.

Fischer, J. (1981) 'The social work revolution', *Social Work*, 26 (3): 199–207.

Franklin, C. and Jordan, C. (1995) 'Qualitative assessment: a methodological review', *Families in Society: The Journal of Contemporary Human Services*, 76 (5): 281–295.

Garfield, S. and Bergin, A. (1986) *Handbook of Psychotherapy and Behavior Change.* New York: Wiley.

Goldstein, H. (1991) 'Qualitative research and social work practice: partners in discoveries', *Journal of Sociology and Social Welfare*, 18 (4): 101–119.

Grinnell, R. (1997) *Social Work Research and Evaluation: Quantitative and Qualitative Approaches.* Itasca, IL: F.E. Peacock.

Guzzetta, C. (1982) 'Research education in social work doctoral programs', in J. Stretch and A. Rosen (eds), *Doctoral Education in Social Work: Issues, Perspectives, and Evaluation.* St Louis: Group for the Advancement of Doctoral Education. pp. 52–65.

Hartman, A. (1992) 'In search of subjugated knowledge', *Social Work*, 37 (6): 483–484.

Haworth, G. (1991) 'My paradigm can beat your paradigm: some reflections on knowledge conflicts', *Journal of Sociology and Social Welfare*, 18 (4): 35–50.

Heineman, M. (1981) 'The obsolete scientific imperative in social work research', *Social Service Review*, 55 (3): 371–397.

Heineman-Pieper, M. (1994) 'Science not scientism: the robustness of naturalistic clinical research', in E. Sherman and W. Reid (eds), *Qualitative Research in Social Work.* New York: Columbia University Press. pp. 71–88.

Hudson, W.W. (1978) 'First axioms of treatment', *Social Work*, 23 (1): 65.

Hudson, W.W. (1982) *The Clinical Measurement Package.* Homewood, IL: Dorsey Press.

Kreuger, L. (1997) 'The end of social work', *Journal of Social Work Education*, 33 (1): 19–27.

Liebow, E. (1993) *Tell Them Who I Am: The Lives of Homeless Women.* New York: Free Press.

Miller, L. and Crabtree, B. (1994) 'Clinical research', in N. Denzin and Y. Lincoln (eds), *Handbook of Qualitative Research.* Thousand Oaks, CA: Sage. pp. 340–352.

Mishler, E. (1995) Transcription advice. November 2. Archives, <Qualrs-L@UGA.cc.UGA.edu>.

Moon, S., Dillon, D. and Sprenkle, D. (1990) 'Family therapy and qualitative research', *Journal of Marital and Family Therapy*, 16 (4): 357–375.

Ogburn, W. (1964) *Social Change.* Gloucester, MA: Peter Smith.

Patton, M. (1990) *Qualitative Evaluation and Research Methods.* Newbury Park, CA: Sage.

Qualitative Research for the Human Sciences. *Qualrs-L@UGA.cc.UGA.edu*

Qualitative Software. *Qual-Software@ mailbase.ac.uk*

QSR NUD*IST Software for Qualitative Data Analysis (1997) Thousand Oaks, CA: SCOLARI/Sage.

Reid, W.J. (1994) 'Reframing the epistemological debate', in E. Sherman and W. Reid (eds), *Qualitative Research in Social Work.* New York: Columbia University Press. pp. 464–486.

Rubin, A. and Babbie, E. (1997) *Research Methods for Social Work.* Pacific Grove, CA: Brooks/Cole.

Ruckdeschel, R., Earnshaw P. and Firrek, A. (1994) 'The qualitative case study and evaluation: issue, methods and examples', in E. Sherman and W. Reid (eds), *Qualitative Research in Social Work*. New York: Columbia University Press. pp. 251–264.

Searight, P. (1988) 'Utilizing qualitative research to self-evaluate direct practice'. Doctoral dissertation, Saint Louis University, St Louis.

Sprenkle, D. (1990) 'Editorial', *Journal of Marital and Family Therapy*, 16 (4): 339.

Sprenkle, D. and Moon, M. (1996) *Research Methods in Family Therapy*. New York: Guilford Press.

12

SINGLE-SYSTEM EVALUATION

Martin Bloom

Unlike Molière's *Bourgeois Gentleman*, a country bumpkin who was astonished to learn that he had been speaking prose all of his life without knowing it, social workers and other helping professionals should not be surprised at the observation that they have always been evaluating their practice as a part of good service. Granted, they may not know the technical vocabulary for discussing objective measures of client outcomes – this is what this chapter (and collateral references) will sketch. However, the fundamental evaluation step is first taken when professionals learn to define clearly the client's problems, target the issues of highest priority, use specific interventions known to be useful in resolving these kinds of problems or challenges, and then proceed to monitor how the problems change (and the other strengths do not change) during and after the service programme. Good problem-solving practice intrinsically involves good evaluation procedures.

Introduction to single-system designs

Kazi and Wilson (1996) report a straightforward single-case evaluation (among other topics) in a British social work agency that will service as a multi-purpose introduction to this methodology. SH, an 11–year-old girl, was reported having difficulty settling into a new school. She was described as 'weepy', crying often both at home and at school to the extent that she was unable to sleep at night and was refusing to go to school. The parents tried unsuccessfully to help, and finally turned to a social work agency. 'The social worker's intervention programme consisted of a plan to enhance SH's importance in the school, combined with frequent counselling, involving both the social worker and relevant teachers' (1996: 13). Within four weeks of the beginning of service, crying had ceased at home and in school.

Let's first examine this situation for its essential practice and evaluation ingredients. Other cases will be more complex, but complexity is a matter of degree, and is not qualitatively different from a simple case. Clearly, the crying behaviour was dysfunctional for the child and problematic for parents and in the classroom. No other problems were mentioned by Kazi and Wilson, and so crying becomes the sole target behaviour. Crying is easily recognized, and so the social worker (whom I will call the practitioner/evaluator because I want to emphasize the joint roles being performed) chose to measure it, with both the form teacher and SH herself reporting crying episodes.

In order to know if the problem behaviour is improving or not, it is necessary to 'start where the client is' – that is, to have a point of reference or baseline. In this case, SH had been crying a considerable amount for a long period of time, according to parents and teachers. So, rather than taking more time to directly document the problem – which is the usual procedure when we are not certain of the exact nature of the problem – the practitioner/evaluator chose to estimate the baseline rate of crying. This is called a retrospective baseline, and it consisted of recalling when SH had been crying, and then plotting on a graph when these times occurred (see Figure 12.1).

The graph is simply a drawing in which the amount or intensity of some target behaviour is indicated on the vertical column (for example the number of times a person cries), and time indicated on the horizontal line as regular intervals (for instance, days or weeks in which some behaviour may occur). Rather than record each specific instance of crying – which could be done with some effort, such as measuring the number of times SH cried each day, or the duration of each occasion of crying –

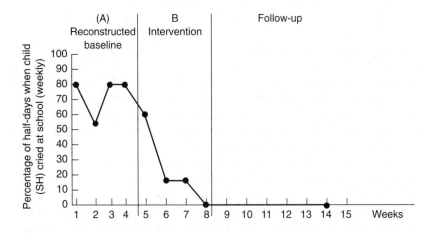

Figure 12.1 *Percentage of half-days when child (SH) cried at school, per week (adapted from Kazi and Wilson, 1996)*

the practitioner/evaluator chose to measure a larger unit, the percentage of half-days per week when SH cried in school. Collecting information and recording it on a graph is always a balance between how much time the rater has available and what degree of completeness of information is desirable. What we see in Figure 12.1 is a reconstructed baseline of four weeks, followed by the direct collecting of information each week of the intervention period. This characterizes a basic single-system design usually labelled as the AB design, where A is always a baseline (a no-service observation period) and B is a distinctive intervention. One can also introduce additional interventions C, D, E . . . , or one can modify the existing intervention, B^1, B^2, etc. Each of these becomes a distinctive design because it changes the logical arrangements among parts.

A line is drawn *between* weeks four and five, since the intervention began in week five and we want to contrast it with the baseline period, weeks one to four; that is, we wanted to contrast the whole of the non-intervention baseline period with the whole of the intervention period. Each dot on the graph represents the intersection of the target problem (occurrences of the target behaviour per week, using the unit of half-days when SH cried in school) and time (weekly units, recorded at the end of the week). So, on week five, she cried 60 per cent of the half-days; then on week six, she cried 20 per cent. These record objective events and thus add a bit of starch to the comment that the child is 'improving'.

As we can read from the graph (Figure 12.1), there appears to be a clear difference between the reconstructed baseline level of crying behaviour (and the pre-existing long-term pattern of crying behaviour that is all too familiar to parents and teachers), and the sharp drop in that problem behaviour to zero that occurs during the intervention period. Then, six weeks later, the evaluator checked back with the teachers to ask how often SH was crying in school. We read that there was no crying in the post-study period, suggesting that the behaviour change was stable and persistent.

Interestingly, since the problem behaviour was also occurring at home, the practitioner/evaluator decided to apply the same intervention at home on a daily basis, without any baseline (see Figure 12.2 where this *daily* monitoring is telescoped into Figure 12.1's weekly monitoring to show the same time periods being represented). This intervention occurs simultaneously with the school intervention in weeks six and seven. Crying stops occurring in the second period of time (corresponding to week seven), while it ceases in the eighth week in school.

Overall, what we see is a successful and persisting outcome of a brief intervention applied to school and home situations. It is very tempting to say that this also shows good practice, but unfortunately we cannot logically make this statement because of the limitations of the evaluation design, as I will discuss shortly. However, the key point is that important changes in client behaviour have occurred. The girl, her parents, and her

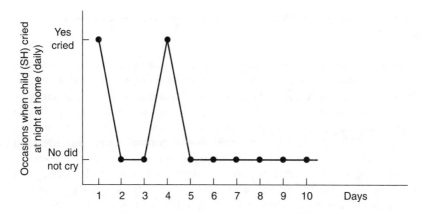

Figure 12.2 *Occasions when child (SH) cried at night at home (recorded on school days of weeks 6 and 7) (adapted from Kazi and Wilson, 1996)*

teachers and peers could not be happier with these constructive out-comes. We could impose some relatively simple statistical analyses (or computer analyses) to demonstrate that these results are also statistically significant at, say, the $p<.05$ level. But the present outcomes are very clinically distinct and do not need statistical support as such; visual analysis will suffice. Most other clinical situations are not as clear, and would benefit from statistical analysis as well (cf. Bloom et al., 1995).

There are relatively few complicated procedures in this level of evalu-ation and analysis, which means that this type of joint practice and evaluation is accessible to practically all social workers and other helping professionals, if they can clearly identify:

1   target events to be changed – which could include strengths to be increased as well as problems to be decreased;
2   clear interventions – so as to be able to know what it is that is associated with a positive change situation and thus be able to use this method again in other cases; and
3   consistent objective monitoring over time so as to be able to compare the reference point (baseline) with the intervention period changes.

It really is a relatively simple matter, even though I have collaborated in writing a 681-page book detailing how these simple procedures can be amplified to fit almost any helping context (Bloom et al., 1995). Critics have written at least an equal amount warning potential users that every choice they make in considering single-system evaluation can lead to hellfire and damnation. The truth is probably somewhere in between these views.

A brief history of evaluation and social services: hellfire and damnation

It might be instructive to look back for a moment at the history of evaluation of social services. In a *Letter to Some Friends of the Poor, in Great Britain* (1795), Casper von Voght gave an account of the management of the poor in Hamburg since the year 1788, including a rough indication of the success of this 'experiment', and hence its value as a model to others worldwide seeking to gain some control over the spiralling problems of pauperism. The Hamburg group used both a centralized secular organization and a policy of personal sustained contact with participants – the hallmarks of modern social services. Using data from later reports, Crooker summarizes von Voght's early evaluations:

> At the end of thirteen years, in 1801, the results accomplished by this system of poor-relief in Hamburg were these: – beggary had been completely extermin- ated; a vast amount of terrible wretchedness had been relieved and much more prevented; many poor had been furnished work, and many had been taught a trade and made self-dependent; while in the free schools, 'gentle means and perseverance got at last the better of a great part of the vices that grow in children who are trained up in beggary.' In 1788 there were 5,166 paupers in a terrible condition; in 1801 there were only 2,689, and these were in a comfortable condition. In 1788 there were 2,225 child paupers; in 1801 there were only 400 child-paupers, and they were being cared for in homes or hospitals, or were being trained in schools. And the amount of money spent annually to give the poor this better care was really not nearly so large as the sum practically thrown away before 1788. (Crooker, 1889: 85)

Even granting some leeway for looseness of language and uncertain definition of terms, these are problems and results that resonated with thoughtful social activists of the late eighteenth and early nineteenth centuries all over the world.

The Hamburg experiment, for example, was very influential on the late eighteenth/early nineteenth-century London magistrate Patrick Colquhoun, whose 1806 treatise on indigence creatively built on von Voght's ideas, as well as those of economists Adam Smith, David Ricardo and Thomas Robert Malthus. Colquhoun clearly identified 'innocent, remedial, and culpable causes of indigence' and identified specific methods to treat or prevent each one. I view these as a beginning point in what is now termed empirical practice, when targets of concern and potential causes to be resolved are clearly identified. Innocent causes such as permanent mental and physical disorders, or the extremes of age, were to be taken care of simply because they were 'the casualties of human life'. Culpable causes of indigence, like laziness, drunkenness or systematic criminality, could only be resolved by improving morals (which leads to increased primary prevention emphasis on education and religion). However, it is with the remedial causes of indigence that Colquhoun is most concerned, such as 'temporary loss of work or sickness', ' a general stagnation of manufactures', or ' lying-in expenses'. Colquhoun's proposed solutions, from welfare to work, national insurance systems, national savings banks, education for labouring people and so forth, sound extraordinarily contemporary as we enter the twenty-first century to address similar problems of the poor.

In Scotland, the Reverend Thomas Chalmers designed rural and urban communal experiments addressing the pervasive conditions of poverty that might be considered an early form of systems theory applied to social concerns. One of his major contributions was a visitation programme that later came to be called 'friendly visiting' in the late nineteenth century and 'social work' in the twentieth. Brown describes this visitation programme as emanating from the pastor's religious duty to visit all parishioners, but when the numbers of the needy greatly expanded, Chalmers developed the idea of visitation by trained helpers to extend aid for material needs (Colquhoun's 'innocent causes'), but also something more:

> Chalmers instructed his [helpers] to visit the homes in their [districts] regularly, and familiarize themselves with all aspects of neighborhood life. They were to discover the character of each inhabitant, and investigate the relationships of kinship, friendship, and prior obligations that existed among their people. They were not simply to wait for the destitute to apply for help, but were to act on rumors, and their own instincts, to seek out the poor who might be too proud or too weak to request assistance. Further, they were to endeavor to close public houses, remove health hazards, strengthen families, and encourage education. In short, they were to be friends and advisors to their [district], but with good intentions firmly rooted in awareness of social realities. (Brown, 1982: 132)

Chalmers engaged in some enthusiastic evaluation of his work and believed that there was evidence of its success – 'assessment-based poor relief had been eliminated, four parish schools established, a chapel built, and an agency of visiting elders, deacons, and Sabbath-school teachers organized and trained' (Brown, 1982: 142). Critics quickly discovered that such statistics cut both ways, and once again found this version of social services wanting. Public accountability is a very old concern for every helping profession, and critics emerge from every nook and cranny.

To conclude this short history of social service and evaluation, many of these ideas were transmitted to the USA where they were first expressed in the New York Society for the Prevention of Pauperism, 1817–23 (Bloom and Klein, 1995–96). A half-century later they were incorporated, without acknowledgement, in 'early' social work agencies (see Chapter 3 by Reid and Zettergren in this volume for an account of more recent developments in empirical practice). Bloom and Fischer (1982) identified in Benjamin Franklin's *Autobiography* (Franklin, 1961) the first explicit use of what must now be called 'multiple baseline single-system evaluation'. What this awkward phrase means will be explained in the next few pages.

Parallel universes: good practice and good evaluation

The basics of single-system evaluation are clear and simple, and they are also potentially very useful to practitioners. This is the reason for their rapid increase in use over the past two decades. Let's list the parallels between good practice and good evaluation procedures:

Steps in good practice	*Steps in good evaluation of practice*
1 Establishing a trusting relationship that the service can help resolve client problems.	1 Establishing a trusting relationship that evaluation of service will help in monitoring and assessing the process and outcomes of the intervention process.
2 Clear definition of presenting problems and of strengths of client and environment.	2 Conceptualizing (in order to make explicit the relevant guiding theory) and translating client problems/strengths into targets of intervention (to decrease or increase, respectively).
3 Establishing client's immediate objectives and long-term goals.	3 Operationalizing objectives and goals as an alternative way of stating targets of intervention.
4 Contracting. Who will do what regarding the problems and/or goals/objectives?	4 Introducing notion of evaluation to client like physician using a thermometer to measure client states of health, at the same time as the intervention is introduced.
5 Assessing client's thoughts, feelings and actions, and the environmental factors involved.	5 Measure baseline conditions as reference point for subsequent changes, using any/all of behavioural observations, individualized rating scales, standardized questionnaires, logs, or non-reactive measures.
6 Practice design. The particular primary prevention, treatment or rehabilitation plan involving client and relevant others in the social and physical environment. This will probably require a training period for the client to understand the intervention.	6 Evaluation design. Draw up evaluation plans involving client, worker, relevant others in social and physical environment. This will probably require a training period for client to understand the intervention and evaluation.

7 Monitoring progress of the client using subjective measures repeated on occasion.

7 Monitoring progress of the objective measures repeated at regular intervals, and plotted on graphs.

8 Decision making, based on subjective, approximate assessment. The worker decides to increase, decrease, or not to change the intervention.

8 Decision making. Based on objective assessment, the worker considers the probabilities of effects associated with the intervention, with regard to making changes or not in the intervention. This information is added to their existing practice wisdom for the actual decision making.

9 Assuming that intervention goals have been met, the worker may introduce a maintenance phase regarding achieved goals, followed by a termination phase.

9 Assuming target objectives have been met on a stable and acceptable level, the worker will introduce a maintenance phase wherein the client is aided to perform the achieved target unaided by the worker, and will eventually begin the termination process.

10 Follow-up if client comes to the attention of the agency.

10 Follow-up included as measure of the staying power of the target achievement.

11 Reports to agency and profession.

11 Reports to agency and profession.

These parallels between practice and evaluation are not perfect, but their similarity is remarkable as we consider the implications of the scientific practitioners in the real world of complex and value-encased human situations.

The real world: 'indeterminate messes'

Unfortunately, life is not always as simple as the SH case, and every time we try to accommodate more complexity in real life situations, the procedures get increasingly detailed, and characterized, in Schon's words by 'indeterminate messes' (Schon, 1983). This complexity may deter potential users, which is a serious problem but not an insoluble one. Research on students introduced to the evaluation methodology shows that they are incorporating parts of the whole process into their practice. That is, students trained in single-system designs perform a number of the steps described above: they specify treatment goals in which clients participate (step 2); operationalize target problems (3); operationalize intervention methods (4); and monitor client change over time (7). Less frequently they use standardized questionnaires or rating forms to measure client change (step 5), graph the monitored data (7), or use statistical techniques to evaluate client change (8) (Blythe and Rodgers, 1993: 110; Gerdes et al., 1996; Richey et al., 1987; see also Reid and Zettergren, Chapter 3 in this volume).

In this chapter I will emphasize basics, and let interested readers explore further. Like many other aspects of life, practice makes, if not perfect, then easier and more useful. Once practitioners master these basic steps, they can continue to use them in their straightforward forms, or, as need and interest demand, they can explore references further for guidelines dealing with more complex situations.[1]

While critics of evaluation suggest that life is too complex, human problems too subtle, and events too changeable to be measured with crude, mechanical instruments and rigid procedures, we have to try our best to capture complexity, subtlety and changing conditions. Society demands an accounting and we had better be able to give it our best attempt. Readers will have to judge for themselves if, for example, the case of a crying child does capture with relatively simple but flexible procedures what is a messy life situation. By having a critical indicator factor, we can document accountability to parents and child, as well as to the school system.

Did evaluation help practice? This is a critical question, and I would suggest that the logical thinking process did help, and that empirical research data would be likely to support claims of accountability. Let me take a parallel instance from research recently conducted in South Africa. Faul, McMurtry and Hudson (1998) suggest that practitioners who used single-system designs and standardized scales showed improved outcomes for clients, compared with those practitioners who did not use these methods. They report tentative but empirically sound results from:

> a small-scale, quasi-experimental study in which one group of clients was served by workers who used these techniques and a second group was served by workers who did not. Findings indicate that clients in the group whose social workers . . . used [empirical clinical practice] techniques showed statistically significant greater improvement on measures of personal and social functioning than clients in the comparison group.

These authors point out the many limitations of their study, due in part to the political, technical and ethical difficulties of conducting research in the field setting. However, they make the interesting point that even though circumstances forced them to use a very weak single-system design (along with quite sophisticated measurement tools), their hypotheses were still supported, thus indicating the robustness of the model. They conclude:

> The results of this pilot study are encouraging in giving preliminary indications that the use of measurement instruments and single subject design

(single-system design) can improve not only the quality of evaluations but the quality of outcomes as well. If similar results occur from subsequent studies that are better able to control for some of the limitations of this study, perhaps it will be possible to resolve some of the arguments for and against the use of empirical practice methods as a regular element of social work services.

Perhaps equally important is the assertion that good practice should incorporate logical thinking. What single-system evaluation contributes to *all practitioners* is the making available of this underlying logic plus the objective documentation of accountability. This combination might contribute to the survival of the helping professions in a time of retrenchment.

The real world revisited: determining some of the indeterminate

With closer inspection of the Kazi and Wilson case example, we can see how much complexity of the situation they were able to incorporate, or we might extend the example a bit, so as to make the complexity clearer. First, even though only one target has been identified, it is obvious that this behaviour creates tensions for the whole family, as well as the girl and the school system. Peers are likely to know what is happening, and this may affect the girl's chances of making friends and participating in a positive youth culture. Picking out a critical target of intervention is likely to be linked to a host of other factors related in systemic fashion. The trick is to be able to pick out the critical target for intervention, the one by which a number of other factors stand or fall. This is where a good practice sense (practice wisdom) is most helpful (Klein and Bloom, 1995).

The practitioner/evaluator chose to look at any instance of crying in school half-days, which may reflect differences in morning versus afternoon behaviour, while not burdening the monitoring persons (teachers and child) with focusing on the negative behaviour *per se*. Indeed, as a general rule, it might have been better to accentuate the positive (non-crying behaviour), especially if the child is collecting data, than the negative.

That the teacher and the child were both monitoring the behaviour has several important implications. First, it provides an opportunity for a reliability check, to make sure we are measuring consistently, by having two different observers compare their data. No information is provided by Kazi and Wilson on this point, but I suspect observer reliability was high, given such an objective event as crying. This objectivity also contributes to a kind of convergent validity, a collective sense that we are in fact measuring what we seek to measure. Secondly, the fact that the child was collecting information provided her with feedback on how she was performing. We assume (a value judgement) that the child was as distressed at crying as were the others around her, and that she preferred not to cry, if given the choice. We know from prior psychological research that feedback is apt to improve performance, and so it turns out that this part of the evaluation procedure may be contributing to the practice goal. Thirdly, it also provides the child with a way of monitoring her own behaviour when the official intervention has ended. The practitioner/ evaluator may have discussed with the child the cues that lead up to a crying episode, and knowing this, as well as what to do about it (from the intervention experience), the child may be able to help herself in the future. This is part of the idea of a maintenance phase in practice (and evaluation). Again, evaluation directly serves practice at this juncture. Evaluation feedback may empower clients in their self-control.

Note that the client was involved in the evaluation as well as in the practice. She was a partner in the process. It was her values (and those of her parents and teachers) that were used to frame the objectives and goals. She was never harmed by the process, even though counselling may have led to some distressing insights – a fact of life that all practitioners experience. There were also compensating efforts, such as helping her recognize her value to the school. The child's involvement was a necessary ingredient both to practice and to evaluation, especially when the child was on her own (after treatment), for her to maintain her achievements.

The practitioner/evaluator has learned some important lessons too. First, there were significant changes in the child's behaviour – but, given the logical limitations of the evaluation design used (the AB design), we can only indicate that statistically significant change occurred, not that the given intervention caused that change. More complex designs can provide the logical basis for asserting causality (such as multiple baseline designs, as in the aforementioned self-report by the venerable Ben Franklin, or repeated measure designs like the ABAB design). However, there is a clear hint for the practitioner/evaluator that his/her practice method repertoire is strengthened by these results, and the practitioner/ evaluator is in a better position to test these methods through future practice choices and learn to what degree they really are what we think (hope?) them to be. I will return to designs shortly.

If you can put up with more discussion of the Kazi and Wilson case example, I will offer some critiques, because they have 'violated' some of the classical assumptions. This is not to be critical as such, but rather to clarify what else might have been possible to make a stronger and more useful evaluation. For example, for statistical reasons it is preferable to have an objective baseline of 10 or more data points, and an intervention period with at least the same number. It might have been possible for the practitioner/evaluator to reconstruct 10 weeks of baseline, and to run the data collection phase at least 10 more weeks. But they didn't, probably because the data were so clear that it was wasteful of time and energy just to fulfil statistical demands. This is a classic conflict between the research-oriented person and the practice-oriented person. The evaluator combines some characteristics of each, because one must be sensitive to client interests, values and behaviours; and yet one must be sensitive to scientific interests to test client outcomes adequately so as to have a solid basis for conducting practice the way we do. Because of increasing time and cost pressures, practitioners are having this dilemma raised several degrees: it is more important than ever to be able to document objective changes in client outcome, but given the limits of time and resources, it is also more important than ever to be sensitive to client need and behaviour within a short time frame.

The Kazi and Wilson statements of practice methods – 'counselling; enhancing SH's importance in the school' – are vague, and inadequate to guide other practitioners. A further use of SSD is to encourage practitioner/evaluators to be specific about what they do, as well as about what is done with and for the client, so that they can know exactly what it is that should be repeated in other cases. We should spend as much time and energy in defining our intervention procedures (so that we may repeat them as desired), as we do in defining the client problems clearly and distinctly.

Creating designs for evaluation

The case of the crying child illustrates an AB design. Let me introduce the labyrinth of design considerations; interested readers may want to pick up the thread of the trail in other books (such as Barlow and Hersen, 1984; Kazdin, 1992). First, practitioners can always begin to act as soon as the client walks in the door. This would be an 'intervention only' design, where there is a quick subjective assessment and simultaneously a choice of intervention that is immediately put into effect. Molière's *Bourgeois Gentleman* would be surprised to learn that this is called a (qualitative and subjective) case study – the workhorse of the helping professions for generations. Depending on how sharp practitioners are in picking up the right clues and putting the story together in a useful way, they may be very 'successful' in helping clients to help themselves. The fundamental problem with case study methods is that we really don't have an objective platform from which to observe changes in the case, and we have no quantitative baseline or reference point, and so we can't document either a significant change – was the client getting better even before he/she came to the practitioner? – or that what we did influenced the change. Of course, we have strong feelings about the obvious 'success' in the case and our part in the process, but the modern world demands objective evidence and this is what single-system evaluation may be able to provide, rather than what might be described by critics as self-serving subjectivity.

The AB design does provide that platform – the baseline – to determine whether or not there was significant change – and a bit of quantitative data comparing this reference period to the whole of the intervention period. Unfortunately, the logic of this design does not exclude the possibility that other factors than the intervention might have been responsible for the results, so we can only say that something changed, not that the intervention alone was responsible for it. Maybe SH, the crying 11-year-old, was bribed by her grandfather not to cry any more. That 'intervention' was not recorded on the graphs, but might have had a stronger effect than counselling. (See Campbell and Stanley, 1966 for the classic statement on alternatives or threats to the validity of findings.)

Other designs offer a foothold on asserting causality. Consider the ABAB design. I will use another example because by the logical nature of the ABAB design, we have to be able to take away the intervention B after it has been successful in achieving the objectives, return to a second baseline observation period (without any intervention – this would be identified as A^2), and then return to the intervention once again (B^2). The logic is based on successively unlikely occurrences: if the target behaviour improves when and only when the intervention is introduced, and grows worse when the intervention is not present, then we can assert that the intervention logically has something to do with the improvement. As an example, consider the study by Thyer and Geller (1987) in which they wanted to increase the proportion of front seat passengers who used seat belts (see Figure 12.3). The logic of their study directed them to see what percentage of front seat passengers ordinarily used seat belts – this is the baseline condition, A^1. Then they introduced an

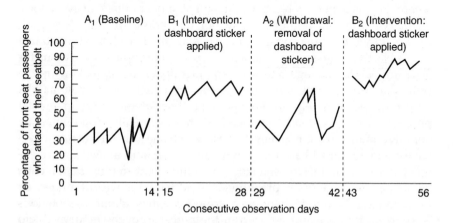

Figure 12.3   *Illustration of an ABAB design: increasing the use of seat belts on passengers using a reminder sticker, 'Buckle Up', on the dashboard (adapted from Thyer and Geller, 1987)*

intervention designed to increase the desired behaviour: they had some drivers attach a small sticker to the dashboard of the car encouraging the use of seat belts. They continued to measure passenger behaviour as before, and found an increased proportion who used seat belts. However, the researchers could not be sure with this AB design that their sticker 'caused' the increased use of seat belts by passengers. So they instituted a withdrawal of the intervention – stickers were removed – and continued the measurement, which indicated a drop in the percentage of passengers who attached their seat belts, even though, on average, there were more seat belt users at time A^2 than at time A^1. That is to say, some front seat passengers seem to have learned and retained the message. In order to encourage a desirable behaviour through the use of an inexpensive method, they reinstituted the dashboard sticker, and were gratified to find improved seat-belt usage. John Stuart Mill's logical method of concomitant variation is clearly visible in these data: high use of seat belts in the presence of the sticker, and lower usage in its absence.

The same logic holds for a multiple baseline design where two or more targets of intervention are engaged at the same time. Baseline periods begin at the same time, but for target 1, the intervention begins while the baseline is continued for target 2 without seeking change in that target, until target 1 is satisfactorily and stably resolved. Then the same intervention is applied to target 2. If this target shows satisfactory and stable improvement when the intervention is introduced, then following the logic of successive unlikely occurrences (where improvement emerges when and only when the intervention is applied and there is no improvement otherwise), we have another way to assert causality. A multiple baseline design is represented in Figure 12.4 (p. 212). Readers will again recognize John Stuart Mill's methods in this logic, which is the historical antecedent of this evaluation method.

It is tempting to use Ben Franklin's wonderful autobiographical example as a study in multiple baseline evaluation. He decided that since he knew right from wrong, he wanted to do more of the former and less of the latter. So he engaged in this 'arduous project' of keeping track of 13 virtues – temperance, silence, order, and so on – using a little notebook in which he put a red dot on each page headed by one of the virtues to indicate where he was not successful. For example, he operationally defined temperance as 'eat not to fullness, drink not to elevation'. And when he succumbed to eating too much or drinking to excess, he gave himself a red mark. Since he was a busy man – readers may recall he had something to do with that war in the colonies – he concentrated on keeping temperate during the first week and letting all the other virtues operate as best they could in nature. In the second week he would concentrate on the next virtue, silence, hoping that the events of the first week would keep his temperance on course, even if he did not concentrate on it.

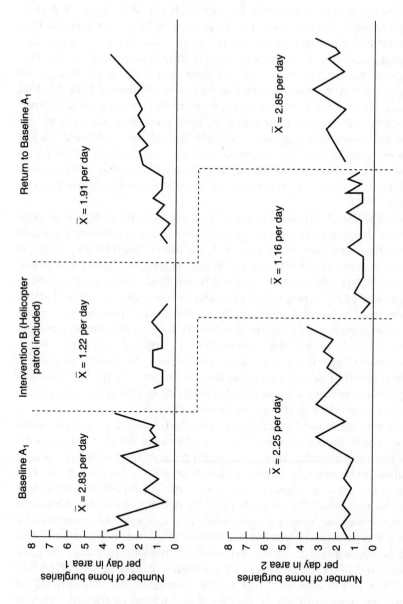

Figure 12.4   Illustration of a multiple baseline design: adding a helicopter patrol to ordinary police activity to reduce home burglaries (adapted from Kirchner et al., 1980)

But . . . this is too complicated (see Bloom and Fischer, 1982: 338–340; Franklin, 1961). Instead, I will present a simpler example of a sequential introduction of the same intervention into two different problem areas, with concomitant success when and only when the intervention is present. (See Figure 12.4, which has the added benefit of including an ABA design along with the multiple baseline design, showing how one may combine single-system designs in many possible combinations.) Here a helicopter patrol was used as the intervention in the case of high rates of home burglaries. This example also shows that burglars can learn from research as well, since in one of the situations the burglary rate increased above the original baseline when the intervention was removed. Reality is messy, no question of it, but at least there is a logical basis for asserting that when the helicopter patrol was active, burglary rates went down, and when the helicopter patrol was absent, the burglary rates went back up – sometimes way up.

There are many other ingenious designs, some of which are logically strong enough to provide the basis for causal inference. The main point is that whatever pattern a practitioner uses, while observing (without intervening) and intervening (with concomitant observing), is, *ipso facto*, an evaluation design. A few observation periods with lots of changes in intervention that follow the vagaries of changes in the client's feelings or behaviours is a design – although probably not an easily comprehended one. There are about a dozen common designs, each with particular characteristics that make it easier or more difficult to use (by placing more or fewer logical demands on the user), and that are more or less ethical (should we leave a client in an unsatisfactory state just because the design dictates the end of service?), and more or less feasible. The general advice is to use the strongest design that is compatible with client agreement and co-operation so as to obtain the clearest informa-tion on helping the client (see Bloom and Orme, 1993, on the ethics of single-system designs).

Social care systems

Evaluation may involve individuals, but it can also be used in collective and aggregate situations. Kazi and Wilson's (1996) paper was a discus-sion of the introduction of single-system designs into a social work agency. Eventually, 21 workers at the agency were involved, using 83 cases. This illustrates the aggregate use of SSD in an agency, working one by one with individual clients, using one or more targets in each case. They report that of the 83 cases, 76 indicated significant improvement on at least one target problem. Forty-one per cent of the designs used were able to provide a basis for logical inference, as well as indications of significant improvements. Overall, this is a remarkable change in objec-tive assessment for a clinical agency in a relatively short space of time.

I would like to give an example of some collective forms of evaluation because the name, single-*system* design, implies that the same methodology applies to any system. Single-system designs have been used with families as a whole, as well as with individual members of families. The work of Reid (1993) is a good example of the various ways to connect single-system evaluation with family groupings. Whittaker et al. (1988) present an instance where multiple indicators of success are used in residential youth care. Researchers such as Benbenishty (1989) have studied the relationship between individual scores and group normative data. Examples are plentiful.

A classic example of the use of the logic of single-system evaluation comes from the work of Dr Joseph Goldberger who was studying the dread problem of pellagra in the 1920s. In one American state institution for children, there was a very high rate of pellagra. Dr Goldberger formulated an hypothesis that something in the diet of these children was causing the disease. He managed to get a government grant to provide enriched foods to these children, and the rate of pellagra dropped dramatically for a period of months. Unfortunately, for political reasons, the grant was not renewed, the institution went back to serving the ordinary food, and the rate of pellagra rapidly returned to its high level. This was in effect an ABA design, one that provides a basis for causal inference; indeed, the pattern of change provided the vital clue to look closely at what is in food, and that led to the eventual understanding and control of pellagra.

Callahan and Redmon (1987) used the single-system approach to study staff utilization and patient waiting time in a paediatric clinic. They examined mean waiting time in minutes for patients (and found it unacceptably high). So they instituted an experimental condition called problem-based scheduling: different categories of patient problems would be likely to require different lengths of service time and, knowing this, patients could be advised to come to the clinic closer to the real time of their visit. Improvements were obtained, and then, following the logic of the ABAB design, to make sure that the experimental condition really was the likely cause of the improvement, they removed problem-based scheduling and went back to the standard time unit for any patient regardless of problem, and the waiting time increased again. So they returned to the experimental condition and the rates once again fell. They ended the project, did a one-month follow-up and found a continuation of the improved waiting time data.

Another large scale example comes from McSweeny's (1978) study of the effects of charging 20 cents for local directory assistance for telephone callers in Cincinnati, Ohio. First, the timespan extended over a 14-year period, and a million callers were involved in this AB study, all of them treated as a single system of people involved in using or not using directory assistance. A parallel AB study was made of long-distance directory assistance for which no additional charges were made. The data indicate a remarkable change in behaviour – some 60,000 fewer calls per day after the local directory assistance charge was introduced, but no significant changes in rates of long-distance directory assistance. The key point is that we obtain meaningful information from both AB designs, but even more important information when we view the two simultaneously. The directory assistance rates were stable for both local and long-distance calls for years prior to the intervention, and then only the local rates dropped. This suggests a tentative logical basis for inferring causality.

A final example of the use of single-system principles on a macro-social level is the paper by Miringoff, Miringoff and Opdycke (1996) where they discuss ways to monitor the social health of a nation. We are familiar with economic reports, from the daily stock market reports to the monthly Consumer Price Index. However, Miringoff and colleagues noted that we lack any comparable measures of social health that could serve as a rational basis for social policy. So they devised a methodology combining 16 leading social indicators, such as infant mortality, child abuse, teenage suicide, high school dropout, unemployment (adult), poverty (over 65 group), food stamp coverage and so forth, using indicators from children, youth, adults and the ageing, as well as measures common to all age groups. They employed the construct of the Model Year, a statistical composite of the best (and worst) performance in each of the 16 areas. This operates like a baseline or reference point, and changes as new best (and worst) performances are recorded for each five-year period. Then, any given year is compared against this Model Year as a percentage of best performance. The 22-year time period shows the pattern of changes in social health as defined above. For this enormously complex index, what we see are equally large social changes, both for the whole index, and for particular items in the index.

An international Index of Children and Youth was developed for UNICEF on an experimental basis (Miringoff et al., 1996). This was a subset of the Index of Social Health plus some additional data, permitting comparisons on 10 nations – West Germany, Japan, Italy, Spain, Norway, Australia, France, Switzerland, the United States and the United Kingdom. Significant improvement was noted in the first five nations listed above; moderate progress in the next three; and substantial declines in the last two. The authors suggest a number of policy implications of these patterns of events.

So, whether one individual is involved, or many millions of individuals, it is possible to use the underlying logic of single-system designs to provide insight and possible directions for future actions.

The future of single-system evaluation

The future isn't what it used to be, and, like everyone else, I hesitate to predict anything (beyond planning how to raise my family, choosing possible directions for my career, buying life insurance, investing in stocks and bonds, and planning for a hale and hardy retirement). However, some factors should be considered. In the United States, schools of social work are now required by their accrediting body to teach students how to evaluate their own practice – without specifying in which of many possible ways this can be done. As a result, many students are learning about evaluation of their own practice, even if they don't use it as much as might be desirable. The spectre of managed care (where bureaucrats determine what services can be reimbursed based on contractual agreements, and where continuation of services depends on documented progress and successful outcomes) also spurs on considerations of objective accountability.

Ethical issues, including the self-empowering client who insists on taking an active role in his/her own helping process, who wants to know specifically what interventions are to be conducted, and who wants evidence that the interventions are helpful, may also influence an orderly, logical and demonstrative process of shared helping. The materials available for considering client consent forms in using single-system designs are reasonably well developed (see Bloom et al., 1995: 637 for a model client consent form), and the ethical issues involved in using single-system designs in practice situations are reasonably well explored (see Bloom and Orme, 1993). Just as we are directly involved in every step of client evaluation, so too are clients involved in every step of their own evaluation, a situation that requires very clear ethical rules to preserve the democratic values of society.

The existence of a journal (*Research on Social Work Practice*) largely devoted to the objective evaluation of practice, including single-system designs, is another encouraging sign of the liveliness of this enterprise. The journals recently have been burning with friendly and hostile discussions of empirical evaluation. And some participants are invited to contribute to research reviews like the one you now hold in your hands.

Yet there are critics aplenty, as you can read in a special issue of *Social Work Research*, 1996, in which three approaches to single-system evaluation were roundly criticized (and defended); see also Rubin and Knox (1996a, 1996b) for another insightful demolition of single-case evaluation (and the equally insightful defences). Critics index the health of a methodology, and by this measure, single-system evaluation is vigorous. Based on these considerations, I would be optimistic about the role of single-system evaluation as a major tool for helping professionals at the beginning of the twenty-first century.

Note

1 See Alter and Egan (1997), Alter and Evens (1990), Alter and Murty (1997), Bloom et al. (1995) and Corcoran and Gingerich (1994). The journal *Research on*

Social Work Practice contains numerous illustrations of single-system designs. See also the special issue of the *Journal of Social Service Research*, 1993, 18 (1/2) entitled *Single-System Designs in the Social Services: Issues and Options for the 1990s*.

References

Alter, C. and Egan, M. (1997) 'Logic modeling: a tool for teaching critical thinking in social work practice', *Journal of Social Work Education*, 33 (1): 85–102.

Alter, C. and Evens, W. (1990) *Evaluating your Practice*. New York: Springer.

Alter, C. and Murty, S. (1997) 'Logic modeling: a tool for teaching practice evaluation', *Journal of Social Work Education*, 33 (1): 103–117.

Barlow, D.H. and Hersen, M. (1984) *Single Case Experimental Design: Strategies for Studying Behaviour Change*, 2nd edn. New York: Pergamon Press.

Benbenishty, R. (1989) 'Combining the single-system and group approaches to evaluate treatment effectiveness on the agency level', *Journal of Social Service Research*, 12: 31–47.

Bloom, M. and Fischer, J. (1982) *Evaluating Practice: Guidelines for the Accountable Professional*. Englewood Cliffs, NJ: Prentice-Hall.

Bloom, M. and Klein, W.C. (1995–96) 'John Griscom and primary prevention at the beginning of the 19th century', *Journal of Applied Social Sciences*, 20 (1): 15–24.

Bloom, M. and Orme, J. (1993) 'Ethics and single-system design', *Journal of Social Service Research*, 18 (1/2): 301–310.

Bloom, M., Fischer, J. and Orme, J. (1995) *Evaluating Practice: Guidelines for the Accountable Professional*, 2nd edn. Boston: Allyn & Bacon.

Blythe, B.J. and Rodgers, A.Y. (1993) 'Evaluating our own practice: past, present, and future trends', in M. Bloom (ed.), *Single-System Designs in the Social Services: Issues and Options for the 1990s*. New York: Haworth Press. pp. 101–119.

Brown, S.J. (1982) *Thomas Chalmers and the Godly Commonwealth in Scotland*. New York: Oxford University Press.

Callahan, N.M. and Redmon, W.K. (1987) 'Effects of problem-based scheduling on patient waiting and staff utilization of time in a pediatric clinic', *Journal of Applied Behaviour Analysis*, 20 (2): 193–199.

Campbell, D.T. and Stanley, J.C. (1966) *Experimental and Quasi-Experimental Designs for Research*. Chicago: Rand McNally.

Colquhoun, P. (1806) *A Treatise on Indigence Exhibiting a General View of the Natural Resources for Productive Labour with Propositions for Ameliorating the Conditions of the Poor and Improving Their Moral Habits and Increasing the Comforts of the Labouring People, Particularly the Rising Generation; By Regulation of Political Economy*. London: J. Hatchward. Reproduced in the Goldsmith's Kress Library of Economic Literature, reel 1888, Item 19292.

Corcoran, K. and Gingerich, W.J. (1994) 'Practice evaluation in the context of managed care: case-recording methods for quality assurance reviews', *Research on Social Work Practice*, 4 (3): 326–337.

Crooker, J.H. (1889) *Problems in American Society: Some Social Studies*. Boston: George H. Ellis.

Faul, A.C., McMurtry, S.L. and Hudson, W.W. (1998) 'Does the use of standard-ized scales and single subject designs improve the outcomes of social work practice?' <Faul@mweb.co.za>

Franklin, B. (1961) *Autobiography and Other Writings*. New York: Signet.

Gerdes, K.E., Edmonds, R.M., Haslam, D.R. and McCartney, T.L. (1996) 'A statewide survey of licensed clinical social workers' use of practice evaluation procedures', *Research on Social Work Practice*, 6 (1): 27–39.

Kazdin, A.E. (1992) *Research Design in Clinical Psychology*, 2nd edn. New York: Macmillan.

Kazi, M.A.F. and Wilson, J.T. (1996) 'Applying single-case evaluation method-ology in a British social work agency', *Research on Social Work Practice*, 6 (1): 5–26.

Kirchner, R.E., Schnelle, J.F., Domash, M., Larson, L., Carr, A. and McNees, M.P.P. (1980) 'The applicability of a helicopter patrol procedure to diverse areas: a cost-benefit evaluation', *Journal of Applied Behaviour Analysis*, 13: 143–148.

Klein, W. and Bloom, M. (1995) 'Practice wisdom', *Social Work*, 40 (6): 799–807.

McSweeny, A.J. (1978) 'Effects of response cost on the behaviour of a million persons: charging for direction assistance in Cincinnati', *Journal of Applied Behaviour Analysis*, 11: 47–51.

Miringoff, M.L., Miringoff, M.-L. and Opdycke, S. (1996) 'Monitoring the nation's social performance: the Index of Social Health', in E.F. Zigler, S.L. Kagan and N.W. Hall (eds), *Children, Families, and Government: Preparing for the Twenty-first Century*. New York: Cambridge University Press.

Reid, W.J. (1993) 'Fitting the single-system design to family treatment', in M. Bloom (ed.), *Single-System Designs in the Social Services: Issues and Options for the 1990s*. New York: Haworth Press. pp. 83–99.

Richey, C.A., Blythe, B.J. and Berlin, S.B. (1987) 'Do social workers evaluate their practice?' *Social Work Research and Abstracts*, 23: 14–20.

Rubin, A. and Knox, K.S. (1996a) 'Data analysis problems in single-case evalu-ation: issues for research on social work practice', *Research on Social Work Practice*, 6 (1): 40–65.

Rubin, A. and Knox, K.S. (1996b) 'Data analysis problems in single-case evalu-ation: a critical look at the single-case design', *Social Casework*, 62: 413–419.

Schon, D. (1983) *The Reflective Practitioner: How Professionals Think in Action*. New York: Basic Books.

Thyer, B. and Geller, S. (1987) 'The "buckle-up" dashboard sticker: an effective environmental intervention for safety belt promotion', *Environment and Behav-iour*, 19 (July): 484–494.

Von Voght, C. (1795) *Account of the Management of the Poor in Hamburg, since the Year 1788. In a Letter to Some Friends of the Poor, in Great Britain*. Reproduced in the Goldsmith's Kress Library of Economic Literature, reel 1588, Item 16814.

Whittaker, J.K., Overstreet, E.J., Grasso, A., Tripodi, T. and Boyland, F. (1988) 'Multiple indicators of success in residential youth care and treatment', *American Journal of Orthopsychiatry*, 58 (1): 143–148.

13

BEHAVIOURAL AND COGNITIVE INTERVENTIONS

Maurice Vanstone

In recent years in the United Kingdom, Canada and many states in the USA, the cognitive-behavioural model has been at the forefront of evidence-based practice with people who persistently offend (Ross and Ross, 1995; Underdown, 1998; Vennard et al., 1997). It is a form of intervention that utilizes a collection of methods drawn from behavioural and cognitive psychology, such as social skills training, self-reinforcement and systematic desensitization (McGuire, 1995). What follows is a critical analysis of the implementation and evaluation of this approach in North America and the United Kingdom and its impact on the shape and structure of both policy and practice. This will be overlaid with an account of the prominent discourses associated with the approach and, given the degree to which research questions impact on the ideas behind official policy, also a critique of the approach in order to identify lessons for future research and practice. The central arguments will reflect agreement with the view that 'evaluation is in itself a critical and inseparable part of being an effective practitioner' (Roberts, 1995: 229), and promote the belief that the disjunction implied in the very use of the phrase 'research and practice' is symptomatic of a central problem of social work practice in this field – the dearth of examples of evidence-based practice.

Accordingly a feature of the chapter will be an exposition of the concept of the social work practitioner as a social scientist. Such practitioners are informed by a theoretical knowledge base, supported by specialist researchers, and respond to the daily problems encountered by clients with a flexibility and sensitivity to needs, while simultaneously contributing to the professional knowledge base. The concept employed fits broadly within the empirical practice model but with the additional principle of feasibility expounded by Reid and Zettergren in Chapter 3 of this volume, and earlier by Smith (1987). The emphasis is on curiosity and the practitioner's commitment to science, not just as a body of knowledge but as a dynamic 'activity, a means of finding out' (Baker, 1988: 42).

From this perspective it can be argued that the practice of social science is unavoidably concerned with answering basic questions which are a reflection of a commitment to both the provision of an effective service and the maxim that doing good requires more than concern for others. Those questions may seem too obvious to mention but, given the apparently low level of commitment to evaluation, require reiteration. They are uncomplicated but integral to good practice and concerned with the nature of problems; the ingredients of their resolution; the appropriateness of those ingredients; their intended and actual effect; how and why those effects may have occurred; and the lessons learned for future problems. Practitioner curiosity, however, is not in itself sufficient; the informed answering of these questions is dependent on the nature of the organization within which practitioners work. A further feature of this chapter, therefore, will be some reflection on the notion of the *learning organization*.

The core themes of the chapter will be presented through an outline of the history and context of research into what works with people who offend. I will describe three examples of cognitive-behavioural programmes: the Integrated Supervision Model from Australia, the Specialized Drug Offender Program from Colorado and the Straight Thinking On Probation (STOP) experiment from Mid Glamorgan in Wales. Concerning the last, in which the author was involved, greater detail will be provided about how the experiment was set up, including what it demonstrated and stimulated, along with a critical look at some of the moral and philosophical objections to the cognitive-behavioural model on which it is based; the extent to which the research design both reflected and influenced the ideas behind the experiment; what was learned; how it could have been different; and the implications for future evidence-based practice.

The historical context of effectiveness research

The history of work with people who offend in the second half of the twentieth century in the United Kingdom and North America can be characterized as one of good intentions – a history of the provision of a 'moral good' only latterly enduring scrutiny driven by the demands of accountability. Until recent years the work of probation officers and juvenile justice workers had survived because of its assumed beneficial effects and the benign social and political climate in which it existed. For instance, in the USA in 1973 the National Advisory Commission on Criminal Justice Standards and Goals recommended a 10-year moratorium on prison building and an increased emphasis on community correctional programmes (Jones, 1990). However, change to the more 'utilitarian, system-oriented goals' of diversion and punishment (Jones, 1990) has been stimulated by adverse research findings on the one hand, and the demands of accountability within criminal justice agencies on the other (Home Office, 1984, 1988; Humphrey and Pease, 1992). If probation officers and juvenile justice practitioners could not influence people to stop offending, so the argument went, they could at least save them from the damaging effects of custody. In the United Kingdom the development of the two most significant community-based innovations of the time, community service and day training centres, was to be driven by that new purpose (Pease et al., 1977; Smith, 1982), while in the USA and Canada the negative research findings resulted in sentencing reforms that undermined the role of rehabilitation in justice and corrections (Andrews et al., 1990). Moreover, the introduction of alternatives to custody and diversion from prosecution had both contributed to an increase in the seriousness of the average criminal profile of the typical person on both juvenile justice and probation caseloads. Ironically, this lessened the likelihood of effective intervention, and stimulated public scepticism about the efficacy of 'community-based corrections' (Conrad, 1991). This combination of factors led to the objectives of effective supervision and protection of the public becoming the central concern of agencies whose responsibility it is to administer and supervise community-based sentences.

Prior to that, the dominant debates were predicated upon questions about the methods used and the values underpinning them, whether social work intervention with offenders was treatment or help, and whether the provision of care was possible within the state apparatus of control (Bottoms and McWilliams, 1979; Bryant et al., 1978; Harris, 1980; Senior 1984). These remain concerns, and no analysis of contemporary social work with offenders should ignore, for example, the prevailing influence of anti-discriminatory and anti-oppressive discourses (Agozino, 1997; Chesney-Lind, 1997; Denny, 1992; Worrall, 1990). The point is that at a policy and political level those issues have been partially eclipsed by the demands for offence reduction and public protection. Coupled with the advent of the managerialism of the 1980s (McWilliams, 1987) and the challenge of 'Nothing Works' research, these changes have increased the pressure on social work agencies within criminal justice systems to expose their practice to the scrutiny of research activity. Therefore, any understanding of the evaluation of cognitive-behavioural work depends on awareness of the issues and processes involved in the slow movement towards evidence-based practice precipitated by that scrutiny.

The beginnings of that process can be discerned in early research on effectiveness in the IMPACT experimental project in the United Kingdom (Folkard et al., 1976). Interestingly (and easy to discern with hindsight) there was relatively less focus on what probation officers actually did with their clients, and more on how the amount of time probation officers spent with probationers might have a positive influence on their propensity to offend. This was an indication, perhaps, of a greater faith in practice methods than prevails now. It is not surprising that the research design mirrored that faith: a potent example, indeed, of research questions both reflecting and moulding the thinking behind policy and practice.

The change to the goals of diversion and punishment, and the concomitant growth in pessimism about the potential of social work intervention to reduce crime referred to above, was stimulated by researchers in the United Kingdom and the USA (Brody, 1976; Lipton et al., 1975). The rehabilitative ideal, if not dead, seemed in need of radical surgery. The negative and generalized message of this research was that nothing could be done by community-based projects to reduce levels of offending. The story, though, is not entirely what it seems: while it is undisputed that the 'nothing works' message had a negative influence and even led to the closure of some projects (McGuire, 1995), it is arguable that its impact occurred more at a policy than a practice level. In the United Kingdom the autonomous practice culture of the probation service survived relatively untouched until the introduction of the *Statement of National Objectives and Priorities* (Home Office, 1984), leaving practitioners to behave as though what they did had a positive influence on people's offending patterns. Practice objectives, encouraged by reports of successful work in other fields, remained rehabilitative and reformative (McGuire and Priestley, 1985; Raynor et al., 1994). Nonetheless, there was little effort to evaluate their achievement, unfortunately, perhaps, because what little evaluation there was provided some reason for optimism (Roberts, 1989).

This apparent aversion to inquiry cannot be explained simply by preoccupation with, for example, the role and function of probation officers (Drakeford, 1983). Different and contradictory arguments have been espoused in the search for a more specific explanation. Research of that era has been described by one commentator as (at least in perception) a one-sided and exploitative transaction in which the practitioners are invariably damned and the researchers glorified (Raynor, 1984). That view has been attacked as an overly defensive response to both negative research findings and the over-reliance on methods drawn primarily from the tradition of anthropological research – a criticism contained in an argument for positivism in research (Sheldon, 1984). While warning against satisfaction with mere good intentions among policy makers and practitioners, Smith (1987) argued that a positivist approach can, because of its demand for scientifically correct experimentation, produce the unintended consequence of deterring practitioners from collaborating with evaluators, and encourage them to shelter under the shadow thrown by vague and subjective claims about effect. Though each of these commentators has a point the problem is, more fundamentally, one of separate development; a history of practice and research as distinct activities which only occasionally coincide. Their proper integration would have had three consequences:

1   human endeavour designed to change or help being firmly committed to a need to know about whether change has occurred or help has been successful;
2   the process of inquiry being as much a practice method as any other;
3   practitioners naturally acting as participant observers (May, 1993).

The reasoning and rehabilitation experiment

Although research projects in the United Kingdom (Raynor, 1988; Roberts, 1989) can be seen in retrospect as a part of the declining subscription to 'nothing works' on the one hand, and the inhibiting of evidence-based practice on the other, it was the 'Reasoning and Rehabilitation' programme in Canada that provided the fulcrum for the emergence of what Pitts (1992) has described as the 'something works doctrine'. The programme was the end result of a review of the literature between 1973 and 1978 which yielded 100 independent studies of varied kinds of success, and clear evidence which challenged the pessimism of the 'nothing works' research (Ross and Fabiano, 1985; Ross and Ross, 1995). What the evidence showed, and subsequent analyses have confirmed, is that successful programmes tend to have the following characteristics (Antonowicz et al., 1994; Lipsey, 1995; McGuire and Priestley, 1995; McIvor, 1990; Petersilia, 1990). They would

- be based on a cognitive-behavioural conceptual model;
- be well structured, properly planned and have clarity of purpose;
- be monitored and effectively supervised;
- be multi-faceted in method;
- focus on offence-related problems;
- be delivered as intended and, therefore, have programme integrity (Hollin, 1995);
- have an emphasis on techniques liable to have an impact on people's thinking;
- target people who persistently offend;
- provide concrete services relevant to people's needs;
- be delivered in a receptive and supportive organizational environment; and
- have an integral evaluation structure.

They contrast with programmes such as those either designed to shock people into going 'straight', or based on traditional psychodynamic intervention and non-directive, client-centred therapy, or aimed at improving self-esteem without attempting to challenge value positions (McLaren, 1992).

The testing of an earlier prototype was undertaken with a group of adolescent female offenders whose disturbed behaviour had remained immune to a variety of treatments. Subjected to this programme their behaviour changed significantly and their recidivism rate dropped to 6 per cent compared to 33 per cent for a matched group. This was followed by what has become known as the Pickering Experiment (Ross et al., 1988), a controlled experiment in which probationers (matched for age and number of previous convictions and, by the use of the Level of Supervision Inventory, for levels of risk and amount of required super-vision) were randomly allocated to either standard probation, life skills training or the Reasoning and Rehabilitation programme. The pro-gramme incorporated such techniques as social skills; interpersonal problem solving; values education; social perspective taking; critical reasoning; and self-control training. A nine-month follow-up revealed significant differences in the offending levels of the groups: 69.5 per cent for regular probation, 47.5 per cent for life skills and 18.1 per cent for the experimental programme. Even starker differences were found in the rates of incarceration for those convicted: 30 per cent for the standard probation group, 11 per cent for the life skills group and zero for the experimental group.

This highly influential experiment, modest though its claims were, not only stimulated a revival of interest in effectiveness but also provided a blueprint for the promulgation of evidence-based practice at an inter-national level. The cognitive-behavioural work at the forefront of this movement, and its evaluation, are exemplified by three examples of programmes which drew their inspiration from this experiment.

The integrated supervision model

This experiment, conducted in the Australian state of Victoria, involved the training of a group of community corrections officers in an integrated model of individual supervision based on the principles of pro-social modelling and reinforcement, problem solving, the use of empathy and a focus on high risk offenders (Trotter, 1993). Examples of pro-social modelling included keeping appointments, being punctual, taking responsibility for one's own actions and understanding others' view-points. The research goals were to evaluate whether the officers in the experimental group implemented the approach, and whether the experi-mental group offended less than the comparison groups. The first comparison group consisted of clients of those officers who did the initial training but did not participate in the experiment, and the second was made up of clients of those officers not trained. A sample of 385 in each of the groups formed the basis of the study.

Because it was not possible to develop a random sample the study adopted a quasi-experimental design in which the experimental and comparison groups were compared on a range of criteria to ensure matching. In a 12-month follow-up it was demonstrated that the officers who implemented the approach, and the experimental group scored significantly less than the control groups in both condition and offence breaches.

The Specialized Drug Offender Programme

This study examined the Colorado Judicial Department's pilot programme for the rehabilitation of drug offenders on probation (Johnson and Hunter, 1995). The Specialized Drug Offender Programme (SDOP) offered more supervision than was normally possible because the programme involved 35 two-hour sessions, and the SDOP caseload was 40 compared to the normal caseload of 160. Seven groups in two districts were run by probation officers who had received three days' training in the approach.

Offenders were screened using an Addiction Severity Index, and those who scored at least five on a nine-point scale (the severe dependency category) were placed in the research pool of 134 probationers, and then randomly allocated to either the SDOP experimental group, the SDOP non-cognitive group, or the regular probation group. The members of the experimental group performed better than those in the control groups in a number of ways, particularly in terms of their significantly lower revocation rates.

The STOP experiment

Like the Colorado project the STOP experiment consisted of the implementation of an amended Reasoning and Rehabilitation programme with 107 probationers. What gives it additional interest is that it incorporated the explicit objective of changing the culture of the organization to embrace the principles of effective practice. The developments required to facilitate such a change involved the consistent application of an evidence-based programme by every team within an evaluative framework. This in turn demanded detailed consultation and preparation, and a research design which ensured that evaluation activity was an inherent part of the change effort.

That process included the appointment of a research consultant to ensure that what Patton (1981, 1982) labelled the 'utility criterion' applied, namely that the evaluation was owned by the organization because of its usefulness to both managers and practitioners. In this sense, the evaluation of the experiment fitted the model proposed by Cheetham and her colleagues. It attempted to take 'account of the complexities of the context, tasks and methods of social work' and produce a study which would be 'seen as comprehensible to the different parties involved in it' (1992: 6). Among other things the process also included the recruitment of a project consultant; cultural sensitization of the Canadian handbook (Ross et al., 1986); the appointment of five extra officers; a staff conference; and a five-day training programme for 45 officers supplemented by two-day familiarization training for managers. Details of the research methodology and the results of the programme can be found elsewhere (Raynor and Vanstone, 1996). Here a summary will suffice.

The purpose of the evaluation was to examine whether the people recruited to the programme were appropriate; whether they completed the programme; how it was viewed by both staff and participants; potential attitude and problem level change, and reconviction in comparison with similar people who had received different sentences. The members of the experimental and comparison groups were matched using the Offender Index (Copas, 1992; Home Office, 1993), and programme integrity was ensured by the monitoring of visual recordings of a randomly selected sample of group sessions. Those who completed the programme showed better than predicted reconviction rates at 12 months and outperformed both other community and custodial sentences; this difference was not sustained, however, over the second 12 months of the follow-up. The implications of this will be discussed later.

Problems, lessons and implications for the future

The above represent interesting examples of cognitive-behavioural work and its evaluation but they are not unique. Over recent years such projects have occurred internationally in a diversity of ways. These range from a car crime project in Northern Ireland (Chapman, 1995) and a diversion from prosecution scheme in Scotland (Kidd, 1995), to programmes for children at risk of delinquency in Spain (Garrido, 1995) and drug offenders in Texas (Cox et al., 1995). This history is interesting in itself but a chapter in a book about social work and evaluation also needs to contribute to thinking about future evaluation and experimental work. So what have these programmes achieved? What can be learned from them, and what are the implications for the next stage in the process of promoting the concept of the social work practitioner as social scientist?

Firstly, they provide a counter to the pessimistic view that nothing can be done about people's offending, and show that it is possible, given the proper approach, to produce and provide programmes for some people who persistently offend which have a positive effect on both attitudes and behaviour. Secondly, they highlight the potential for changing the practice cultures of organizations so that they encompass a genuine curiosity about the impact of the work being undertaken. For instance, in Mid Glamorgan the STOP experiment was (at least partly) instrumental in stimulating a team of probation officers to set up their own controlled experiment in order to test whether they could achieve an organizational objective (Deering et al., 1996). Briefly, this involved the random allocation of probationers to either an experimental programme formulated by the officers themselves or to standard probation supervision, and a 12-month reconviction follow-up. As a result a service-wide experiment has been set up, thus providing a clear example of creative and critical practitioners influencing policy.

Nevertheless the cognitive-behavioural approach has attracted criticism, and the research itself must be open to critical analysis. However, before moving on to some of the moral and philosophical objections, it is necessary to examine what the evidence from meta-analysis – the aggregation and synthesis of the results of a number of studies – actually tells us about 'what works'.

We know that cognitive-behavioural, skill-oriented interventions encompassed in multi-modal programmes produce best results, although it should be noted that one meta-analysis has challenged this assertion (Whitehead and Lab, 1989). We also know that community settings are more often associated with reduction of offending than institutional or residential settings; and that studies using softer outcome criteria, such as client reports or attitudinal measures, have more effect than those using harder data like reconviction rates. Moreover, more rigorous research designs produce lower effect sizes than weaker designs (Losel, 1995). It is well to remember, however, that meta-analysis itself tells us little about finer points such as staff motivations and abilities, or about the characteristics of the people who participate in the programmes, because it can only focus on issues that are reported widely enough in the literature to be combined quantitatively (Lipsey, 1995).

The approach has been criticized for encouraging a focus on the individual to the exclusion of socio-economic, political and cultural contexts. This criticism has been applied most rigorously by those who characterize it as a throwback to individualized and positivistic criminology in which crime is associated with abnormality in the individual, who nevertheless has unconstrained choices (Neary, 1992). Others recognize that it is possible to defend the approach in the event of it being effective, but cast doubt on this possibility because, in general, working methods with people who offend exclude the 'personal, cultural, economic and racial factors' (Pitts, 1992: 138). This criticism has additional resonance when account is taken of the fact that in one of the most comprehensive of recent meta-analyses (Lipsey, 1992) the largest single reduction in offending (35 per cent) was achieved by employment-focused programmes. An interesting but rare example of a project informed by an awareness of the social and cultural context of young offenders' lives is the Turas project in West Belfast (Chapman, 1995). With an unemployment rate of 80 per cent on the estates covered by the project, it was seen as essential that the work should be undertaken within the context of the social consequences of government policy, and what is described as the 'culture of resistance' (amongst young people) versus the 'culture of management'.

Pitts eschews macho-correctionalism and argues for evidence-based practice on the grounds that its concern with the relevance of provision will lead to the widening of the practice focus. He also warns against the danger (inherent in the 'what works' bandwagon) of the deprofessional-ization of the probation officer role, and its degeneration into unthinking application of techniques devised by somebody else. He provides a useful reminder that programmes such as Reasoning and Rehabilitation, when inappropriately applied, can stifle creativity and curiosity in practitioners, and undermine evidence-based practice.

Critics also suggest that interventions cannot be cloned or replicated, and the building of a knowledge base might inhibit the use of discretion amongst practitioners. The critical issue, however, is the nature of that discretion. Effective practice depends on practitioners who are creative and resourceful but who also have an awareness of what they should not change as well as what they should. Thus aware, they would then be more likely to contribute to a scientific model imbued with 'thoughtful and reflective diversity' (Pitts, 1992). This is surely the essence of dynamic scientific inquiry. The problem lies partly with the cognitive-behavioural model to the degree that it encourages a focus on the individual, even though some of its proponents stress the need to address the wider socio-economic problems faced by people who offend. But it also relates to its application being limited to 'offenders', and not applied in any meaningful way to the management and practice activities surrounding it (Thurston, forthcoming).

This deficit is inevitable if research design excludes those activities as irrelevant. The STOP experiment lends itself to an illustration of this point. It was a systematically applied project with an appropriate level of resources, but the research included only a partial focus on management and practice matters. This limited the questions addressed by the research, which in turn contributed to a problem and a missed opportunity. The problem is the lack of sustained application of the problem-solving and thinking skills learned in the programme to the post-group transactions between probation officers and STOP participators. This may well account for the decline in the positive impact on offending rates in the second year of the follow-up period because it diluted reinforcement and the potential for more effective intervention in the wider context of the participants' lives. By and large the research questions were limited to the groupwork programme and its impact, directly affecting the design of the intervention by emphasizing the groupwork component and placing subsequent supervision in the shadows. They also implicitly encouraged practitioners to isolate the groupwork programme from that supervision. Nonetheless it was the existence of an evaluation process and its impact on the culture of the organization that led to a policy of promoting probation orders involving the permeation of cognitive-behavioural methods through the whole period of supervision (Harry et al., 1998). In this sense it provides us with an example of evaluation negatively influencing policy and practice but encouraging reflection and problem-solving processes which have reshaped future policy and practice.

The key to how this might have been avoided in the first place lies in the missed opportunity for a fuller focus on the impact of the experiment upon the organization itself. We know that evaluation has the potential to influence the culture of an organization by its impact upon attitudes towards evaluation and information, and its effect on levels of awareness about members' contribution to knowledge, skills and innovation. In so doing it can neutralize the deterrence effect on practitioners described by Smith (1987). Evidence of this kind of influence emanating from the STOP experiment has been referred to above (Harry et al., 1998), but the partial examination of the organizational process of implementing the experiment itself contributed to the slippage in the reduction of offending. Future evaluation designs need to focus on the culture of the organization in a much broader sense (Thurston, forthcoming). They would then include not only the client group and practitioners but also the practice and management culture as legitimate subject matter. This would improve the prospect of the structures, systems and policies of organizations becoming 'target systems' for change in the way long ago advocated by Pincus and Minahan (1973). Scrutiny of this kind might encompass problem-solving methods, decision-making processes, values, anti-oppressive practice, management style, the use and abuse of power, and the degree to which the organization as a whole acts as a model of the thinking and behaviour it is attempting to inculcate in its client group. An organization that is uncommitted to learning and empiricism cannot engage clients in effective learning processes.

Conclusion

Hopefully, this chapter is consistent with that principle in so far as it is a contribution to a continuing process of reflection on, and evaluation of, an experimental project and the broad approach upon which it was based. So what has that approach achieved?

Prior to its advent in the late 1980s the positive impact of research on policy and practice in work with people who offend had been minimal.

What research there had been was broadly pessimistic in its conclusions and had been ignored by a generation of practitioners. Moreover, it was open to charges of remoteness, a lack of relevance and obfuscation. It is indisputable, however, that further light can be thrown on the effectiveness and quality of practice if that practice 'is more widely subjected to systematic evaluation of its effectiveness' (McIvor, 1995: 210). Research into cognitive-behavioural work with people who offend forms only part of the case for evidence based practice; effective work must include broader strategies on issues such as poverty and unemployment. However, it has provided the key to the door of that systematic evaluation.

The opening of that door depends on the extent to which policy makers and practitioners retain a commitment to evaluation with the following features:

- the involvement of practitioners who behave not only as effective helpers but as social scientists;
- partnerships with researchers in higher education as participant consultants;
- a focus on the process as well as the content of evaluation;
- a realistic eye on both the minimum level of evaluation that is necessary, and the maximum that is desirable to improve the quality of practice;
- information systems that facilitate practice as well as management, and which have the inbuilt capacity to evaluate critical aspects of services at appropriate times – what Patton (1982) calls 'situational responsiveness';
- a corollary capacity for continuous evaluation as opposed to a closed project approach;
- the provision of a self-critical and self-reflective model for those whose practice is under scrutiny; and
- specific, understandable and useable feedback.

Paradoxically, perhaps, another achievement of the approach rests on the degree to which it has exposed its own limitations. Within the context of the contribution of social and economic policy decisions of governments of both the left and right wings of political ideology, it has demonstrated only one small aspect of effectiveness in reducing crime. In so doing it has run the risk of encouraging the fantasy that the cure for crime lies in the hands of social work practitioners and managers within the criminal justice system. Although it represents just one way of working with offending it has come perilously near to minimizing the importance of more general work on structural problems such as poverty and unemployment. At times, through its emphasis on forms of service delivery, it has led to the eclipse of some issues that might have been brought into the light by wider examination of the process of evaluation; for example how the attitudes and values of members of an organization might influence the structure, content and flow of programmes developed within that organization.

Despite these reservations, the evaluation of cognitive-behavioural work in the criminal justice system has made a highly significant contribution to the development of evidence based practice, and provided a template for a practice premised on a constant desire to satisfy professional curiosity and enhance the professional knowledge base.

References

Agozino, B. (1997) *Black Women and the Criminal Justice System*. Aldershot: Ashgate.

Andrews, D.D., Zinger, I., Hoge, R.D., Bonta, J., Gendreau, P. and Cullen, F.T. (1990) 'Does correctional treatment work? A clinically relevant and psychologically informed meta-analysis', *Criminology*, 28: 369–404.

Antonowicz, D. and Ross, R. (1994) 'Essential components of successful rehabilitation programs for offenders', *International Journal of Offender Therapy and Comparative Criminology*, 38: 97–104.

Baker, T.L. (1988) *Doing Social Research*. Singapore: McGraw-Hill.

Bottoms, A.E. and McWilliams, W. (1979) 'A non-treatment paradigm for probation practice', *British Journal of Social Work*, 9: 159–202.

Brody, S.R. (1976) *The Effectiveness of Sentencing*. London: HMSO.

Bryant, M., Coker, J., Estlea, B., Himmel, S. and Knapp, T. (1978) 'Sentenced to social work', *Probation Journal*, 38: 123–126.

Chapman, T. (1995) 'Creating a culture of change: a case study of a car crime project in Belfast', in J. McGuire (ed.), *What Works: Reducing Offending*. Chichester: Wiley. pp.127–138

Cheetham, J., Fuller, R., McIvor, G. and Petch, A. (1992) *Evaluating Social Work Effectiveness*. Buckingham: Open University Press.

Chesney-Lind, M. (1997) *The Female Offender: Girls, Women and Crime*. London: Sage.

Conrad, J.P. (1991) 'The pessimistic reflections of a chronic optimist', *Federal Probation*, 55 (2): 4–9.

Copas, J.B. (1992) 'Statistical analysis for a risk of reconviction predictor'. Report to the Home Office, University of Warwick (unpublished).

Cox, F.A., Gingerich, D.M., Magliolo, D.M., Harris, P.M. and White, B. (1995) 'Reasoning and rehabilitation in Texas', in R.R. Ross and R.D. Ross (eds), *Thinking Straight*. Ottawa: AIR Training and Publications. pp. 237–248.

Deering, J., Thurston, R. and Vanstone, M. (1996) 'Individual supervision and reconviction: an experimental programme in Pontypridd', *Probation Journal*, 43: 70–76.

Denny, D. (1992) *Racism and Anti-Racism in Probation*. London: Routledge.

Drakeford, M. (1983) 'Probation: containment or liberty?' *Probation Journal*, 30: 7–10.

Folkard, M.S., Smith, D.E. and Smith, D.D. (1976) *IMPACT Vol. II*. London: HMSO.

Garrido, V. (1995) 'R and R with Spanish offenders and children at risk', in R.R. Ross and R.D. Ross (eds), *Thinking Straight*. Ottawa: AIR Training and Publications. pp. 359–382

Harris, R.J. (1980) 'A changing service: the case for separating care and control in probation practice', *British Journal of Social Work*, 10 (2): 163–184.

Harry, R., Hegarty, P., Lisles, C., Thurston, R. and Vanstone, M. (1998) 'Research into practice does go: integrating research within programme development', *Groupwork*, 10 (2): 107–124.

Hollin, C.R. (1995) 'The meaning and implications of programme integrity', in J. McGuire (ed.), *What Works: Reducing Reoffending*. Chichester: Wiley. pp. 195–208.

Home Office (1984) *Probation Service in England and Wales: Statement of National Objectives and Priorities*. London: Home Office.

Home Office (1988) *Punishment, Custody and the Community*. London: HMSO.

Home Office (1993) *The National Risk of Reconviction Predictor*. London: Home Office Research and Planning Unit.

Humphrey, C. and Pease, K. (1992) 'Effectiveness measurement in the probation service: a view from the troops', *Howard Journal of Criminal Justice*, 31: 31–52.

Johnson, G. and Hunter, R.M. (1995) 'Evaluation of the specialized drug offender programme', in R.R. Ross and R.D. Ross (eds), *Thinking Straight*. Ottawa: AIR Training and Publications. pp. 215–236.

Jones, P.R. (1990) 'Community corrections in Kansas: extending community-based corrections or widening the net?' *Journal of Research in Criminology and Deviance*, 27 (1): 79–99.

Kidd, W.B. (1995) 'The dissemination of reasoning and rehabilitation in Scotland', in R.R. Ross and R.D. Ross (eds), *Thinking Straight*. Ottawa: AIR Training and Publications. pp. 343–350.

Lipsey, M. (1992) 'Juvenile delinquency treatment: a meta-analytic inquiry into the variability of effects', in T. Cook, H. Cooper, D.S. Cordray, H. Hartmann, L.V. Hedges, R.L. Light, T.A. Louis and F. Mosteller (eds), *Meta-Analysis for Explanation: A Case-book*. New York: Russell Sage Foundation. pp. 83–127.

Lipsey, M. (1995) 'What do we learn from 400 research studies on the effectiveness of treatment with juvenile delinquents?' in J. McGuire (ed.), *What Works: Reducing Offending*. Chichester: Wiley. pp. 63–78.

Lipton, D., Martinson, R. and Wilks, J. (1975) *The Effectiveness of Correctional Treatment*. New York: Praeger.

Losel, F. (1995) 'The efficacy of correctional treatment: a review and synthesis of meta-evaluations', in J. McGuire (ed.), *What Works: Reducing Offending*. Chichester: Wiley.

May, T. (1993) *Social Research: Issues, Methods and Process*. Buckingham: Open University Press.

McGuire, J. (ed.) (1995) *What Works: Reducing Offending*. Chichester: Wiley.

McGuire, J. and Priestley, P. (1985) *Offending Behaviour: Skills and Stratagems for Going Straight*. London: Batsford.

McGuire, J. and Priestley, P. (1995) 'Reviewing "what works": past, present and future', in J. McGuire (ed.), *What Works: Reducing Offending*. Chichester: Wiley. pp. 3–34.

McIvor, G. (1990) *Sanctions for Serious or Persistent Offenders*. Stirling: Social Work Research Centre.

McIvor, G. (1995) 'Practitioner evaluation in probation', in J. McGuire (ed.), *What Works: Reducing Offending*. Chichester: Wiley. pp. 209–220.

McLaren, K. (1992) *Reducing Reoffending: What Works Now?* Wellington, NZ: Department of Justice.

McWilliams, W. (1987) 'Probation, pragmatism and policy', *Howard Journal of Criminal Justice*, 29: 14–24.

Neary, M. (1992) 'Robert Ross, probation and the problem of rationality'. Unpublished paper distributed at the 'What Works' conference, Salford University.

Patton, M.Q. (1981) *Creative Evaluation*. London: Sage.

Patton, M.Q. (1982) *Practical Evaluation*. London: Sage.

Pease, K., Billingham, S. and Earnshaw, I. (1977) *Community Service Assessed in 1976*. Home Office Research Study No. 39. London: HMSO.

Petersilia, J. (1990) 'Conditions that permit intensive supervision programmes to survive', *Crime and Delinquency*, 36: 126–145.

Pincus, A. and Minahan, A. (1973) *Social Work Practice: Model and Method*. Itasca, NY: F.E. Peacock.

Pitts, J. (1992) 'The end of an era', *Howard Journal of Criminal Justice*, 31: 133–149.

Raynor, P. (1984) 'Evaluation with one eye closed: the empiricist agenda in social work research', *British Journal of Social Work*, 14: 1–10.

Raynor, P. (1988) *Probation as an Alternative to Custody*. Aldershot: Avebury.

Raynor, P. and Vanstone, M. (1996) 'Reasoning and rehabilitation in Britain: the results of the Straight Thinking On Probation (STOP) programme', *International Journal of Offender Therapy and Comparative Criminology*, 40: 279–291.

Raynor, P., Smith, D. and Vanstone, M. (1994) *Effective Probation Practice*. Basingstoke: Macmillan.

Roberts, C. (1989) *Hereford and Worcester Probation Service Young Offender Project: First Evaluation Report*. Oxford: Department of Social and Administrative Studies.

Roberts, C. (1995) 'Effective probation practice and service delivery', in J. McGuire (ed.), *What Works: Reducing Offending*. Chichester: Wiley. pp. 221–236.

Ross, R.R. and Fabiano, E.A. (1985) *Time to Think: A Cognitive Model of Delinquency Prevention and Offender Rehabilitation*. Johnson City, TN: Institute of Social Sciences and Arts.

Ross, R.R. and Ross, R.D. (eds) (1995) *Thinking Straight*. Ottawa: AIR Training and Publications.

Ross, R.R., Fabiano, E.A. and Ross, R.D. (1986) *Reasoning and Rehabilitation: A Handbook for Teaching Cognitive Skills*. Ottawa: University of Ottawa.

Ross, R.R., Fabiano, E.A. and Ewles, C.D. (1988) 'Reasoning and rehabilitation', *International Journal of Offender Therapy and Comparative Criminology*, 32: 29–35.

Senior, P. (1984) 'The probation order: vehicle of social work or social control?' *Probation Journal*, 31 (2): 64–70.

Sheldon, B. (1984) 'Evaluation with one eye closed: the empiricist agenda in social work – a reply to Peter Raynor', *British Journal of Social Work*, 14 (6): 635–637.

Smith, D. (1987) 'The limits of positivism in social work research', *British Journal of Social Work*, 17: 401–416.

Smith, L. (1982) 'Day training centres', *Research Bulletin* (Home Office), 14: 34–37.

Thurston, R. (forthcoming) *The Impact of Organizational Factors on the Effectiveness of Practice*. Report to the Probation Studies Unit, Oxford.

Trotter, C. (1993) *The Supervision of Offenders – What Works? A Study Undertaken in Community Based Corrections, Victoria*. Melbourne: Social Work Department, Monash University and the Victoria Department of Justice.

Underdown, A. (1998) *Strategies for Effective Supervision: Report of the HMIP What Works Project*. London: Home Office.

Vennard, J., Sugg, D. and Hedderman, C. (1997) *Changing Offenders' Attitudes and Behaviour: What Works?* Home Office Research Study, 171, London: Home Office.

Whitehead, J.T. and Lab, S.P. (1989) 'A meta-analysis of juvenile correctional treatment', *Crime and Delinquency*, 26 (3): 276–295.

Worrall, A. (1990) *Offending Women: Female Lawbreakers and the Criminal Justice System*. London: Routledge.

INDEX